The Underground Railroad
in Floyd County, Indiana

To all African Americans both past and present
who have lived in Floyd County, Indiana,
and to all of the freedom seekers who have passed this way.

The Underground Railroad in Floyd County, Indiana

by
PAMELA R. PETERS

McFarland & Company, Inc., Publishers
Jefferson, North Carolina, and London

```
977.2 P483u

Peters, Pamela R., 1940-

The underground railroad in
 Floyd County, Indiana
```

Library of Congress Cataloguing-in-Publication Data

Peters, Pamela R., 1940–
The underground railroad in Floyd County, Indiana /
by Pamela R. Peters
p. cm.
Includes bibliographical references and index.
ISBN 0-7864-1070-1 (softcover : 50# alkaline paper) ∞
1. Underground railroad — Indiana — Floyd County.
2. Fugitive slaves — Indiana — Floyd County — History —
19th century.   3. African Americans — Indiana — Floyd
County — History — 19th century.   4. Antislavery movements —
Indiana — Floyd County — History — 19th century.   5. Floyd
County (Ind.) — Race relations.   6. Floyd County (Ind.) —
History — 19th century.   7. Historic sites — Indiana —
Floyd County.   I. Title.
F532.F6P48   2001   977.2'1903 — dc21   2001031291

British Library cataloguing data are available

©2001 Pamela R. Peters. All rights reserved

*No part of this book may be reproduced or transmitted in any form
or by any means, electronic or mechanical, including photocopying
or recording, or by any information storage and retrieval system,
without permission in writing from the publisher.*

Manufactured in the United States of America

Cover images: Outbuilding at River Road and Five Mile Lane, with a hidden room
at the lowest level, at the right (courtesy Jennifer Suzanne Vezner).
Underground Railroad document in the family of Burrell Stapleton Grundy.

*McFarland & Company, Inc., Publishers
Box 611, Jefferson, North Carolina 28640
www.mcfarlandpub.com*

Contents

Acknowledgments	vi
Preface	1
1 Conditions During the Antebellum Period	3
2 The Anti-Black Bias	15
3 Anti-Slavery Sentiment: Political and Social	26
4 Anti-Slavery Sentiment: Religious	38
5 The Free African American Community	59
6 Underground Railroad Escape Routes	84
7 Specific Underground Railroad Sites	99
8 Key Individuals	120
9 Final Comments	131
Epilogue	134
Appendix A: Transfers to Second Presbyterian Church, 1837–1852	141
Appendix B: Sneed Anti-Slavery Memorial, 1840	143
Appendix C: Floyd County African American Heads of Households, 1830	147
Appendix D: Floyd County African Americans in the Civil War	149
Appendix E: Freedom Papers, Bills of Sale, Deeds of Manumission	151
Notes	171
Bibliography	203
Index	211

ACKNOWLEDGMENTS. This book has been a joint effort, and I am grateful to many people for their assistance. In particular, I wish to thank the members of "Coterie" for their interest in my project. Although their names are too numerous to list, I am very grateful to all of them for their help and continued support. I acknowledge the work that Sally Newkirk and Suellen Wilkinson at the Carnegie Center for Art and History, Dr. John Findling at Indiana University Southeast, Thomas "Tim" Moody, and my daughter, Stephanie Carlson, put into reading the manuscript and for their helpful comments. I am grateful to the Carnegie Center for Art and History for its support of me as the primary researcher on an Underground Railroad research project in 1998–99, which was funded by the Indiana Humanities Council. I also acknowledge here their permission to publish the research which forms the basis of this book.

Others in the community who have shared their private letters, papers and family oral traditions, all of which have been invaluable for "telling the story," and who have generously given me permission to publish are: Grace McKee for sharing her grandfather's Civil War letters; Mary Stewart and her daughter, Janel J. Harris, for sharing their photographs and collected material on Sweet Gum Stable; Pearl Grundy Kimbrough, Webster Lee Harraway, Dr. Ben Reid, Barbara Clayton Clark, Donna M. Byrd, John Bezy, Frank Didelot, Joanne Hale, Edward Pinaire and Ruth Bledsoe for sharing their family oral histories and other pertinent information; Albert and Suzanne Kaegi for help in locating African American historical sites and George Yater for sharing his vast knowledge. The staff at various libraries have been invaluable for their cooperation, and I hereby acknowledge their permission to publish: the Amistad Research Center at Tulane University; the Roy O. West Library at DePauw University; the Filson Club Historical Society; the Ohio Historical Society Library and Archives; Nancy A. Harper, clerk of the presbytery of Ohio Valley; Brenda Callahan of inter-library loan services at Indiana University Southeast; the Duggan Library staff at Hanover College; Louisville Presbyterian Seminary Library staff; Robert French at the Louisville Music Academy; and Yvonne Knight, administrator of the Howard Steamboat Museum in Jeffersonville, Indiana. I thank Pen Bogert of the Filson Club Historical Society for sharing his research and Jeffrey Mauck for sharing his skill and expertise as a researcher — in particular his newspaper research from the Civil War years.

Of special mention for their outstanding help, support and permission to publish are the following: Timothy Kate Sorrow for her invaluable collection of family letters and papers which represent the heartbeat of the Whig/Republican attitude in New Albany during the Civil War period — something that otherwise would have been difficult to obtain; Associate Director Lee Fletcher at the New Albany–Floyd County Public Library along with the staff of the Stuart B. Wrege Indiana History Room, including Darlene Adair, Donna Foster, Patricia Foster, Cynthia Froman, Bonita Mason, Betty Menges and Lynn Ruef. Jennifer Vezner's photographic work for this effort has been exceptional. Finally, I am indebted to my husband, Curt Peters, who has given me ongoing assistance throughout this project, and without whom it could not have been completed. His knowledge of things known and unknown have created a wonderful atmosphere in which to complete this undertaking.

Preface

My interest in Floyd County, Indiana, and its antebellum history of runaway slaves' flight through this region began when I moved to New Albany, the county seat of Floyd County, with my husband and children in 1976. Of particular interest to me were the ensuing complications involved in the fact that Floyd County's southern border, consisting of thirteen miles, ran along the Ohio River and was thus in a direct path lying north of the City of Louisville in the slave state of Kentucky. I was left with unanswered questions. Where did runaway slaves go once they reached the river's edge on Indiana soil? Did they have to hide and, if so, why? Wasn't Indiana free soil? How did they get out of the Southern Indiana area, and who helped them? This study attempts to answer those questions and to uncover and expose the various attitudes prevalent in Floyd County during the antebellum and Civil War years. It examines the early African American community and other segments of the community where anti-slavery sentiment would have been prevalent, in an attempt to ferret out information about the Underground Railroad in the area.

My research began in 1996 when I delivered a paper on this topic to the "Coterie," a Floyd County study group that has been in existence since 1898. After the initial research, I realized how much information was missing about runaway slave activity in Floyd County and I have, therefore, continued a search that appears to have no end. That search, for example, led me in 1998 to the Freedom and Manumission Papers stored in the Recorder's office. Nothing has excited me more than the discovery of these records. These legal documents, which are dealt with in the Epilogue and Appendix E, are a detailed record of the many people who came through the Floyd County court system to obtain or to register their freedom. It is impossible to read them without being touched by their heart-rending details.

This study is not meant to be a definitive answer to the question of the Underground Railroad and runaway slaves in Floyd County, Indiana, and it is assumed that new information will continue to appear. The main purpose of this document has been to share information. I have attempted to present the material while remaining honest to both written and oral history, without forming opinions that would tend to exclude new and useful information which might still surface. Perhaps, this study of the Underground Railroad and antebellum attitudes toward slavery in Floyd County will contribute to the public's general understanding of it in Floyd County, in the State of Indiana and the country as a whole, and others will be stimulated to continue the search in their own region.

It has sometimes been assumed that once a slave seeking freedom was able to cross over the Ohio River into a non-slaveholding state, freedom was secured and the person was free to come and go without hindrance. As this study points out, however, arrival on Indiana soil only meant a continuation of the struggle for freedom. Local, state and federal laws worked against African Americans, both slave and free, to keep them from remaining in Indiana and from making any advancement socially, politically or economically. Free African Americans living on Indiana soil, some of whom had never been enslaved, knew what this struggle was. They had to register with the local authorities, pay a bond in the event they became a burden to the community and, if they lived within New Albany city limits, were generally "forced" to live in designated areas of town. They were denied certain rights and privileges and suffered under constant scrutiny and degradation. And yet slaves as well as free people continued to arrive. Some came secretly and attempted to lose themselves within the existing free black community. Others arrived and left for areas farther north just as soon as their feet hit the shore. Still others pursued freedom for themselves and their loved ones by attempting to purchase it through the Floyd County court system. The focus of this book is on the "freedom seekers," those who risked everything—even at times their lives—to attain that goal.

Chapter 1
Conditions During the Antebellum Period

Because (1) Indiana was a free state from its very conception and because (2) New Albany is situated along the banks of the Ohio River that divided a slave state from a free state, (3) the Indiana community of New Albany in Floyd County naturally was a good place for the runaway slave to come.[1]

So one might think. But of the three commonly held beliefs expressed in the foregoing sentence, only the second one, that of New Albany being situated along the banks of the Ohio River, can be made with full certainty and without any qualifiers attached.

Indiana had slaves despite federal and state laws that made slavery a violation of the Indiana state constitution. In 1800 there were at least 175 slaves in Indiana, and slavery continued openly for at least another forty years. In 1803 the Indiana governor and judges adopted an old Virginia law permitting lifetime contracts between masters and servants. In some cases this was thought of as the system of indenture, but in other cases it was still out-and-out slavery. "Thus slavery continued among a select few in the Indiana Territory, to the annoyance of the majority."[2]

Because Floyd County was situated on the border of a slave state, it was not unusual for this community to number slaves in the population. Ruth Bledsoe, a New Albany resident, had a grandmother, Mariah Gray, who was a slave in Madison, Indiana, and was first freed at the close of the Civil War. One of Mariah's tasks as a young girl was to make scouring powder by pounding bricks on the back steps of her master's kitchen in Madison. A search of the Floyd County newspapers and court records also shows several incidents of slavery in Floyd County. In 1811 John Oatman, whose family ran the ferry below New Albany from 1805 to 1811, paid a tax of $1 on one slave.[3] Even in 1860 it was reported by the local newspaper that the slave of Jacob L. Smyser of the State Street Mill in New Albany was killed by a slave of Mr. Tinsely.[4] The last will and testament of George Wheeler of Floyd County, signed February 6, 1828, states that "Negro Harry" was to be passed down to George's wife, Mary, and that she was to give him his freedom.[5] In her will, Mary Rice of Floyd County instructed her heirs to sell "her negroes" at public auction.[6] Ann Kirkwood, a resident of Floyd County, left to her husband, William Kirkwood, "My negro boy Richard now hired to Dr. Miller of Oldham County, Kentucky."[7] This hiring back and forth from slave state to free state was not an uncommon practice. Not only did Indiana slave owners "hire out" their slaves to residents of Kentucky, but Louisville owners were also in the habit of sending their slaves across the river into New Albany on business.[8] In this way some slaves were able to gain their freedom by running away.

The state-sanctioned system of indenture usually took the form of an apprenticeship in order for the young person, often a very young child, to learn a job skill. For the girls it was usually a "housekeeping" indenture. For the boys it could have been that of a servant, blacksmith, farmer or other skilled laborer. The Floyd County indenture records located in the recorder's office begin in 1832 and continue through 1915. Indentured servants in Floyd County were both Caucasian and African American. Normally they were children who had come from the county poorhouse, slaves who had arrived in Floyd County from another state with or without their owners, orphans, or children who had come from families too poor to care for them themselves. A list of the Floyd County indentured servant records involving African Americans includes the following:

(1) The indenture of "Betsy Jane," a poor mulatto girl, age nine years, by the Overseer of the Poor to William B. Hendrick, to be instructed in the business and duties of a household servant, November 24, 1832.[9]

(2) The indenture of Barbara Ann Neil, age three years, by the Overseers of the Poor, to James Baker, to learn the art of housekeeping, from December 3, 1847, to December 3, 1862.[10]

(3) The indenture of Nancy Hawkins, a "colored" girl, age nine years, by her father, Cupid Hawkins, to George Lyman on September 14, 1848, as a house servant.

(4) The indenture of Maria Hawkins, a "colored" girl, by her father, Cupid Hawkins, to Lorine Matthews, on September 22, 1848, as a house servant.

(5) The indenture of Rebecca Clipper, a poor "colored" girl, by the Overseers of the Poor in Greenville Township, age eleven years and eight months, to Robert Scott, from May 19, 1849, to September 23, 1855, to learn the art and mystery of housekeeping. Robert Scott will at the time of her eighteenth birthday give her a good bedstead and a cow.

(6) The indenture of Robert Findley, son of Mahala Floyd, apprenticed to Solomon Byerly on September 8, 1849.

(7) The indenture of Ann Dungen, a "colored" girl, age nine years, to Henson McIntosh, African American, from July 9, 1850, to December 1, 1858, to learn the art of housekeeping.

1. Conditions During the Antebellum Period 5

(8) The indenture of Matilda O'Neal to Rev. Samuel K. Sneed, to learn the art of housekeeping, on August 3, 1850.

(9) The indenture of Moses Mitchum by his father, Isam Mitchum, to Lewis H. Naghal, on October 24, 1850.

(10) The indenture of Sarah Roberts by her father to William S. Culbertson, on December 25, 1850.

(11) The indenture of John Graham, a "negro," to James H. Marshall on September 28, 1865.

With respect to the commonly held assumption that New Albany was a good place for the enslaved to flee for temporary safety, this is only partially true. After the War of 1812, soldiers returned home to the South bringing news of Canada and of their surprise at finding former slaves fighting among the ranks of the British. Those still held in slavery overheard this piece of information, and began their northward search for freedom in Canada.[11] Runaway slaves started crossing the Ohio River and passing through New Albany as the town was being established. This "crossing over" the ribbon of water became a "rite of passage" for the slave who risked being caught and suffering bodily harm and even death to escape slavery and attain freedom.[12] If the runaway slave was able to reach Floyd County, he or she quickly discovered that it was not necessarily a safe place, and the journey had to be continued farther north.

This "run for freedom" was the beginning of what eventually came to be called the "Underground Railroad." This system of escape was not an underground conveyance or a series of tunnels. As the enslaved attempted escape from bondage, he or she met people along the way who responded with food, shelter, money and transportation. The "cart" has often been placed before the "horse" in describing the Underground Railroad, and many have thought that Quakers and other humanitarian and religious people established "safe houses" initially, and then the slave made a run for those places of safety. But as a normal rule the slave who ran away from bondage used his or her own initiative and headed in a northerly direction, seldom having knowledge of a safe path. If the person was lucky, he or she met up with helpful people along the way. Particularly in the border states, the Underground Railroad was often loosely organized, was extremely clandestine and was spontaneously played out just as often as it was planned.

When examining runaway slaves' flight through New Albany–Floyd County, it is important to know what was happening just south in Louisville, Kentucky. Slave trade was concentrated in Louisville because it was the largest Southern city bordering the Ohio River for hundreds of miles. Also, over a period of time the large tracts of land purchased by Kentucky pioneers were broken down into smaller farms and slaves were no longer needed. After a state law prohibiting additional slaves from being brought into Kentucky was repealed in 1849, the slave trade took off with a vengeance. It became especially lucrative to sell off slaves to meet the growing needs of the Southern cotton market. As this cotton market continued to expand, Kentucky became a state filled with slave traders.

This buying and selling was indeed legal, and the Louisville slave markets were located in the heart of the downtown area. The Arterburn Slave Pens, which are designated with a historical marker, were located on the east side of First Street between Jefferson and Market; it had pens and a jail yard. The Arterburns published numerous advertisements in the 1840s and 1850s. Matthew Garrison, also a notorious dealer, had pens on the east side of Second Street between Market and Main.[13] Garrison employed a "runner," William W. Wilson, who was paid $20 for every African American person he brought to Garrison. Free men and women from both north and south of the Ohio River were sometimes taken back into slavery in this way. The *New Albany Daily Ledger* published the following warning as late as 1862:

> **Kidnapping.** We learn that recently a pretty extensive business is being done by certain parties in Kentucky and Indiana, in the way of kidnapping free negroes and contrabands and carrying them into Kentucky for sale. Two or three free negroes have lately been thus kidnapped from this vicinity [New Albany–Floyd County], and, we are informed, taken into Kentucky and sold into slavery. We hear, also, that a large number of contrabands, gathered up at Cairo and other points, have been transported through this state, contrary to all law under pretext that they were property of loyal Missouri owners who feared an emancipation law in that state and were taken into Kentucky and sold again into slavery. It is bad enough to steal a negro slave; but it is infinitely more outrageous to kidnap men born free, and those who [*sic*] by due process of law, and sell them into slavery. The authorities of Indiana should at once look into this matter, and see that laws of the state are no longer violated by the outrageous proceedings of these kidnappers. Some of the gang are said to be residents of this city, others reside at Louisville, Owensboro, and other towns in Kentucky and Indiana. The matter demands immediate investigation.[14]

Other slave pens were located on the south side of Jefferson Street between Fourth and Fifth streets, on Market between Fifth and Sixth streets, and on Sixth Street between Market and Main until 1852 when the owners, Benjamin and Thomas Powell, sold the business to Garrison.[15] Slaves were kept in pens until they were sold to individual buyers or taken by wagon to Portland, in west Louisville, where they were shipped to New Orleans for sale. There were many small-time operators who had no pens but only locked rooms and coops. Slave auctions took place in Louisville on the courthouse grounds or in the middle of Market Street between Fourth and Fifth streets. In the 1850s, a white youngster recalled how he and his friends were intrigued by "Garrison's nigger pen" containing human merchandise.[16]

Slave-holding and slave trade continued, in fact, in Kentucky and Louisville until late in 1865. President Lincoln's Emancipation Proclamation of 1863 did not

1. Conditions During the Antebellum Period

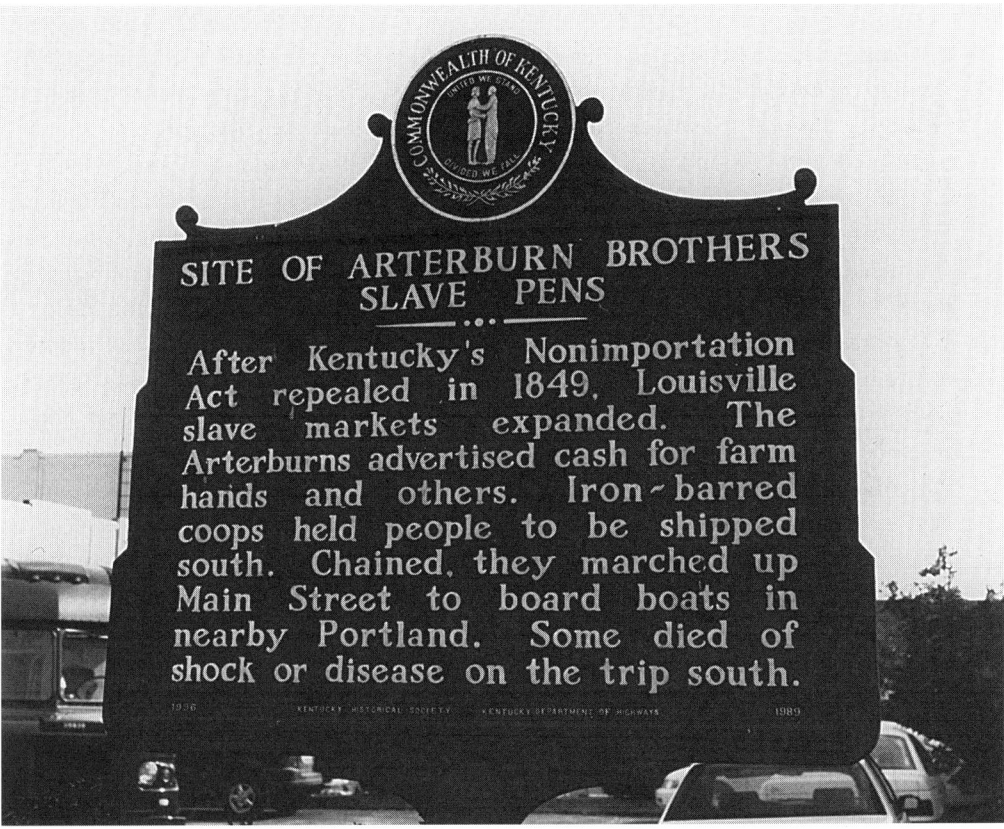

Historical marker at the site of the Arterburn Slave Pens on First Street between Jefferson and Market streets, Louisville, Kentucky. (Photograph courtesy Jennifer Suzanne Vezner)

apply to slaves in Kentucky. Lincoln's Proclamation applied only to those states in rebellion against the Union. He was afraid that if he abolished slavery in Kentucky, he would anger slaveowners and lose the state to the Confederacy. Therefore, slavery was not legally abolished in Kentucky until December 18, 1865, when twenty-seven of the thirty-six states ratified the 13th Amendment.

By the Civil War, Louisville was a city of 69,739 inhabitants with 62,888 whites, 1,948 free blacks and 4,903 slaves.[17] Escape for Jefferson County slaves was tempting since it appeared that the Ohio River was the only barrier between them and a new and better life. Slavery within an urban setting took on a much different personality than slavery as it was found in rural areas. Slave owners within a city were not able to exercise as much control over their slaves as in the countryside where slaves lived together in comparative isolation. For example, Louisville slaves were scattered throughout the city, generally living in small houses or outbuildings behind their owners' houses. Slaves tended, therefore, to socialize with free blacks on the streets, in the black churches, in the homes of free blacks or in taverns. Yater wrote, "There was fear of crime and fear that free blacks would implant notions of escape in the minds of slaves. This fear was reinforced by the many runaways from the interior who used Louisville as the springboard to freedom."[18] Though free blacks living in Louisville did not have an easy existence, their presence created a constant, gnawing fear in white owners who felt them a threat to the retention of their slaves.

Moreover, city life for the slave was not as demanding as that of plantation life. Frequently, slave owners would allow their slaves to "hire themselves out" to others who needed the extra labor. This freedom of movement in Louisville encouraged slaves to attempt escape. The gentleman's agreement, or unwritten understanding, along the Ohio River allowed a slave to cross over into Indiana and work for his owner by transporting goods or hiring himself out during the day as long as he was home by curfew in the evening. A rather unusual set of circumstances surrounded a case heard by the Kentucky Court of Appeals in October of 1844. The case had originated in the Chancery Court of Louisville and involved a Kentucky owner, Mr. Graham, who allowed his slaves to move to Louisville and study music with William Williams, a free African American. The slaves, Reuben, Henry and George, were then allowed to travel around the country with Williams and for two years were given as much liberty as they required in order to earn money that they then shared with their owner. As musicians, they performed in Madison, Indiana, as well as on several occasions in New Albany, often without Williams being present. In January of 1841 these men had been given permission to take the steamboat *Pike* into Cincinnati from Louisville. They left the *Pike* in Cincinnati and in this way escaped to Canada. The slaves' owner, Graham, filed legal action against the owners of the *Pike*, Misters Strader and Gorman, for the unauthorized transportation of his three slaves. Graham spent between $700 and $1,000 in a fruitless effort to recover the men. The Court of Appeals passed down a verdict for the complainant and awarded Graham $3,000 in damages. (It was estimated that Reuben, Henry and George were each worth $1,500, so he was not awarded their full value.)[19]

As the black population increased on both sides of the Ohio River, so did the tension. This tension was built on fear, and it translated into the harsh "Free Negro Law." The law was enforced in the Commonwealth of Kentucky to restrict nonresident, free blacks from coming within its borders. Even though Kentucky slaves were sometimes allowed to cross over into Floyd County to do business for their owners, free African Americans from Floyd County were harshly treated if they set foot on Kentucky soil. The law stated that any free black who was not a resident of Kentucky but who came into the Commonwealth "for any purpose, or upon any pretense whatever, unless in obedience to the process of a Court" would be charged as a felon and, if convicted, sent to the penitentiary for not less than one or more than five years. For example, a New Albany resident, Jacob Mitchum, had gone to Portland to procure a job on the steamer *B. J. Adams*. Under "Sec. 2" of the law enumerated above, Mitchum was arrested and placed in jail.[20]

1. Conditions During the Antebellum Period 9

There is also evidence in both Louisville and New Albany newspapers, as well as court records, of slaves giving important assistance to other slaves willing to risk a run for freedom. One example is that of Ralph, a slave of Bishop Martin J. Spalding of Louisville (fourth bishop of Louisville from 1850 to 1864), who was supposedly working with a New Albany white man named William Hosea.[21] Hosea, a driver of the New Albany stage, or omnibus as it was called, crossed the Ohio River on a regular basis carrying people back and forth on the ferries between Louisville and Southern Indiana. On a Sunday afternoon in January, 1857, Hosea was arrested by a Louisville police officer on suspicion of attempting to "run off" slaves, *i.e.*, to work actively at transporting slaves to free territory. Hosea had been in communication with Ralph, whom he met in an alley. He was noticed by the officer for nearly two hours dodging about, evidently looking for someone. Others testified to seeing Hosea frequently at corners looking up and down streets, evidently very anxious and uneasy. The Louisville police force was already suspicious of Ralph for helping other slaves to run away. So Hosea was brought before Louisville police court. He was "proved to be a most excellent character" by several witnesses, including Mr. Gruyan, the Marshal of New Albany, who attested to his good behavior. Gruyan testified that he was of the opinion the suspicions against Hosea were ungrounded. Hosea also testified that he was in the daily habit of going about looking up his passengers at unusual times in certain sections of Louisville. The *New Albany Daily Ledger* feigned outrage at this arrest, claiming that no one in New Albany would ever suspect William Hosea of "running off" slaves or committing any other unlawful act. The *Ledger* chided Louisville for the hasty way in which they made arrests. Hosea in fact had been arrested in Louisville the year before on a charge of selling a fraudulent 120-acre land warrant and representing himself as an Indiana lawyer. The Louisville newspaper intimated that his mind had been impaired by alcoholism.[22] Hosea was eventually discharged, but in the final analysis, Hosea's character was not as unblemished as the New Albany newspaper made it out to be. It seems the newspaper protested so much in order to defend a New Albany resident who was in actuality breaking the law.

This account of Hosea and the slave, Ralph, also serves to illustrate another point. Because of New Albany's close proximity to a slave state, constant border problems occurred between the two communities. Not only was there a competitive nature to the relationship, but there existed a long-standing rift between Kentucky and Indiana over the slavery issue. This is shown by one John Brown, who recorded a conversation he had in Portland, Kentucky, with a tavern keeper on March 4, 1822. A Mr. Owen related to John Brown that dissension existed between Indiana and Kentucky "on account of slaves who had escaped to the former and were protected by them."[23] The diary entry also illustrates that runaway slaves were crossing the Ohio River at a very early date.

Another illustration of the tension between Kentucky and New Albany concerns two white brothers, Peter and Porterfield Devore, twins, who lived on Water Street in New Albany near the Ohio River and the mouth of Falling Run Creek in the southwest part of town. They were arrested by the sheriff of Breckinridge County, Kentucky, August 8, 1860, on suspicion of "running off" slaves.[24] An eyewitness testified he saw Peter in a skiff late at night at the river's edge. The *Ledger* chastised Kentucky law enforcement for arresting the boys who were ostensibly at Cloverport, Kentucky, on a job search. The New Albany newspaper stated the family had at one time resided in Kentucky and, therefore, "had nothing against slavery." It is just as likely, however, that the Devore family had moved to New Albany, Indiana, from Kentucky, to get away from slavery. It is a strong possibility that these brothers were employed by the Anti-Slavery League, which owned boats along the Ohio River to assist escaping slaves to cross the river.

By its very nature, the Underground Railroad operation had to remain veiled in secrecy for the protection of the runaway slaves and of those who helped them. Because of this secrecy, due both to the danger involved in being on the border of a slave state and the lack of recorded data, the conclusion has sometimes been reached in the Floyd County area that "it didn't happen here." Several well-known sources on the Underground Railroad, including Wilbur Siebert's *The Underground Railroad* and Levi Coffin's *Reminiscences*, deal with interviews of white people in Ohio and other parts of Indiana but don't look much at the black communities or at southern Indiana.[25] Moreover, New Albany has always been painted as a "Southern city" with its economic and social ties more closely associated with Louisville, Kentucky, than with the northern part of the state. B. F. Scribner, in his 1887 book written about the Civil War period, *How Soldiers Were Made*, described New Albany as being a place where "the public sentiment of the majority sympathized with the South.... If the South was forced to separate, the dividing line should be drawn north of New Albany."[26]

This attitude was characteristic of some in the community, especially because the livelihood of many depended directly on the steamboat industry, which had business ties to the South. However, that attitude was representative of only a portion of the people. At the start of the Civil War, farmers, for example, were prohibited from using the New Albany wharf to cross the river and sell their goods in the Louisville (Southern) market. Cincinnati put pressure on the citizens of Ohio River communities not to sell supplies and produce through Louisville because they would be supplying the Southern rebels through the Louisville and Nashville Railroad.[27] James R. W. Smith, writing from New Albany to his New Jersey brother, Samuel Leigh Southard Smith, reported to him, "Provisions have been stopped from going to Louisville. You cannot carry the smallest article across the river without being watched."[28] He continued,

> Mr. Bucks [?] has been compelled to leave the city [New Albany] on account of his sentiment. He was insulted daily. He was uneasy both with regard to himself and family as his life and residence were in danger. There is a spirit here that shoots

a traitor as if he was nothing more than a dog. All river business is suspended. The citizens will not permit a steamer to leave the port. Many boats are here.... Companies are on the street drilling almost constantly.... Uncle Obe ["Obe" was a merchant in Louisville] was over the other day when several companies were on the street. He says you do not see anything of the kind in Louisville.[29]

If Mr. Bucks was compelled to leave New Albany because of his "Southern" sentiment, conversely, J. B. Boyet of Ellaville County, Sligh, Georgia, upon arriving in New Albany, was made to sign a statement before the Floyd County Recorder, Josiah Gwin, certifying that he would henceforth faithfully support, protect and defend the Constitution of the United States and the Union and "abide by and faithfully support all proclamations of the President made during the existing rebellion, having reference to slaves."[30]

There are reasons, of course, why much of the information about slaves' entry onto Floyd County soil has been lost to us. First of all, it was against the law to aid or harbor runaway slaves. The Federal Fugitive Slave Act of February 12, 1793, Article IV, Sec. 2 of the Constitution of the United States, authorized an owner or his agent to secure the arrest of fugitive slaves in *any* state or territory. The act also designated penalties for those who harbored escaped slaves. A person aiding the escape of a fugitive was subject to $1,000 fine and six months in prison in addition to $1,000 civil damages payable to the owner. The United States Supreme Court in 1842 weakened the execution of the 1793 Act when it ruled that the federal statute could not compel state officials to assist in recovering runaways. But Southern representatives in Congress secured a compromise in the September 18, 1850, Fugitive Slave Act. This statute provided that U.S. Commissioners as well as the courts could issue warrants for the arrest of runaway slaves. The term "runaway slave" now became retroactive and included those slaves who had fled in the past and had since established themselves in free territory. If the U.S. Marshals failed to execute warrants, they were subject to a $1,000 fine.[31] If arrested, the runaway slave was not allowed to testify on his own behalf.

The 1850 Fugitive Slave Act was put to the test for the first time in Indiana in New Albany itself. On November 12, 1850, Judge Jared C. Jocelyn heard a case brought before him by Plaintiff Dennis Framell, who had traveled to New Albany from Arkansas to take possession of three people he claimed were his property. The three, comprising a woman, her daughter and grandson, had been confined in the New Albany jail until called before Judge Jocelyn for a hearing. Interest in this case was particularly high, not only because it was the first case to be tried in Indiana under the new law, but also because the alleged runaways appeared to be white. They had been living in New Albany about four months. The boy had been attending the city schools "mingling with white children, no one suspecting him of being aught else than white like ourselves."[32] The oldest woman said she was a native of Baltimore but that many years before, her husband had been killed by Indians and she and her daughter captured. They had continued living with the Indians, most recently in Arkansas, but had never been treated by them as slaves.

This case received coverage in newspapers as far away as New York, Washington, Philadelphia and other Eastern states. The best attorneys volunteered their services on behalf of these people. Meanwhile, the case was appealed by a writ of *habeas corpus* to Judge Huntington of the United States Court of Appeals with the belief that a delay, allowing evidence from the runaways' former residence to arrive, would postpone the trial indefinitely.[33] On November 29, 1850, Mr. Merideth, the United States Marshal for the District of Southern Indiana, arrived in New Albany with an order from Judge Huntington to deliver the three to the claimant, Mr. Framell, since no evidence had been produced from their former home showing them to be who they claimed. They were then taken from the New Albany jail to Louisville where they were temporarily housed in the slave pens belonging to Benjamin and Thomas Powell on Sixth Street. The New Albany newspaper claimed,

> We suppose Judge Huntington's decision was in accordance with the law but not with justice. Our citizens exhibited a good deal of feeling when the facts became known, not because of any general sympathy with runaway slaves but because they believe the persons of the Anglo-Saxon race had been unjustly deprived of liberty.[34]

Eventually, the family was released. Citizens in both Louisville and New Albany raised the $600 demanded by Framell for settlement of the case and the three returned to New Albany.[35] This first case to be tried under the Fugitive Slave Act in Indiana proved to be an instrument that turned people against it as they saw firsthand that under this new law the victim was not allowed to testify on his own behalf.[36] The Fugitive Slave Law was again challenged in 1854 in New Albany by the editors of the *Tribune,* a Whig/Republican paper, who wanted to re-open the issue, and by the Southern Indiana Methodists at their quarterly conference held in Indianapolis in that same year.[37]

Besides the fact that assisting escaping slaves was illegal, another reason for lack of documentation on runaway slaves and the Underground Railroad is that crossing the Ohio River onto Indiana soil was not the freedom the escaping slaves hoped for and, therefore, runaways were soon on their way farther north. Many of them passed through New Albany as quickly as possible, leaving no trace of their presence. Remaining in Floyd County for any length of time was dangerous because of the slave catchers hired by owners to find their property. Some citizens who lived in the border counties of Floyd, Clark and Harrison earned a living by catching runaways and, of course, slave catchers from Louisville crossed to Indiana easily by using the ferry transportation system. The *New Albany Daily Ledger* continued to make reference to slave hunting occurring on Indiana soil even after the Civil War began.[38] Though James Smith of New Albany wrote in a letter to his brother Sam that "Several slaves have passed through Indiana enroute for Canada from seceding states and no one pretends to stop them,"[39] the newspapers of that day reported many instances of slaves making the attempt to cross the Ohio River only to be caught in the process. For example, on April 16, 1861, the local newspaper reported:

> We understand three slaves escaped from their owners in Kentucky, who live a few miles below Louisville, on Sunday and fled to this state. Our informant states that they crossed the river a short distance below this city [New Albany] in a skiff, and that one of them was captured and returned to his owner. The other two have not been heard from, and a reward of $100.00 each is offered for their apprehension. We have heard nothing definite about the matter more than a fisherman by the name of Fipps, living in the vicinity of Clarksville, [Indiana, next to New Albany] caught one of the runaways.[40]

Another report stated:

> We are informed that numbers of runaway slaves have lately attempted to escape from the lower counties of Kentucky into this state. But few however have succeeded in their design they being arrested on this side of the river and returned to their masters or lodged in jails in Kentucky. An officer of this city informs us that not less than 20 runaways have been thus arrested and returned from the neighborhood of this city [New Albany] since the first of January.[41]

And yet another asserted that a "slave woman, said to be the property of a Mr. Dixon of Louisville, Kentucky, was captured in this city [New Albany] yesterday, by our city officers and returned to him."[42]

Rev. Benjamin Franklin Crary, who was pastor of Wesley Chapel Methodist Church in New Albany, 1856–1857, reported slave catchers had been seen coming across the river with dogs hunting for their prey.[43] Rev. John Bishop, pastor of Second Presbyterian Church in New Albany from 1846 to 1850, made reference in a letter to the American Home Missionary Society to the fact that many early settlers coming into the outlying areas of Southern Indiana and the Northwest Territory from the South had themselves been slave catchers and would have introduced slavery into the Territory if they had their own way.[44]

Slave catchers were active in all of the communities along the Southern Indiana shore. In 1903–1904 John Howard of the Jeffersonville, Indiana, shipbuilding family wrote his "Memoirs." As a young man, he and his friends had an encounter with a slave catcher on the Indiana shore at Jeffersonville, which is less than six miles upstream from New Albany. That portion of his "Memoirs " reads as follows:

> In those days, we did not thin[g] [sic] anything of crossing, or going anywhere on the Falls with a skiff. The danger was not so great as afterwards when the U.S. Government began to build dams and improve the Falls. They were, however, always a terror to strangers.
> Dan and I and others, when young men, made trips to Louisville every week

at night, sometimes going on the last ferry boat, which left Jeffersonville at 7 o'clock P.M., and returning in a skiff at midnight or later. We never failed finding some kind of an old skiff on the Kentucky shore, opposite the ship yard, and sometimes paddled over without oars.

The greatest difficulty was crossing in a fog. Have been frequently lost, and then the Falls was a dread, until we tried the expedient of tying a deck plank, or long strip of pine, to the stern of the skiff. Then we started in the direction we wanted to go, and keeping our eye on this strip, which would show the least turn of the skiff, and there was no trouble in keeping a direct course, even with the fog so dense that sometimes we could hardly see the strip.

Once three of us landed just below the ship yard, in an old leaky skiff, half full of water, about half past one o'clock at night, and in a dense fog. I was rowing, the other two bailing. When I stepped ashore, I was immediately grabbed by a big man, old Joe Reeder, who said with an oath, "I've got you." They took us for runaway niggers, having heard of three who expected to cross that night and they mistook us for the runaways. When they found their mistake, they were raving mad, and there came very near being trouble. Old Joe Reeder and others were always on the lookout for runaway slaves, and made a good deal of money returning them and getting the reward.[45]

Documentation has also been lost since by law enslaved persons were not allowed to learn reading and writing, and a formal education for free blacks was difficult to obtain. Additionally, out of fear neither slave nor free would have wanted to record Underground Railroad activities. Instead, some stories survived through oral tradition.

Yet another reason for the lack of preserved information involves John B. Norman and the *New Albany Daily Ledger*. Norman, as editor of the *Ledger* from September 27, 1849, to his death on October 31, 1869, was a Democrat, deeply partisan, a strong foe of abolitionism and notorious for his constant degradation of African Americans. He printed very little, if any, positive information about blacks.

Despite this lack of recorded data, when the information about the Underground Railroad and runaway slaves is gathered and put together in one document, much is actually available to us. It is evident that a considerable amount of runaway slave activity did occur in New Albany and Floyd County, with many of the slaves being apprehended before they could get out of the area. As one historian put it,

> It has been stated that probably more negroes crossed the Ohio River at two or three places in front of Louisville than any place else from the mouth of the Wabash River to Cincinnati, the reason being that the three good-sized cities [Louisville, Jeffersonville and New Albany] at the falls furnished good hiding places for the runaways among the colored people.[46]

We now turn to an examination of the most prevalent attitudes regarding slavery that existed in Floyd County prior to and through the Civil War. In the following three chapters, we will look at the anti-black bias, the anti-slavery sentiment, which took various forms, and the free African American community.

Chapter 2
The Anti-Black Bias

New Albany–Floyd County was a community that was split over the slavery issue, and it was not just a matter of ethics. New Albany's very existence hinged on its riverboat industry and economic ties to the South. Many in Floyd County believed the Union should be saved at all costs, and if this meant leaving slavery undisturbed, so be it. But the feelings and opinions aroused over the slavery issue among Floyd County citizens were very diverse. Even if a pro-slavery attitude was not prominent in this Southern Indiana community, New Albany possessed a definite anti-black bias, as is evidenced by articles published in the New Albany daily newspapers during the antebellum years. If the system of slavery were to be demolished, African Americans in great numbers would undoubtedly move into the state, and this was something many in Indiana did not want. The *Louisville Daily Courier* often reported on Kentucky slaves running away from Louisville and crossing the river at New Albany. It praised the "honest" New Albany citizens who captured them.[1]

There are references to Floyd County citizens as slave catchers as well as reports of incidents where the New Albany police assisted in capturing runaway slaves. One such example of New Albany police involvement was reported in very critical terms in the *Jeffersonville Republican,* a newspaper edited by Dr. Nathaniel Field. It was reprinted in the *Ledger* as follows:

> John Talson (a free man of color) was recently arrested in the neighborhood of New Albany by a police officer of that city by the name of Ray upon suspicion of his being a fugitive slave, conveyed to Kentucky and thrown into the Louisville jail, where he still remains awaiting the pleasure of his captor. This Mr. Ray had no authority under the sun for this tyrannical act. Testimony has been forwarded to this place from the State of Virginia confirming the statement of Talson that he is a free man. Two of our citizens visited New Albany a few days ago and informed Mr. Ray of this fact yet he showed no disposition to release Talson from imprisonment. His behavior on this occasion was in perfect keeping with his occupation. His perfect indifference about the matter proves a necessity of holding such men to a strict account of their acts. It is to be hoped there are men in New Albany to vindicate the rights of the oppressed, and bring this police officer to justice.[2]

Another incident involving the police occurred during the Civil War. Fifteen slaves, who had been "stolen," according to the *Ledger,* from their masters in the neighborhood of Lexington, Kentucky, and brought to Louisville by a Michigan regiment, were ordered out of the lines by General Gordon Granger, Commander of the District of Central Kentucky, and crossed the river from Louisville to Indiana "to take the Underground Railroad for the north,"[3] as the newspaper expressed it. Six of them were arrested by the sheriff at Silver Creek almost immediately. The *Ledger* claimed that the hiding place of the remaining nine was known and their arrest was imminent. (Silver Creek runs along the eastern border of Floyd County, separating Floyd from Clark County; it flows into the Ohio River.)

Still another account involving the New Albany police and a slave who ran away from his owner in Danville, Kentucky, happened on Wednesday, November 14, 1862. The slave was discovered to be in New Albany with a horse and buggy on his way north. Marshall Akers arrested the slave and returned him to his owner. "The parties implicated in aiding the slave were forced to pay expenses incurred in the pursuit and capture of the property and the owner did not prosecute further." No mention is made of the names of the parties implicated in helping him.[4]

Free African American citizens of Floyd County experienced a constant struggle with racism. In January of 1861, David Caution, an African American from Louisville, was convicted of attempting to rape a white woman and was executed at Louisville in the presence of 10,000 to 12,000 people.[5] A few days later, five white men were charged in New Albany with ravishing a "Negro woman," fined $5 plus costs and, in default of payment, sent to jail for fifteen days.[6] Black churches constantly dealt with racism and violence. The African church in West Union was burned in 1841[7], and in October of 1862, the newspaper reported that the "African church" had been robbed.[8] One night in 1865 during a worship service, white citizens fired guns at the "African Church in West Union."[9] The worshippers asked them to leave. The troublemakers headed for a saloon farther out the "turnpike" (known today as State Street) and returned to the church drunk. They again fired at the church, but this time the shots were returned. In all some 30 to 35 shots were fired by both parties. One of the African Americans had his finger shot off. No one was arrested but both sides were encouraged by the judge to be more tolerant.

John B. Norman, editor of the *New Albany Daily Ledger* for more than twenty years, was a spokesman for the many who held an anti-black bias. Contemporary historian Henry E. Cheaney claims the *New Albany Daily Ledger* was one of the most irreconcilable newspapers in the state on any issue involving blacks.[10] Norman was fond of using a "tongue in cheek" method of reporting news as it occurred in the African American community. And if he wasn't ridiculing, he was reporting the unpleasant things that took place there. Yet despite his reputation of being biased against Republicans, the anti-slavery movement and abolitionism, the black community and the idea of more blacks moving into the state, he also had a reputation of being one of the most capable and well-known journalists in Indiana.[11] Norman exerted a lot of influence on New Albany and the surrounding area because of the *Ledger's* wide readership. His hostile and uncompromising attitude, therefore, became widely known, giving readers a somewhat distorted picture of New Albany as a place that held the black person in low esteem. Norman would stir up feelings among the white citizens by printing small infractions committed by black citizens that emerged from the police court records such as "[___] (colored) was arrested today for stealing someone's chicken and things."[12] Or he would incite white citizens against the black population by instilling fear of job competition, claiming the influx of blacks would take available jobs away from the general population. The fact that any slave from Kentucky who chose to run off was only hours away from New Albany fed this fear and encouraged the *Ledger* to stress over and over the theme of barring them from coming into Indiana.

Not all newspapers published along the Ohio River border were in accord with the *New Albany Daily Ledger*. Some were either "anti-slavery" in spirit, Republican or simply expressed a kinder attitude toward blacks. A Salem, Indiana, paper called the *Salem Weekly Times*, published in 1858 by Mr. Hicks and a Quaker by the name of Mr. Trueblood,[13] was described as being "Black Republican" by the *New Albany Ledger*.[14] Jeffersonville, seven miles northeast of New Albany, published the *Jeffersonville Republican*. The *Cincinnati Herald*, as well as the *Republican*, were printed in Cincinnati. New Albany had its Whig/Republican *Tribune* for a short time between 1852 and 1854, which regarded slavery as "a very great evil, morally, socially, and politically."[15] *Tribune* Editor Gregg expressed remorse for free blacks in the North, claiming that life for them was a less happy condition than that of the poor slave.[16] The *Tribune* also called Norman a "mean man," one who was neither respectable nor decent.[17]

Throughout the antebellum years, the *New Albany Daily Ledger* voiced its anti-abolitionist sentiment. This became more pronounced the closer the country came to war and included denouncing intellectual societies in town whose membership embraced "pillars of the community." It criticized the committees of the Young Men's Christian Association and the Mokuna Society (a literary club) for inviting such "obnoxious" abolitionists as Wendell Phillips to town. No evidence has been found to verify that Phillips accepted the invitation to speak in New Albany. (Phillips was often called the "golden trumpet" of the abolitionist cause.) The *Tribune*, which was the Whig/Republican paper, accused the *Ledger* of bigotry and narrow-mindedness since "Wendell Phillips is a splendid lecturer ... and could lecture in South Carolina without giving offense because he stays away from politics and religion."[18] According to the *Tribune*, the *Ledger* believed that if these societies continued to convert the lecture series into an abolition propaganda platform, they would soon lose their constituents.[19]

Those who were against slavery were not necessary all abolitionists (*i.e.*, immediatists). Norman attempted to paint all anti-slavery people as abolitionists—even President Abraham Lincoln, who was not an abolitionist.[20] In September 1862, Norman attacked President Lincoln when the preliminary Emancipation Proclamation was announced:

> The proclamation of the President, announcing the abolition of slavery in all the rebellious states on the first of January next, was read with astonishment and grief by thousands of loyal men yesterday. It struck like a death knell upon the hopes of very many, who despairing of justice and sound common sense in other quarters, were disposed to place faith in the moderation and patriotism of the President.... We would willingly cast the mantle of charity over this last act of the President, if we could believe there was even a decent pretext for it. But there is none, worthy a president or a man, that he can make, that we can imagine.[21]

A poem, supposedly written by Norman, and published after Lincoln's Emancipation Proclamation of January 1863, in the form of a flyer for distribution to subscribers, shows his bias and reads in part:

> 'Tis a delicate task, my friends, we confess,
> To please all our patrons in a New Year's Address.
> We must not speak of him who's the head of the Nation,
> Except in terms of the greatest laudation,
> Nor say aught against the great Proclamation
> That looks to gradual emancipation;
> Nor speak of the army, to give information,
> We've learned from officers lofty in station;
> Or say anything else to create a sensation,
> Or else we will find by a forced gravitation,
> 'Tis *Fort Lafayette*, and only one ration.
> When such is the case, friends, what can we say,
> When our tongues and our pens are tied up in this way,
> And we know not the consequence, perhaps it may
> Take us off in the barracks almost any day.
> Why we hardly dare ask if Cassius M. Clay,
> As General and Minister, draws double pay,
> Or why General Fremont roves about o'er the land,
> And a dozen more Generals are without command,
> Why the President preached at his inauguration
> To Congress assembled and to the whole Nation,
> A doctrine opposed to his late Proclamation;
> Of the pressure he's had from the friends of the nigger,
> Who have forced him at last to "go the whole figure,"
> And their pledge of support is made on condition
> That he stands by the doctrine of slave abolition.[22]

An additional problem Norman created was his "sin of omission." Because of his anti-black attitude, he failed to print positive information about African Americans. There were no births or marriages listed, and only an occasional obituary of

2. The Anti-Black Bias

a well-known African American was printed. As a general rule he printed only the bad news, seldom the positive. This total neglect of the good and emphasis on the bad became a tool that constantly worked at separating the races, causing anxiety between them and building up fear, prejudice, suspicion and animosity.

Victor M. Bogle claimed, "The editor of the *Ledger* reflects, for the times, a ... probably majority attitude of New Albany citizens toward the Negro in the immediate pre–Civil War years."[23] However, community pressure must have been put on Norman from time to time to change. Occasionally during the Civil War period, an editorial in the *Ledger* stated that the paper did not believe there was a citizen of New Albany who could justly complain of the conduct of the black soldiers in the city hospitals. "We have several times commended their orderly behavior through these columns, as creditable in the highest degree to them ... the conduct of these soldiers has, so far as we have ever heard, been unquestionably good."[24] It goes on to complain that some white people have been known deliberately to walk along the streets, armed with brass "knucks" or a sling shot in order to assault sick and wounded black soldiers.[25]

> [These people — the perpetrators] are scoundrels of the lowest degree, who should not be countenanced or tolerated in any decent community, and will not be — they are of the same character precisely as the man who, with a little brief authority, uses it to oppress and domineer over those who are so unfortunate as to be under him.[26]

Norman's variation in attitude makes one wonder what kind of pressure may have been brought to bear upon New Albany's leading newspaper. It seems to show that he, as editor-in-chief, was not always reflecting the attitude of the entire community and that there was an element present in Floyd County that sought to defend blacks against Norman's biased rhetoric.

An illustration of Norman's modifications on another point and an indication that not everyone in New Albany agreed with him may be found in an incident of mid–April 1861. In a letter written from his parents' house on Upper Main Street[27] in New Albany, James Smith informed his brother, Sam, living in New Jersey at the time, that

> Indiana is upside down! New Albany is boiling over with rage and indignation. The people are wild. Gillespie's Border Rangers, the Anderson Guards and the Morrison Light Guards have all formed to assist in subjugating the south. The people here, though on the border of a slave state, are wild with enthusiasm.[28]

Smith claimed that among the "Border Rangers" were deserters from the Southern traitors who left because they refused to fight under any other banner than the "Stars and Stripes." A Southern steamer from Memphis, *Commercial*, attempted to land at New Albany's wharf with its "ignoble flag of the southern traitors" flying, only to be met with jeers and threats from a crowd of New Albany residents who forced the captain to pull off and leave the New Albany dock. With strong anti–Southern feelings running high, none other than John B. Norman was threatened with assassination. James' letter continued with the following astonishing news:

> John B. Norman, the senior editor of the *Ledger*, was hung in effigy on last Sunday at the junction of Main and Pearl streets. Since then he has returned to his allegiance as he was threatened with assassination. He is now a strong union man simply because he cannot be anything else.[29]

Obviously, this piece of news was not published in the *New Albany Daily Ledger*.

Norman's anti-black attitudes were reflective of many in Indiana as is evidenced by the passage of the Exclusion Act in 1851, which was adopted to prevent further settlement of blacks in the state. Isaac N. Akin, Clerk of the Floyd Circuit Court, published a notice prior to the county election in August of 1851, which stated in part, "A vote will be taken on the adoption or rejection of the new or amended Constitution, and on the adoption or rejection of the separate article thereof, relating to the exclusion of negroes and mulattoes from this State."[30] Indiana voters approved the Exclusion Act with a vote of 109,967 for and 21,066 against.[31] The Exclusion Act was still in effect fifteen years later and was not nullified until 1866. Though this law was to have been taken out of operation at the time of its nullification, the offensive language of the clauses prohibiting blacks from settling in the state was actually not eliminated until March of 1881. This 1881 action finally brought Indiana into conformity with the Federal Constitution.[32] Therefore, as more and more blacks attempted to enter and settle in Floyd County, the *New Albany Daily Ledger* protested vehemently against this with almost weekly, and sometimes daily, editorials, reminding those who had settled previous to November 1, 1851, of the requirement to procure from the clerks of the Floyd Circuit Court a certificate of the fact, "in order that their contracts with each other and with the whites may be valid."[33] Many restrictions had been placed on free African Americans entering the state before the Exclusion Act was passed, such as having to register with the authorities and pay a bond of $500 as security for good behavior. This law was difficult to enforce, but attempts to do so were made from time to time. In August of 1850, the authorities in neighboring Clark County began compelling free blacks who had not already done so to pay their fee. When they were not able to come up with the money, some were afraid, and they crossed over into Floyd County, a fact that troubled the *Ledger*.[34] Other restrictions involved the prohibition of mixed marriages. In 1850 a black man was tarred and feathered in New Albany for living with a white woman.[35] The "Floyd County Marriage Record Index" records that the Justice of the Peace refused to marry Jack Gaston and Polly Smith because Gaston was black and Smith was white.[36]

As the country moved closer to war, the exclusion of blacks from Floyd County continued to be an issue. "Our readers will be glad to learn that the negroes who are here in violation of the law are leaving in a peaceful manner. Twenty-one were seen passing the prison at Jeffersonville yesterday in a wagon bound northward," gloated the *Ledger*.[37] A few days later it was evident that some of the new immigrants had remained in Jeffersonville. A public meeting was held and a committee was appointed to give them notice they could not stay there.[38]

Historian Emma Lou Thornbrough states:

> Although some Negroes left the southern counties of Indiana, many more continued to arrive. Some of them were fugitives from Kentucky who came on their own initiative; others were so-called "contrabands," slaves who fell into the hands of members of the Union Army and were sent by them to the free states. As the war progressed, the number of Negroes sent North by members of the army also increased. In October, 1862, it was reported that Army officers had brought ten or twelve Negroes to New Albany. The following month several more Kentucky slaves who had been freed by an Illinois regiment were instructed to go to Indiana.[39]

Before the Emancipation Proclamation of January 1, 1863, Union soldiers acted without any legal authority in freeing the slaves, and the *New Albany Daily Ledger* protested in vain that sending them to Indiana was a violation of the State Constitution.[40]

> We understand that several more strange negroes, besides those we mentioned a few days ago, have been sent to this city. The law strictly forbids this, under heavy penalties, and those employing negroes who have come into the State contrary to law are also liable to heavy fine. The following is the law on this subject, which we quote from an act entitled "An Act to Enforce the Thirteenth Article of the Constitution, approved July 18, 1852," which may be found on page 444 of the 1st volume of *Gavin & Hord's Statutes of Indiana:*
>
> > Sec. 1. Be it Enacted, & c., That it shall not be lawful for any negro or mulatto to come into, settle in, or become an inhabitant of this State.
> >
> > Sec. 7. Any person who shall employ a negro or mulatto, who shall have come into the State of Indiana, subsequent to the 31st day of October, in the year One Thousand Eight Hundred and Fifty-One, or shall hereafter come into said State, or who shall encourage such negro or mulatto to remain in the State, shall be fined in any sum not less than ten dollars nor more than five hundred dollars.[41]

Other sections of the Exclusion Act forbade residents to carry on business with blacks who came into the state illegally and made it the duty of all officers to arrest and prosecute any person or persons found violating this statute. "Will our officers do their duty in this particular, before the city is overrun with worthless runaway slaves?"[42] chastised the *Ledger*. Any and all fines collected in Indiana for violations were to be appropriated for the colonization of African Americans and their descendants who were willing to emigrate to Liberia.

All of this is an indication that not all runaways and newly freed slaves who came into Floyd County slipped through and left in the dead of night. Some stayed and attempted to become a part of the established black community. Although the newspaper complained loud and long, there was really no way of strictly enforcing the Exclusion Act.

Though settlement in Indiana by blacks was not legal after 1851,[43] the reports in local newspapers suggest that the black population figure in Floyd County continued to rise as the nation came closer to war and as the institution of slavery began falling apart. The 1860 Floyd County census, however, does not show much growth. The jump from 1850 to 1860 was relatively small and showed an increase of only 175 African Americans. This number may have seemed enormous to the biased *Ledger,* but it may also indicate some inaccuracies. The census takers may have had a problem with an accurate count of blacks during this time period for several reasons. Not all former slaves had surnames and in any case many whites assumed they had none. Therefore, inconsistencies in the use of particular names developed. Often several families were crammed into small dwellings making it difficult to know who belonged to whom. We know for a fact that many names were misspelled. Inaccuracies in census records of blacks may also be indicative of the fear and misunderstanding that existed between the races at the time, a fear perpetuated by the fact that many blacks lived in isolation from the white community. Additionally, some new arrivals were on Indiana soil illegally with no permanent address and evaded being counted in the census. The census count may also indicate that blacks were on the move, coming into Indiana through Floyd County but, after remaining temporarily, moving farther north. The 1870 census shows a bigger jump in the black population, up from 757 in 1860 to 1,210 ten years later. The greater share of newcomers were moving into the upper parts of the first, third and fifth wards where there was already a concentration of blacks.

Perhaps no other event shows the racial difficulties in New Albany at that time more than the race riot of 1862. Racial tension had been growing during the decade before the Civil War, and the attempts made to keep the black population under control also kept the fears of the biased, white population at bay, at least temporarily. But any tranquility there might have been was swept away by the 1860s. In August of 1860 a crowd of young men gathered at the Market House with the intention of heading for West Union, home to most of the city's African Americans, in order to inflict punishment on the African Americans for apparently disobeying the Exclusion Act of 1851. The town marshal, Thomas Akers, was able to calm the crowd by promising he would have posters printed cautioning "runaway and freed negroes" from moving into town and warning those already living in New Albany from harboring newcomers. Marshal Akers' poster read:

> *Caution to Negroes.*— As the residence of many persons of color in this city and vicinity, is in violation of the constitution and laws of Indiana, and their recent imprudent conduct has become the occasion of a good deal of excitement in our

midst, and given some apprehensions of violence against them, I call upon all our citizens to contribute their influence to the maintenance of order and quiet, and the prevention of violence, and I request and admonish all negroes of the class above referred to, that they seek safety by leaving this city and vicinity within three days from August 8, 1860, or they will be dealt with according to law; and other persons of color are hereby cautioned against harboring any negroes who may be here unlawfully.
Thomas Akers, City Marshal
New Albany, August 7, 1860[44]

Tension continued to mount during the Civil War as Union troops moved through the South, liberating slaves, more and more of them crossing state lines to reach the north side of the Ohio River. Some arrived under deplorable conditions and in every stage of hunger, sickness and destitution. In the Tuesday paper of July 22, 1862, the *New Albany Daily Ledger* reported that two white men had been shot, one of them killed, at the hands of one or more "negroes" the night before. The *Ledger*, in denouncing the act of violence, blamed it on the "unhappy condition of the country and the discussions in Congress of the rights and wrongs of negroes," which the editors believed unquestionably inspired a portion of the "negro" population with an "exalted idea of their own importance." The newspaper goes on to say:

> The number of colored persons whose lawful home is in this city is not large, and we do not believe, as a general thing, they are vicious. There are a number of negroes here, however, — who do not belong here; who are in the State in violation of law. These can be removed peaceably and effectually, without a resort to violence, and this should be done.
>
> The man who killed Locke and shot at Lansford, we doubt not, will be arrested and punished. But, even in a moment of just resentment, and when the whole community is justly incensed at this atrocious murder, let us sincerely hope the innocent will not be punished for the deeds of the guilty.[45]

However, the newspaper's warning went unheeded and crowds of men and young boys began gathering on the corners and moved about New Albany in search of blacks. At approximately 8:00 a.m. on that same day, July 22, two African American men were captured on Market Street near the Market House and were beaten in a dreadful manner. They were able to escape with their lives, but a few hours later, two more were attacked with stones and clubs on Market Street near Lower Second and were so dreadfully beaten that one of them died.

At the same time, a large and excited crowd gathered and started toward "Daytown," a northern suburb of the city, where they found several other African American men, all of whom were attacked and beaten with clubs and bricks. One was shot and killed. Around 12:00 noon a black man who worked on the ram *Monarch*, and who had been sick in the hospital, was attacked on Market Street. He was beaten in such an inhumane manner that his face and head were literally "pounded into a jelly."[46] Somehow he was able to reach safety in a house in that vicinity and thus escaped death. A black man boarding at the Israel House was attacked and "shockingly pounded," but he escaped inside. The mob pursued him, but Mrs. Israel barred the doors and refused to allow the crowd entrance.

The rioters continued to pick up white men and by 2:00 p.m., nearly 200 men and boys headed for West Union where most of the blacks resided. Here three or four "negroes" were found and cruelly beaten. They were pounded with clubs, bricks and boulders until they were near death. Adding insult to injury, they were left to the mercies of a gang of nine- to twelve-year-old boys, who pelted them with stones, yelling, "'We'll kill the d__d niggers,' and so forth."[47]

While this was going on, the crowd found a black farmer at work in his field in West Union, stacking barley. He was up on the stack, where he sat for some time amid a shower of stones. The crowd called him down from the stack, but somehow he was able to talk himself out of any further harm or danger. The newspaper reported that to their knowledge, this was the only black who escaped a beating throughout the entire day.

At 4:00 p.m., another black man was returning from Louisville with a load of stone, driving his team of horses along State Street toward his home in the north end of town. He was attacked by the mob, dragged from his wagon and fearfully beaten. He managed to escape and ran for his life, pursued by the crowd, down Oak Street to Lower Second and, at the corner of Lower Second and Spring Street, he took refuge in a house. The mob dragged him out and would have murdered him except for Mayor Alexander S. Burnett, a native of Virginia who lived nearby at 277 Market Street, and Benjamin Lockwood, a Presbyterian and tanner from Delaware, who both came to his rescue. Lockwood soon retreated amid a shower of stones, but Mayor Burnett, who was not a young man (63 years of age), persisted, managed to pick the man up, protect him with his own body and lock him in jail for safety. The man, however, did not survive his injuries. The mob continued to roam the city of New Albany. In the evening they headed for the homes of other black residents who lived outside of the restricted African American "ghettos." They visited the home of George Washington Carter on Upper Eighth Street. The family stayed behind locked doors in safety, but the mob ruined their garden and vineyards.[48]

A patrol of armed soldiers was called in to guard New Albany during the night, but despite that, the mob gathered at the jail and demanded the keys so they could get at the black prisoners and the guns that were inside. They threatened to batter down the jail door with a cannon but were not successful. The rioters continued their rampage into the next day, destroying the property of blacks until the riot finally abated after thirty hours of killing and wanton destruction.

A week after the race riot, the *Ledger* began denying that any black women or children had been molested or injured as had been reported earlier. They changed their story to suggest that perhaps in one or two instances women and children had been injured but only one seriously. They also reported that Mr. Lansford, the white man who was shot and injured, was recovering slowly from his wound. The riots in New Albany created a panic among blacks, particularly the men, and many families began their exodus out of New Albany. At least thirty families were counted leaving the city, and a large number of young people who held jobs on the river changed their residence from New Albany to Louisville. The newspaper took this opportunity to blame the race riot on the abolitionist movement by stating: "They fly to a slave state to enjoy that liberty and security which is denied them in a free state, and this is one of the legitimate, the inevitable results of the efforts of the abolitionists for an equality of the races."[49] At this time the fear and panic also spread to black communities north of New Albany such as that of Lick Creek near Chambersburg, which experienced a mass exodus. A black resident from New Albany traveled north to Bedford during the last week of July 1862, to visit one of his black friends. He was urged to leave town immediately, but even so, a crowd followed him into the country and beat him in a terrible manner.[50]

Again, on the night of May 18, 1863, there was fear of a race riot in New Albany. Alexander Martin, a lifelong member of Third Presbyterian church, lived at the corner of Oak and upper Tenth Street. He was captain of the 38th Indiana Volunteers, Company H, under B. F. Scribner, and home on medical leave recuperating from an injury suffered during the Civil War. Martin intervened on behalf of an African American in order to protect him from assault by a crowd that was stoning him near Martin's house.[51]

Other isolated, racially motivated incidents continued to occur after the Civil War in New Albany, some of which nearly erupted into full-scale riots. On December 26, 1865, race riots nearby occurred in Jeffersonville; fighting in Corydon, Indiana, broke out several days later.[52]

The controversy over the slavery issue in the political New Albany newspapers gives us a vivid picture of attitudes of the editors and many constituents in the New Albany community toward slavery in general and blacks in particular. In southern Indiana the *Ledger* was the most widely read newspaper of the day. Its broad subscription base certainly had a negative influence on readers' attitudes about blacks—runaway slaves or free. The New Albany police force also saw it as their duty to uphold the Exclusion Act and keep new African Americans from settling within the boundaries of Floyd County and the State of Indiana as a whole. There were those in Floyd County, however, who did not agree with the attitudes expressed by the *Ledger*. We turn now to an examination of a variety of anti-slavery attitudes and efforts that also existed in Floyd County, some of which were more humane and concerned about African Americans as people than were others.

Chapter 3
Anti-Slavery Sentiment: Political and Social

Presidential candidate Stephen A. Douglas[1] spoke in Louisville at the end of September in the year 1860 and came through the New Albany train station on his way to Chicago. "Some people beat on his back, pulled at his coat and jeered him, all the while cheering for Lincoln in his ears."[2] Douglas apparently did not have any Democrats around him at the time for protection, and the New Albany citizens who abused him may have been among those who were critical of his support of the Kansas-Nebraska Act, believing he was only attempting to get the Southern vote.[3]

The anti-slavery issue was a complicated one and had many different meanings. A slaveowner who saw slavery as being economically inefficient, *i.e.,* his slaves became sick and died or they ran away, could be called "anti-slavery." There were those who called themselves "Free Soilers." They were people who wanted to leave slavery alone in the states where it already existed but did not want to see it spread to the new territories. There were those who spoke out against it from a political perspective or from the pulpit but who, when faced with the opportunity, would not become personally involved. At the end of the spectrum were the activists. The "gradualists" thought slavery should be done away with step by step. The "immediatists" or "abolitionists" were those who were fanatical and would go to any length to abolish slavery. William Lloyd Garrison, a white leader in the abolitionist movement, was such an individual. His followers became known as "Garrisonians."

That there was a strong core of Republican Lincoln supporters in Floyd County is evidenced by the fact that New Albany had a company of "Wide Awakes."[4] The Wide Awakes were composed of young Lincoln supporters who dressed alike in colorful uniforms and marched in parades at Republican rallies carrying torches and flags. Often roman candles and rockets were set off as they marched along the streets in parade. The first Wide Awake chapter began at Hartford, Connecticut, and spread quickly over the country. The Wide Awakes could often be heard chanting, "Free Soil, Free Labor, Free Men, Fremont!" as they marched.[5] James Smith, whose family belonged to Second Presbyterian Church and whose father, Isaac P. Smith, was the architect and builder of that church, wrote a letter to his brother Sam in 1860. He stated that he had knowledge of a man connected with the *Ledger* office who had been converted from being a "Douglas man" to being a "Lincoln supporter" after hearing a strong Republican speech given in New Albany by Caleb B. Smith (no relationship to the Isaac P. Smith family). "I know others who have changed their opinions, some of whom you are acquainted with and would be astonished if I was to mention their names. The Republicans in this section of the country are awake and doing…."[6] Nevertheless, because of the widely read *New Albany Daily Ledger,* the anti-slavery citizens of Floyd County did not have a published voice that spoke for them as did those with pro-slavery views.

Probably the earliest anti-slavery movement in Indiana was that which was directed toward preventing the introduction of slavery into the Indiana Territory. Wesley G. Scott, son of John Scott, authored the Scott family memoirs, which speak of the struggle these early Floyd County settlers had in dealing with the idea of introducing slavery into Indiana Territory.[7] It would, of course, be easy if we could label people and draw a box around those who were anti-slavery and another around those who were pro-slavery. Unfortunately, things are not that simple, particularly when dealing with a sensitive issue such as slavery. John B. Norman, the *Ledger* editor, with his strong anti-black bias, for example, was typical of many citizens of the time in that he was also extremely pro–Union. Most likely his pro-slavery attitude sprang from the belief that the breakup of the slavery system would threaten the Union.

An example of the ambiguity involved here is that of Seth Woodruff, sometimes referred to as the "Father of New Albany" because of his versatility in helping New Albany establish itself. Seth Woodruff came from New Jersey to the "Falls of the Ohio" in 1817. He traveled by stage to Pittsburgh with his wife and five children and on to Louisville by flatboat. Written history tells us that "He was strongly opposed to slavery and outspoken on the subject as well. He did not find Louisville to his liking and crossed to New Albany in the fall of 1817. He was a most versatile man who served as magistrate, tavern keeper, harness setter, bricklayer, stone mason and Baptist preacher."[8] Records show that in 1821 citizens of New Albany, led by Judge Seth Woodruff, rescued a free African American by the name of "Moses" (no surname given), who was also a citizen of New Albany, from the hands of a Kentucky posse of forty-three armed men. They represented Abraham Fields of Kentucky who claimed Moses was his runaway slave.[9] Woodruff suspected there would be trouble and requested that Colonel Paxson, part of the Indiana militia, have a group of armed men present to preserve order. Woodruff was determined that Moses should have a fair trial. When Moses showed proof that he was born in Clark County, Indiana, and had never been a slave, Squire Bassett pronounced him a free man. A fight ensued between the Kentuckians and a gathering of interested New Albanians, and the Kentuckians were forced to retreat without their man. "Subsequently," reported L. A.

Williams in his history of the county, "the negroes, understanding that they would find protection in New Albany, flocked in there in such numbers that they became a nuisance, and the people at one time gathered and shipped a squad of them down the river with positive instructions not to return."[10] This story shows the early presence of an anti-black bias along the northern shore of the Ohio River. For all his strong community presence and influence, Woodruff was not able to bring his "antislavery" influence to bear on every incident. Further research on Woodruff turned up some revealing and contradictory information about him in the Floyd County court records. On February 5, 1839, Seth Woodruff purchased one Jemina Stubblefield from Jane Van De Graff of Fayette County, Kentucky, and brought her to Floyd County as his property. He did not formally set Jemina Stubblefield free until April 16, 1850.[11] Woodruff died on August 12, 1852. He presents for us an example of how complicated the issue of slavery became for those living in a border state.

Hinton Rowan Helper

Abolitionism had other sides that affected attitudes in Southern Indiana. In 1857, a white man by the name of Hinton Rowan Helper published a book titled *The Impending Crisis of the South: How to Meet It*. Helper lived in North Carolina in relative poverty and did not own any slaves. He was an abolitionist who believed the inefficiency of slavery was causing an economic decline in the South. He set out to prove that fact through the use of statistics. Because the South drew a line between the races, Helper's attitude was alarming to the Southerner because he drew a line between upper- and lower-class whites. His key to "class" was whether or not one was a slaveowner. Although an "abolitionist," Helper had a strong anti-black bias and supported the idea that slavery should be abolished and blacks deported. His ideas, though extremely controversial, were picked up by the Republican Party and used for political purposes. The first session of the Thirty-sixth Congress dealt with Helper's writings when congressmen from the new Republican party sought to receive endorsement of Helper's book so that it could be distributed in the border states. Since *The Impending Crisis* was written for Southerners, and many Southerners had moved into the Old Northwest territory, the heavy distribution of the book there was important to secure the Republican vote. Sixty-eight Republican congressmen signed their names to the endorsement of the distribution of *The Impending Crisis*.[12] Much political confusion resulted, but with the endorsement and support of publications such as the *New York Tribune*, copies of Helper's book were liberally distributed by the Republican Party, with special attention being given to the border states. Fifty thousand copies of Helper's *Compendium of the Impending Crisis of the South*, written in 1860, were distributed in the Old Northwest by that fall.[13]

Helper emphasized several points in his "war" against slavery. They included the idea that non-slaveholding whites should organize themselves politically and work toward making slaveholders ineligible to vote. He believed that slaveholding merchants should not be patronized and neither should one share in religious fellowship with slaveholders. He advocated that a tax be applied to slaveholders for each and every slave in his possession and that that money be used for colonization of blacks. He believed that slavery should be abolished immediately.[14]

Helper's scheme of abolishing slavery caught on. Harriett Beecher Stowe's *Uncle Tom's Cabin* had been a best seller in Indiana. By 1859 *The Impending Crisis* came in second in the state of Indiana for nonfiction books.[15] The ideas found in "Helperism" were not new to the southern Indiana area. Cassius M. Clay, a strong anti-slavery advocate from Kentucky, had already advocated these ideas in a column of the Lexington-based *True American*. Clay sought to organize the non-slaveholding whites against the slaveholder. "In his contention that slaveholders were the natural enemy of the yeomen and poor whites, he was the forerunner of Helper."[16]

Daniel Worth (1795–1862), a native of North Carolina who had moved to Indiana and become a Methodist preacher, was accused of distributing copies of Helper's book to individuals in North Carolina. *The Impending Crisis* was labeled an "incendiary publication" and was, therefore, prohibited by state law. Worth, who had returned to North Carolina from Indiana, was brought into court and formally charged in 1860. He was placed under a $3,000 bond, eventually paid for by Northern abolitionist friends such as Lewis Tappan.[17]

"Helperism" did indeed infiltrate Floyd County. Cassius M. Clay spoke in New Albany in 1860, according to the *Ledger*.[18] Among Republican Isaac P. Smith's documents and papers was a tract titled "The Poor Whites of the South: The Injury Done Them by Slavery," which espouses Helper's philosophy. Though the tract is left unsigned, it was distributed by the Republican Party in Indiana.

On May 19, 1860, the *New Albany Daily Ledger* gave an account of a New Albany resident who had gotten himself into trouble in Hopkins County, Kentucky, on account of "Helferism."[19] A slave owner, Edward Sloan, from the Madisonville, Kentucky, area, observed a white stranger in a clearing near his home in earnest conversation with Sloan's slaves. As soon as Sloan approached them, the man rode off into the woods. Sloan noticed that he was riding with heavy saddlebags across his horse. He demanded of his slaves to know who the man was and what he had wanted. Only one slave, Sam, would divulge that the man had wanted the slaves to murder Sloan and his family, burn all the buildings, take the best horses and meet a band of "Helperites" on the Ohio River bank across from Evansville, Indiana, where they would receive help getting across. Sloan later learned that there were at least fifteen "Helperites" in Hopkins County, Kentucky. An alarm was sounded and the stranger was soon captured at the home of a free black. He admitted to being a "Helperite" and gave his name as "Sanders" (Saunders) from New Albany. When the contents of his saddlebags were examined, it was discovered they were full of Hinton R. Helper

> ☞ A careful perusal of the following is commended to all who feel an interest in the elevation of the white as well as the colored race. It is a very clear exhibition of the condition of the mass of the white population in the slave States.

THE POOR WHITES OF THE SOUTH.

THE INJURY DONE THEM BY SLAVERY.

"Be the sin, the dangers, and evils of Slavery all our own. We compel, we ask, none to share them with us."—*Letter of Governor Hammond of South Carolina to Thomas Clarkson.*

The number of slaveholders in the slave States of this Union, as ascertained by the census returns of 1850, was three hundred and forty-seven thousand five hundred and twenty-five. An average of five persons and seven-tenths to a family, as assumed by the Superintendent of the Census, would give 1,980,894 as the number of persons interested as slaveholders in their own right, or by family relation. The whole number of whites in the slaveholding States being 6,222,418, the slaveholding proportion is a fraction short of 32 per cent.

The Superintendent of the Census, Professor De Bow, says of the number, 347,525, returned slave-owners. Alabama, Mississippi, and Louisiana, with 897,531 slaves, return 73,081 slave-owners. The relative excess of slave-owners returned in Virginia, Maryland, and the District of Columbia, must be attributed, in part, to the inclusion of a relatively larger number of "slave-hirers." Upon the whole, it may safely be concluded that at least seven-tenths of the whites in the slave States are not slave-owners, either in their own right or by family relation. The number of white males in the slave States, aged twenty-one years and upward, in 1850, was 1,490,892.

Considering that the number of 347,525, re-

Mid-nineteenth century tract distributed in the border states by the Republican party. It espouses the doctrines of Hinton Rowan Helper. (Courtesy Isaac P. Smith Letters and Papers)

books, *New York Tribunes* [20] and William H. Seward speeches.[21] After this story was released, the *Ledger* editor claimed it was probably a hoax as "there are few of the abolitionist stripe in New Albany and the doctrines of that faction meet with no favor from our citizens."[22]

Tabloid journalism was popular during this time, and this story suggests that such was used. If the story is true, however, the encouragement toward violence was undoubtedly a direct result of Helper's vitriolic philosophy. In his *Impending Crisis*, Helper demanded of the slaveowner,

> It is for you to decide whether we are to have justice peaceably or by violence, for whatever consequences may follow, we are determined to have it one way or the other. Do you aspire to become the victims of white nonslaveholding vengeance

by day, and of barbarous massacre by the negroes at night? Would you be instrumental in bringing upon yourselves, your wives and your children, a fate too horrible to contemplate?[23]

Furthermore, it is said that John Brown had ordered copies of Helper's *Compendium*, giving Brown the impetus he needed to carry out his violent raid in Virginia.[24]

Although the Republican party thought that spreading the ideas of Helper in the border states would assist them in getting the vote, it is difficult to say how much of an impact Helperism actually had in Floyd County. It was not a topic broached much by the Floyd County newspapers during that time. It is doubtful the *Ledger* editor had even read Helper's books since he used the word "Helferism" rather than "Helperism." Additionally, the same editor said, "There are few of the abolitionist stripe in New Albany and the doctrines of that faction meet with no favor from our citizens," which probably shows he did not have a deep understanding of Helper's particular brand of abolitionist philosophy.

The American Colonization Society

The American Colonization Society, an organization that sought to resettle free blacks in Liberia, was founded in 1816–17. It was popular among many anti-slavery people throughout the country as a way of ending slavery. Particularly in Indiana, it met with a favorable reception because of state legislation that already excluded blacks. The effort continued and by 1829 the Indiana Colonization Society had come into existence, though it did not receive financial support from the state until 1851.[25]

In 1836 a formal colonization society was established in New Albany by R. R. Gurley, secretary of the American Colonization Society.[26] Trotter states in his book, *River Jordan,* that interest in the movement generally declined by 1840 as the abolitionist and anti-slavery movements gained momentum.[27] The fact that a colonization society in New Albany had its beginning in 1836 may be an indication there was no abolitionist or anti-slavery effort moving forward there. There was some Floyd County interest in colonization before 1836, however. First Presbyterian Church records show that collections were taken for the "Colonization Society" and the sum of $13 was given in 1832.[28] In 1833 Robert Downey, a New Albany resident, presented the idea that much money could be raised for the colonization effort by selling shares at $1 each. The New Albany *Gazette* endorsed the idea. Downey believed that as much as $10 million could be raised by this method. But only $115 was raised in New Albany as a result of the "Downey Plan."[29]

Financial support from the state in 1851 must have been the impetus behind a public meeting held at the courthouse in New Albany "for those who favor a national plan of colonizing Africa."[30] James Mitchell, a black Methodist minister from

Indianapolis who was active in the state colonization effort, published the following notice, which appeared in the New Albany papers on a daily basis for a period of time. It preyed upon the sentiments of religious and patriot folk.

> Colonization Notice
>
> The ministers and churches of Indiana will please remember the Fourth of July celebration, in aid of the colonization enterprise, and on the Sabbath following the anniversary of our National independence, take up a collection in such churches as regard this work with favor.
>
> The State Society stands much in need of funds to carry on the work within our own State and we now respectfully pray that good men will come to our aid, and enable us to meet the many calls that colored men make on our Society for a passage to Liberia.
>
> James Mitchell, agent
> Indianapolis
> July 2, 1851[31]

Mitchell supported this notice by publishing excerpts of letters from blacks who had emigrated. The letters that were printed in the *New Albany Daily Ledger* generally showed the colonization effort in a flattering light. The "colored convention" held in Indianapolis August 1, 1851, however, adopted by an overwhelming majority a resolution stating that should the laws of Indiana become so oppressive as to be intolerable, "people of color" were encouraged to emigrate to Canada, Jamaica, Mexico, New Granada or Central America, but not to Liberia. The Indianapolis *State Journal* reported that there was a great prejudice in the minds of the members of the convention against Liberia.[32] In 1852, however, James Mitchell claimed he had letters of application from seventy-five people in Indiana willing to leave for Liberia. But there is a lack of evidence showing how many actually went in that year.[33] In 1853 it seems thirty-three blacks left from Indiana, and in 1854 fourteen left the state for Liberia.[34] Over the years several white preachers also came to New Albany attempting to sell the idea of colonization. The primary mover in this endeavor was Rev. W. W. Hibben, a Methodist preacher from Madison, Indiana. He was an agent of the American Colonization Society of Indiana who frequently visited New Albany after the Civil War started. When in New Albany, he normally spoke at Centenary and Wesley Methodist churches regarding the emigration of blacks.[35] Henry Ward Beecher also supported the movement, traveled to New Albany and spoke on colonization from time to time.

The colonization society in New Albany was made up of religious people who probably meant well, thinking colonization would not only emancipate the slaves but also give them a new start in a "homeland" where they could govern themselves and live in freedom. But colonization efforts there, as well as elsewhere, were tinted with an anti-black bias. In the end, the colonization effort was a failure. Many blacks were against the idea because they wanted their rights on American soil — not foreign soil. Frederick Douglass, for one, was against the idea of colonization.[36] His friend, Byrd

Parker, pastor of the African Methodist Episcopal church in New Albany from 1850 to 1853, supported Douglass in his anti-colonization stance.[37] In the State of Indiana, as well as other states, only a very few chose to emigrate, and there is no record of any leaving for Liberia from Floyd County.

The American Anti-Slavery Society

During the 1830s, anti-slavery organizations began springing up in the Northern states. As early as 1831, the New England Anti-Slavery Society was formed, and in 1833 the American Anti-Slavery Society was founded.[38] These organizations became stronger primarily after the passage of the Fugitive Slave Law of 1850 and centered their activities particularly where a free state bordered a slave state. Theodore Weld, leader of the 1834 student revolt at Lane Seminary near Cincinnati, formed a band of young followers who assembled in New York in the early 1830s for an intensive training session before being "turned loose to win the West." Out of Weld's efforts, an anti-slavery campaign evolved in all of the Eastern seaboard states, including the state of Maine, which is of particular interest because of a man by the name of John Dole. Dole, who was from Lincoln County, Maine,[39] and worked as a guard for the American Anti-Slavery Society along the Ohio River, was eventually assigned to work as an anti-slavery guard in New Albany.

The Maine Anti-slavery Society was established in October of 1834, and by May of 1838 the state had forty-eight abolition organizations. From the beginning, leaders of the American Anti-Slavery Society felt the best means of increasing opposition to slavery was through the use of paid agents.[40] Henry B. Stanton, also a leader in the Lane Seminary walk-out, was commissioned along with Weld to raise funds and to search for new agents for the society. He began giving anti-slavery lectures in May of 1836. That fall Rev. David Thurston, a Congregationalist preacher from Winthrop, Maine, became one of the driving forces of the anti-slavery movement in that state. His efforts for the cause of the slave appeared to be tireless as he lectured several nights in one place, making converts and establishing new societies in counties along the southwest coastal areas of Maine.

> Thurston was using the tactics of Theodore Weld, the primary voice of the agents' convention. Weld believed in staying in a community and lecturing day after day until a core of abolitionists could be created and induced to establish an anti-slavery society. Thurston was the first agent in Maine to go to so many small communities and lay the foundation for abolition....[41]

An anti-slavery organization was established in Lincoln County, Maine, on March 13–14, 1838, and there is evidence that Lincoln County residents assisted runaway slaves as they came through Maine on their way to New Brunswick.[42] Thurston had lectured in the Lincoln County villages of Wiscasset, Sheepscot, Alna, New Castle and Damariscota. Somewhere in the audience, John Dole,[43] probably from Alna, listened and was converted to the anti-slavery movement. He was eventually hired as an agent of the American Anti-slavery Society. Ichabod Codding may also have influenced Dole. Codding was recruited by Theodore Weld, commissioned in 1836 and assigned as an agent to Maine in 1838. Both Codding and Thurston were present at Wiscasset when the Lincoln County Anti-Slavery Society was established.[44] Codding later led the movement in Illinois. It is possible that Dole accompanied him there since the first mention we have of Dole's work was in Cairo, Illinois.

The first anti-slavery groups formed in Indiana were in the counties of Decatur, Jefferson and Wayne in 1836.[45] Rev. John S. Weaver, a Presbyterian pastor from Decatur County, helped form one of them. A group in Jefferson County was made up of students at Hanover College who organized on March 8, 1836. The major anti-slavery societies in the state of Indiana during that time were: Whitewater Society, Middle Fork, Wayne County; Fall Creek Society in Madison County; Western Anti-slavery Society in Morgan County and the Anti-slavery Society in Jefferson County.[46]

John Dole, employee of the American Anti-Slavery Society, assigned to work in New Albany. (Source: William M. Cockrum, *History of the Underground Railroad*)

Marion Clinton Miller, in his dissertation "The Anti-Slavery Movement in Indiana," claims that the impulse for the formation of a state society may have come from Gamaliel Bailey of Cincinnati, editor of the *Cincinnati Weekly Herald and Philanthropist*.[47] On September 12, 1838, at Milton, Indiana, men from the counties of Decatur, Wayne, Cass, Franklin, Union, Jay, Jennings, Dearborn, Fayette and Jefferson[48] met to form an anti-slavery society. James Morrow from Jefferson County was elected President, Dr. Luke Miensell, Vice-President, and Rev. A. T. Rankin and William Beard, Directors. The gatherings were called "library meetings" for the protection of the participants. There is no evidence that an anti-slavery organization existed in Floyd County, although we have the testimony of William Cockrum that the Eastern Anti-Slavery Society sent workers such as John Dole into the border counties to assist runaway slaves.

Abolitionist missionaries from the East worked the states of Ohio, Indiana and Illinois, establishing anti-slavery societies as they traveled. Charles C. Burleigh, one of Weld's group, came to Indiana and endeavored to lecture in Wayne County in the northwest part of the state, but his effort failed.[49] A representative of the American Anti-Slavery Society who also came to Indiana was Arnold Buffum.[50] He gave lectures on tour in the central, eastern and southeastern parts of the state in 1841 and established the first successful anti-slavery newspaper in Indiana, *The Protectionist,* which was published at New Garden in Wayne County. According to Cochrum, the Society was active on both sides of the Ohio River from above Pittsburgh to Cincinnati and down to Jeffersonville and New Albany on the north side of the river, Louisville on the south side, as well as the Indiana counties of Harrison, Crawford and Vanderburgh, continuing down to the Mississippi River. Cockrum claimed that there were men on duty who moved up and down the river disguised as teachers, map-makers, surveyors, peddlers, lumbermen, naturalists and geologists. The Presbyterians also sent out colporteurs to distribute Bibles and Christian literature. While carrying on their various occupations and becoming acquainted with the area, they would use their knowledge for work as spies for the Anti-Slavery Society. The colloquial language used to describe their work was "running off slaves." There was a superintendent for each of the four states—Illinois, Indiana, Ohio and Pennsylvania, who managed the men working in the assigned state. The superintendent of Indiana was J. T. Hanover, alias John Hansen.[51]

Cockrum wrote the following:

> While John Hansen was working for the Anti-Slavery League he was for two or three days every two weeks at my father's house, where he boarded off and on for five years. He was a naturalist and one time was near what is known as Snaky Point now on the Evansville and Indianapolis railroad, two and a half miles northeast of Oakland City. He was bitten by a snake and remained at my father's house for two and a half months, and came very near dying. During the time he was there, much of his mail accumulated at Princeton (just north of Evansville). I was sent there many times for it and did much of his correspondence. While he was there sick, young men came to see him from Princeton, Booneville, Petersburg, and many other places. These men were all in the employ of the Anti-Slavery League. I am yet in possession of a diary kept by Hansen during that period, also a key which was used by Hansen in making his report. Without this key, nothing in the work could be unraveled.[52]

Hansen worked and traveled over the southernmost three or four tiers of counties of Indiana pretending to represent an Eastern real estate firm from which he received large packages of mail at many of the county seats and large towns all along southern Indiana. The young men assigned to do this hazardous work under him were men who could be depended upon so as not to arouse suspicion. They were a very disciplined group and, as in any secret organization, had a code language. All that was said or done was by a number, the numbers referring to land, towns, ranges, sections and acres. The routes these men were on were called by names of timber native to the area, such as linden, oak, maple, hickory, walnut, dogwood, sassafras and beech.[53]

John Dole's role was that of an anti-slavery guard who was sent by Superintendent Hansen to New Albany. Dole had been working for the Anti-Slavery League in Cairo, Illinois. Many of the lumbermen who worked along the river supplying firewood for the steamboats were Northerners who detested slavery. Dole had previously worked in a logging camp in Maine until he was hired to come west and work for the Anti-Slavery League. After working in Illinois for a time and having trouble with a tough element in Cairo, he was sent to Evansville with a letter of introduction to Superintendent Hansen stating, "If you have any need for someone to do some real fighting, call on Dole. He has the ability and the will to do a good job."[54] Cockrum devoted an entire chapter in his book, *The Underground Railroad*, to John Dole and his anti-slavery work.[55] When Mr. Hansen sent Dole on to New Albany, he felt, "He had grit and did whatever he attempted to do well. I have no data of his work after he reached New Albany from Evansville but I feel certain that he made good wherever he was sent."[56]

To give an idea of how the American Anti-Slavery Society employees apprised slaves of the Underground Railroad, Cockrum related that they would travel south of the Ohio River, thereby carrying out the most dangerous part of the work. In many cases these men would pose as peddlers who carried large leather packs on their backs containing various small items to sell, such as jewelry, ribbons, clothing and cutlery. The employees had to be clean-cut, intelligent and sensitive and would first work their way into the confidence of the lady of the house. After asking permission to show their goods to the slaves, they would do so, bringing their merchandise back again and again over a period of time. In this way they covered a large area of the country and became acquainted with the white owners and their slaves, as well as the roads and waterways in a particular territory. After getting to know the area, they would select a slave who they felt could be trusted and talk to him about gaining his freedom. The commissioned agent would pay the slave to go out at night and speak to other slaves in the area about escaping. When two or three were ready to go, they would agree on the time and place. The peddler, working with another agent, would head for one of the crossing places on the Ohio, hopefully reaching the river before morning light.[57]

The American Anti-Slavery Society, which received its funds from wealthy supporters in the East, owned boats along the Ohio River. Several places were assigned as regular crossing points. New Albany was such a crossing point. For example, at midnight on May 14, 1855, someone from New Albany attempted to rescue slaves from the riverbank at Portland. Henry, his wife Violett and their two children were caught by a night watchman as they were waiting in a hack near the "lower ferry" for a skiff to take them to the Indiana shore. "At this juncture a skiff was seen rapidly nearing the Kentucky shore apparently from New Albany. The occupant became alarmed and fled back again to the other side of the river before any attempt could be made to catch him."[58] Another crossing place was at the mouth of Indian Creek in Harrison County.[59] There the refugees were ferried across, then conveyed to friends near Corydon, who carried them a little farther north across Washington County and a corner of Jackson County to Jennings County, then through Decatur, Rush and Fayette counties into Wayne County, "where they had an innumerable host of friends among the Quakers where they were then conveyed up to Lake Michigan and freedom."[60] Through Theodore Weld's connection with and influence in the Society and his experience at Lane Seminary, employees may have looked to the New Albany Theological Seminary student body and other Presbyterians for support. This leads us to examine the anti-slavery sentiment found within religious organizations in Floyd County including the Presbyterian and Methodist churches as well as the New Albany Theological Seminary, which existed from 1840 to 1856.

Chapter 4
Anti-Slavery Sentiment: Religious

After President Lincoln gave the Emancipation Proclamation in January of 1963, Levi Coffin, the Quaker who has been called the "Head of the Underground Railroad," came to New Albany in hopes of raising money for assisting the newly freed slaves. When he reached New Albany, he went directly to the Rev. John Guest Atterbury, pastor of Second Presbyterian Church.[1] Coffin was living in Cincinnati at the time, helping former slaves and runaways in that place. He would have known that he could find support at Second Presbyterian Church as well as from others in New Albany. We now take a closer look at a very influential segment of the early Floyd County population.

The Presbyterians

There is a strong oral tradition that associates Second Presbyterian Church with hiding fugitive slaves in the undercroft of the building. The church, constructed in 1849–1852,[2] is located on the banks of the Ohio River at the southeast corner of Third and Main (High) streets. The building was purchased in 1889 by a group of African Americans who formed Second Baptist Church,[3] and it is still used by that Baptist congregation today. The Second Presbyterian Church group had broken away from First Presbyterian Church in 1837 for reasons that are no longer entirely clear. Nevertheless, some important features of that split can be known.

At the time Second Presbyterian Church was formed, the Presbyterians had divided into the New School (N.S.) and the Old School (O.S.). First Presbyterian Church remained with the Old School, but Second Presbyterian aligned itself with the New School.[4] A mere city block separated the two churches. The New School was generally progressive in its social orientation and more consistently forthright about abolishing slavery. Additionally, New School Presbyterians were more supportive of the religious revivalist movement that took root and spread in the 1820s and 1830s with the opening of new territories in the West. Out of the religious fervor of this revivalist movement sprang temperance and benevolence groups, which in turn led to the establishment of abolitionist and anti-slavery organizations. After the passage of the Fugitive Slave Law in 1850, the law "was denounced from the pulpit by many New School Presbyterian clergymen."[5]

The revivalist movement is relevant to the present study because in 1837 Rev. Samuel K. Sneed (Snead) was called away from First Presbyterian Church in New Albany to serve the newly formed Second Presbyterian church. He was a major force in establishing "Mt. Tabor," the area north of town where revivals were held. As early as June, 1838, Second Presbyterian session records speak of converts from the Mt. Tabor revival meetings.[6] This spirit of revivalism touched members of Second Presbyterian church as well as others in New Albany and likely influenced their attitudes about social reform, benevolent activity and the anti-slavery movement. That differences between the Old and New School in Southern Indiana on the issue of slavery did exist is brought out in a letter written by Sneed to the American Home Missionary Society. It reads in part:

The Rev. Samuel K. Sneed, pastor of Second Presbyterian Church, 1837–1843. (Courtesy Stuart B. Wrege Indiana History Room, New Albany–Floyd County Public Library)

> With regard to the counties bordering on the Ohio River, we cannot do much there at present; there are old and new school Presbyterian churches in every village on the Ohio River. The majority of new school are antislavery but are waiting for the action of the General Assembly to set them free from all possible upcoming action. The old school are antislavery also but wait for God to sanctify and purify his church from all sin of slavery as well as other sins when he will think fit to do so.[7]

Sneed's observations show that the Old School Presbyterians approached slavery more cautiously than the New School. The Old School was dragging its feet on the whole issue, possibly out of fear of giving offense to Southern brothers and sisters who owned slaves. From 1850 to 1861, the New School Presbyterians were completely engrossed in the slavery issue because of the internal problems slavery was creating.[8] At their General Assembly meeting in 1857, they moved to cut off their relationship with slaveholding congregations in the South.[9] However, Second Presbyterian Church (N.S.) session records in New Albany during the Civil War period, as well as histories published in newspapers and pamphlets after the Civil War, do not

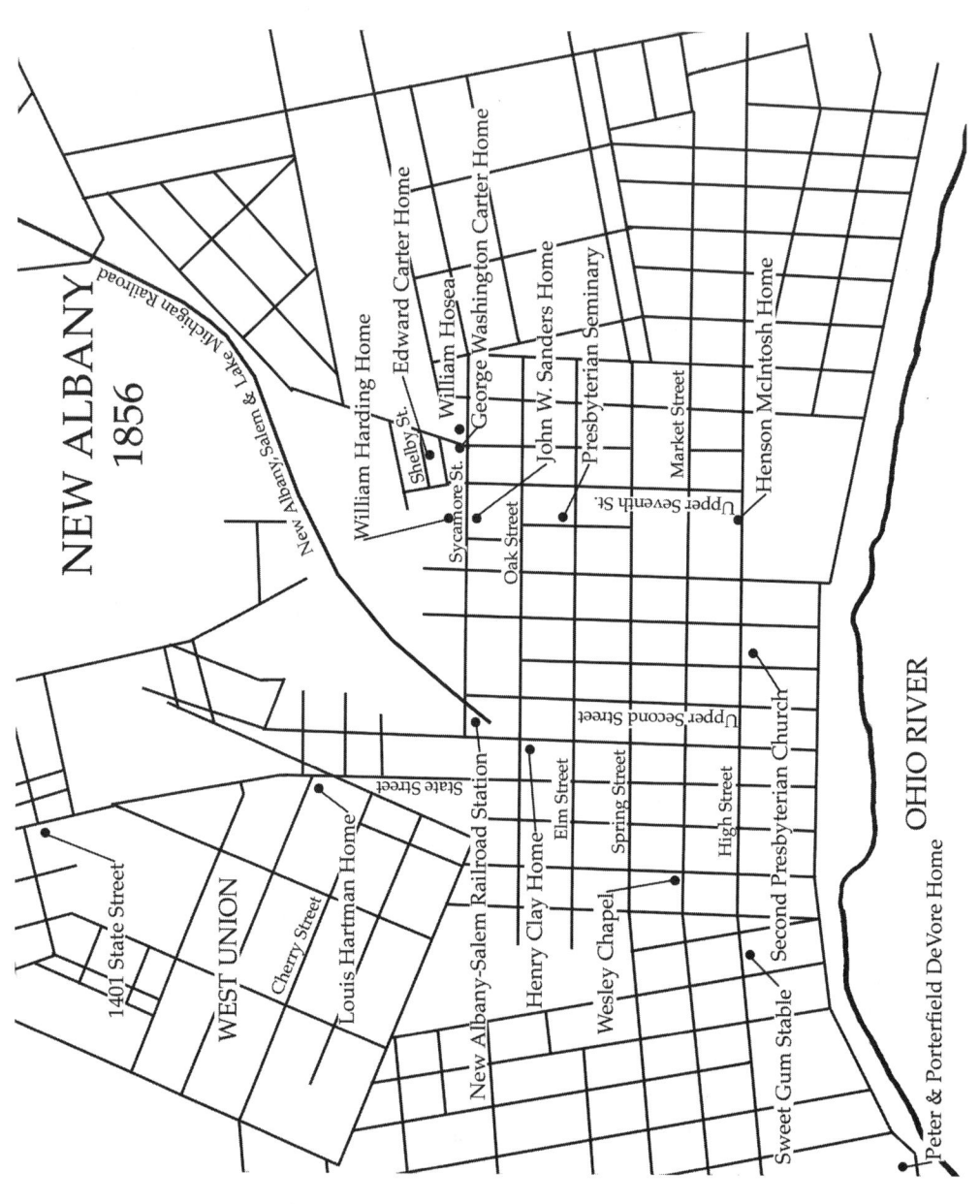

broach the subject of slavery. Occasionally, an obscure sentence such as that recorded on August 29, 1847, is included, and one can only guess at its meaning: "A number of meetings of session have been held recently, of which no record was kept, at which business pertaining to the welfare of the church was transacted."[10] This complete silence on slavery, the heart and center of controversy in the Presbyterian Church during that time, was apparently an attempt to throw a veil of obscurity over the true personality of this parish and to protect it and its members from the scathing rhetoric of the *Ledger* and worse, from the accusing finger of its neighbor across the river— Louisville, Kentucky.

On the presbytery level, however, the New School expressed its anti-slavery views openly. During Sneed's ministry in Southern Indiana, he was a strong spokesman against slavery. For example, in 1840 he and his elder, John Loughmiller, attended the Presbytery of Salem (N.S.) meeting in Brownstown. There Sneed presented, to be sent on to the General Assembly, an anti-slavery memorial that he himself had drafted and edited. The memorial was unanimously adopted and contains succinct anti-slavery, if not abolitionist, language. It speaks of the equality of the Caucasian and African races, of the institution of slavery as being in violation of Christian doctrine and goes as far as to encouraging total emancipation.[11] (See Appendix B for the full text of this memorial.) Furthermore, in April of 1841, the Salem Presbytery (N.S.) sent out its own request asking all presbyteries to answer the question, "Shall the sin of slavery be tolerated in the Presbyterian church?" with the intent of sending the answers to the General Assembly. Even though Sneed was the one who brought up the issue of slavery often at the presbytery meetings, there is no sign in the session records that show he or his elder, John Loughmiller, brought this ultimate question in the form of a resolution back to Second Presbyterian church.[12] It is difficult to believe, however, that he kept silent about it on his own turf.

Many of the Presbyterians who settled the New Albany–Floyd County area were against slavery. Unlike Hinton Rowan Helper, who came from Southern, impoverished back country, these people came from Northeastern free states or moved to the area from slave states where they felt uncomfortable. Nearby Springville in Clark County was also a center for abolitionism.[13] They were attracted to the Old Northwest and New Albany in particular, because the Scribner brothers, educated people from Albany, New York, and Morristown, New Jersey, had begun to circulate a handbill in an attempt to attract the merchant class and other Presbyterians like themselves. The handbill read in part,

> New Albany. This town is just laid out, with spacious streets, public squares, markets, etc. It is situated on the bank of the Ohio River, at the crossing place from Louisville to Vincennes, about two miles below the falls, in the Indiana Territory, and affords a beautiful and commodious harbor.... July 8, 1813[14]

Opposite: **Map of New Albany, Indiana, circa 1856.**

The language in this handbill is typical of others distributed at the time, but it must have been influential because in response to its circulation, many Easterners headed west to the newly formed "New" Albany. (See Appendix A for a list of people transferring to Second Presbyterian Church.)

Ashbel S. Wells, an early Presbyterian missionary to reach the area and one who worked for the American Home Missionary Society,[15] wrote Rev. Absalom Peters at the home office in New York about conditions in New Albany:

> With regard to the state of things in this place,.... There has been a steady advance in piety, knowledge and benevolent action among the members of the church. The attendance in public worship is becoming more general and the fixed attention given to the preached word is such as to justify the expectation that the present is a seed time and that in due season we shall reap if we faint not. At our next communion it is expected that several will join us by profession and certificates so that there will be between 70 & 80 members in regular church standing. The religious influence now felt in this place from the operation of the various Societies and churches is seen in the quiet and peaceful conduct of our citizens and in the observance of the Sabbath in a very happy manner.... Since my arrival the Furnaces and Boxing Mills have been stopped on the Sabbath and far less work if any is done in the ship yards on that day.[16]

We have made the point that Sneed was a presbytery leader in anti-slavery discussions. But he presents another example of the complexity surrounding the subject of slavery in Floyd County. The fine line between the systems of slavery in the South and indenture north of the Ohio River showed itself in Sneed. He was from Kentucky and grew up in a family that owned slaves. While living in Kentucky, he was a member of the Transylvania Presbytery before becoming pastor of the First Presbyterian Church in New Albany in 1832. When Sneed moved from Kentucky to Indiana, he brought with him a slave, Elsie Willett, then an eleven-year-old girl. She lived with and worked in Sneed's home, ostensibly as an indentured servant, from 1832 until July 4, 1839. When she turned eighteen years old, under the indenture agreement, she was to become a free woman. However, Sneed did not go through the Floyd County court system to legally grant Elsie her freedom until December 9, 1858. Sneed stated in the document that "The said Elsie Willett was taken by me to Indiana with a knowledge of the laws of said state upon the subject of slavery — and with the intent that said Elsie Willett should be and become free."[17] One could say that Sneed "bought Elsie into freedom," but it took him more than eighteen years after her release from "indenture" to publicly grant her that freedom. The slavery issue must have presented a personal dilemma for Sneed. Whether or not he ever admitted he "owned" Elsie to his parishioners and to the presbytery remains a mystery. He may have rationalized that Elsie was his indentured servant and never applied the whole issue of slavery to his own situation. A parallel case was found in Harrison County, Indiana, and involved John George Pfrimmer, a minister in the United Brethren in Christ denomination. He immigrated from France to a farm near Corydon,

Indiana, in 1808 and purchased a slave, Betsey, and her child, Letina, from John Elliott of Knox County, Kentucky, in 1811. Ten years later he represented Indiana at the Indiana State General Conference, which passed a resolution "That all slavery, in every sense of the word, be totally prohibited ... in our community."[18]

Following Sneed at Second Presbyterian, the reverends E. R. Beadle and John Black, doctors of divinity, served only a short time, each resigning due to ill health. John Bishop, formerly a pastor in Plymouth, Indiana, was installed at Second Presbyterian on November 1, 1846. He remained in New Albany until October 21, 1850, when the American Home Missionary Society assigned him to the Indiana counties of Lawrence, Jackson, Crawford, Dubois and Monroe.[19] Bishop attended Lane Seminary. His father, Dr. Robert H. Bishop, a strong anti-slavery man, was President of Miami University in the 1830s, and a trustee at Lane Seminary. After he left New Albany, John Bishop felt free from his mission station in Bedford, Indiana, to write the following confidential letter to the Society:

> From our geographical position we have received much detriment from slavery since the southern parts of Indiana and Illinois were originally settled by Southerners of the most bigoted sort. This class still furnishes the most intolerant defenders of slavery and opposers of Emancipation. Many have been slave catchers and would have introduced slavery itself into the Northwest Territory if they had had their way. Religiously, these people were associated with the Baptist order — Regular, antinomian, two-seed Baptists, or as they are now generally designated Whiskey Baptists. But new settlers are improving this society. Another important issue is the relation of the border Presbytery to the South and Slave states. I wish the Society had not a man in the South. But slavery will fall eventually, like the walls of Jericho. Then it will be well to have an army camped outside, for when the final shout is raised every man may go right up before him and possess the land.[20]

In another letter written August 2, 1852, he asked for additional help — a man who would work with him and be capable of conducting revivals. "I believe firmly that such a man, just now, might turn Southern Indiana into a Western New York."[21]

Following Bishop, John Guest Atterbury, from Detroit, Michigan, was installed as pastor of Second Presbyterian Church, the same day as the dedication of the new edifice. He served from August of 1851 to July, 1866.[22] Sneed, Bishop and Atterbury continued to have a relationship with each other in the presbytery, since the two former pastors remained in the area working for the American Home Missionary Society. Additionally, John Atterbury's brother, William Atterbury, was pastor at Second Presbyterian church (N.S.) at Madison, Indiana, from 1854 to 1865. This continued contact with one another could have helped to strengthen these pastors in their anti-slavery views and give their church members support in their own anti-slavery attitudes in an otherwise hostile place.

We catch another glimpse of the anti-slavery personality of Second Presbyterian Church from Atterbury and his work in New Albany. Shortly after his installation, a religious revival took place at Second Presbyterian.[23] The guest preacher during this week-long meeting was the Rev. Henry Little. Little was a very strong anti-slavery man who spoke out openly against slavery. His home base was Madison, Indiana, but he, too, was an agent of the American Home Missionary Society. His letters to the society back in New York expressed his anti-slavery views on a regular basis. He wanted to continue working on the north side of the river in Indiana and Ohio, claiming he would rather not go into the slave states (January 1, 1845). In August of 1845 he reported to the home office that he had visited the most anti-slavery portions of his field and that the Presbyterians there thought the Society "has gone as far against slavery as can be expected of an organ of the Congregational and Presbyterian Churches. If the New School Assembly does not go further against slavery at the next meeting, both the Assembly and the American Home Missionary Society will lose some men and some churches."[24] Little, therefore, expressed the wish that the New School would take an even stronger stand against slavery. In October, 1845, he again wrote Milton Badger at the home office saying the Presbyterian statement on the slavery questions was weak and that "the American Home Missionary Society statement is about half as bad." Several years later Little brought a missionary named John G. Fee to the attention of the Society. Fee, an outspoken and militant abolitionist from Lewis County, Kentucky, was also serving as an employee of the Society. He later resigned to protest the failure of the General Assembly to take a stronger anti-slavery stand.[25] Little wrote that he supported Fee and implied in his letter that he would support abolitionists generally on pragmatic grounds.[26] Little's presence as a guest preacher for a week-long revival at the invitation of Atterbury is indicative of the anti-slavery, if not abolitionist, attitudes present at Second Presbyterian.

As the Civil War began, Second Presbyterian established a mission church in New Albany. It was located on State Street between Green and Clay in the area of West Union, where the majority of blacks lived. Atterbury had reported on May 25, 1861, that a committee making home visits in anticipation of starting the mission had discovered the painful fact that a large number of families had been entirely excluded from all the evangelical influences of the New Albany churches. As a result, on February 3, 1862, E. Mann was appointed superintendent of the new mission. The women of the church began sewing garments. Poor children in New Albany were thus provided with clothing and shoes.[27] This endeavor continued after the Civil War when, in addition to that ongoing mission effort, a member, Emma Graham, began teaching in Atlanta for the Western Freedmen's Aid Society. On October 3, 1870, the elders and deacons met and appointed committees to canvass the church for additional funds for the West Union mission. This is due, no doubt, to the fact that there was another influx of blacks at that time; a new and larger building for the mission was completed July 5, 1871.[28] It is believed that this work, both before and after the Civil War, was tolerated by the *Ledger* and those who supported its ideas because it

4. Anti-Slavery Sentiment: Religious

The Rev. John Guest Atterbury, pastor of Second Presbyterian Church, 1852–1866. (Courtesy Stuart B. Wrege Indiana History Room, New Albany–Floyd County Public Library)

was considered charitable mission work and did not, therefore, place the members in the same category as that of abolitionists.[29]

There was clearly great concern at Second Presbyterian over the plight of slaves and blacks. Powerful testimony is found in a sermon preached by Atterbury at the height of the Civil War, November 27, 1862, and recorded in part below. The sermon was titled "God in Civil Government." In view of its anti-slavery content, Atterbury was brave to deliver it publicly.[30] It was an even braver thing to publish it, which he did at the request of his elders. He set a strong example for people living in a town with a newspaper that was so viciously anti-black biased. A portion of that sermon reads:

We cannot discriminate between the acts of the national government and the state government. They are all part and parcel of one great wrong. Standing here on free soil, I am less concerned to point to the cruel laws of the south, than I am to the cruel contempt of the people and laws of the north. Many seem to associate all oppression with the south. But without the law of slavery have we not the spirit of it in the manner in which the blacks are treated? ... Do not the recent anti-negro riots in several of our northern cities, such as that whose disgrace we feel [he is referring to the race riot in New Albany that took place that summer in July 1862], indicate a wide-spread contempt and hatred, which constitute the bitterest oppression? ... How can we appeal to the air of freedom and benevolence, the recognition of the common brotherhood of man, in our constitution, when we are violating it in our treatment of the colored race? It will not be enough that we are educated, as the phrase is, "up to emancipation," if we have the spirit of oppression for the emancipated.... If we would have God's favor with us as a nation we must be right. To be right we must do right. *Right does not depend on color. God is no respecter of persons or races. He has made all of one blood, and he seeks the good of all and we must seek the good of all within our province*[31] [Emphasis added].

Other relevant facts show that Second Presbyterian Church had a relationship with the black community. After President Lincoln signed the Emancipation Proclamation on January 1, 1863, Levi Coffin, "Head of the Underground Railroad," as he was referred to, traveled around Southern Indiana soliciting funds to help contraband soldiers, their families, and newly freed and runaway slaves. It was previously mentioned that the first person he went to for help in New Albany was John Guest

Atterbury of Second Presbyterian Church. Together they visited ministers of the other New Albany churches. Interested members met at Centenary Methodist Episcopal Church to hear Coffin speak. The sum of $237 was collected for the cause.[32] Also, church records that survived from immediately after the Civil War show that Second Presbyterian supported the Freedmen's Association financially (July, 1867). The New Albany Presbyterian "Committee on the Freedmen" reported in 1872 that their denomination had the following "negro church officers" in service in the South: seventeen ordained ministers, four licentiates, five catechists and eleven teachers.[33] "Credit is due a religious group which had the pride and courage to acknowledge its interracial work in a community where the hostile *Daily Ledger* was published," said Dr. Cheaney in his study of attitudes in the press and pulpit in Indiana toward blacks.[34] Moreover, it is no coincidence that it was an African American congregation, made up primarily of former slaves, that purchased the church building from the Presbyterians in 1889. No doubt they already had a relationship with that church — both its members and the building.[35]

A brief look at some of the members of Second Presbyterian Church is helpful and sheds additional light on the personality of this church family. Session records reveal that a number of African American citizens belonged to Second Presbyterian and were ministered to by the pastors.[36] "We find the Africans 'at our doors' and are laboring as hard to convert them here on the banks of the Ohio River as ever did an agent of the Missionary Society to convert the 'Black Republicans' on the banks of the Niger," wrote the *Ledger* sarcastically.[37] John Bishop baptized a black woman on her deathbed on May 17, 1848. Floyd County court records show that the Presbyterian ministers performed marriage ceremonies for African Americans. Hannah Johnson was received into membership at Second Presbyterian in 1842 and was buried by Atterbury on January 21, 1856.[38] Levi Welch, born in Maryland in 1770, and his wife, Harriett, born in 1790 in South Carolina, transferred their church membership from Second Presbyterian to the "Colored Baptist Church" in 1845.[39] Amanda Finney, born in Massachusetts in 1814, was a servant of Dr. William Ashbel Clapp. She belonged to Second Presbyterian although Dr. Clapp was a member of First Presbyterian. Amanda lived in Clapp's home, as did another African American servant, Josephine Mitchum.[40] Amanda transferred her church membership to the "Colored Baptist Church" in 1845 along with the Welches. Harriett Hill Carter, a part of the George Washington Carter household, joined the church on October 28, 1838, and transferred to Third Presbyterian Church in April 1858.[41]

Besides the African Americans referred to above, several white members are also important for their contribution to anti-slavery attitudes in New Albany. The architect of the Second Presbyterian Church building was member Isaac P. Smith, who lived across the street and two blocks east of the church at 513 East Main Street. Smith was born in Newark, New Jersey, March 22, 1808, and married Abby H. Campbell on January 1, 1835. The Smiths came west to New Albany in 1837. Upon arrival they joined First Presbyterian church but transferred to Second Presbyterian in 1853 and remained members there. During the Civil War, Smith was quartermaster of the 23rd Regiment of Indiana Volunteers. While his regiment was stationed near Vicksburg, Tennessee, a slave, Patsy Lindsey, came into the camp for protection. Smith and others befriended Patsy. Another member of the regiment, James A. Doll, was a neighbor of Smith's and a fellow member of Second Presbyterian Church. With arrangements made by Smith, he managed to take Lindsey north with him to New Albany, though this trip would have been dangerous and difficult. It is believed Doll traveled with her by boat from Vicksburg to Memphis, to St. Louis and then up the Ohio River by steamboat to New Albany under the protection of the Union Army. The Smith family took Lindsey in and she remained at their home for some time. Abby Smith was known for her deeds of kindness and charity among the poor and needy of New Albany. "She gave of her time, heart and service to laboring among the neglected classes. The men of the city ... had unbounded confidence in her motives as well as in her judgement and cheerfully supported her in her efforts for the neglected ones by the free gifts of their money and goods," stated her obituary.[42] Isaac Smith was a political leader in first the Whig and then the Republican party; the *Ledger* called him a "Black Republican."[43] If John B. Norman exemplified the pro–Union Democrat, Isaac Smith was the exemplification of the pro–Union Republican. The First Ward meeting of the Whig party convened at his shop. He was elected chairman of the Lincoln Campaign Club, the local committee formed to elect Abraham Lincoln as President.[44] Isaac and Abby's family correspondence and a collection of political papers, sermons and speeches, some from Newark, New Jersey, reflect an interest in the politics of the day from the side of the Republican and anti-slavery sentiment.

    James Brooks, who had been converted through a revival led by Rev. Ashbel Wells, joined the Presbyterian church on September 19, 1830, and became an ordained ruling elder of Second Presbyterian Church in 1837. He was also the clerk of session from 1837 to 1851, when he was forced to step down because of problems facing him regarding the financial status of the New Albany–Salem Railroad. James Brooks, first president of the New Albany–Salem Railroad, which was formed July 1, 1847, held that position until his resignation October 1, 1858. The New Albany–Salem Railroad eventually ran all the way from New Albany to Michigan City, making the entire trip for the first time on July 4, 1854. The railroad line is a verified escape route of slaves who traveled both in the cars and followed the rails on foot as they headed north.[45] Politically, Brooks was a staunch Republican. On April 2, 1862, the Secretary of War, Edwin M. Stanton,[46] appointed him assistant quartermaster of volunteers with rank of captain. In this position he became a confidant of Stanton in matters dealing with the United States Ram Fleet and the Mississippi Marine Brigade. He generally made his headquarters in New Albany because of its strategic place on the Ohio River. He purchased steamboats, had gunboats built, ordered coal and other supplies, and

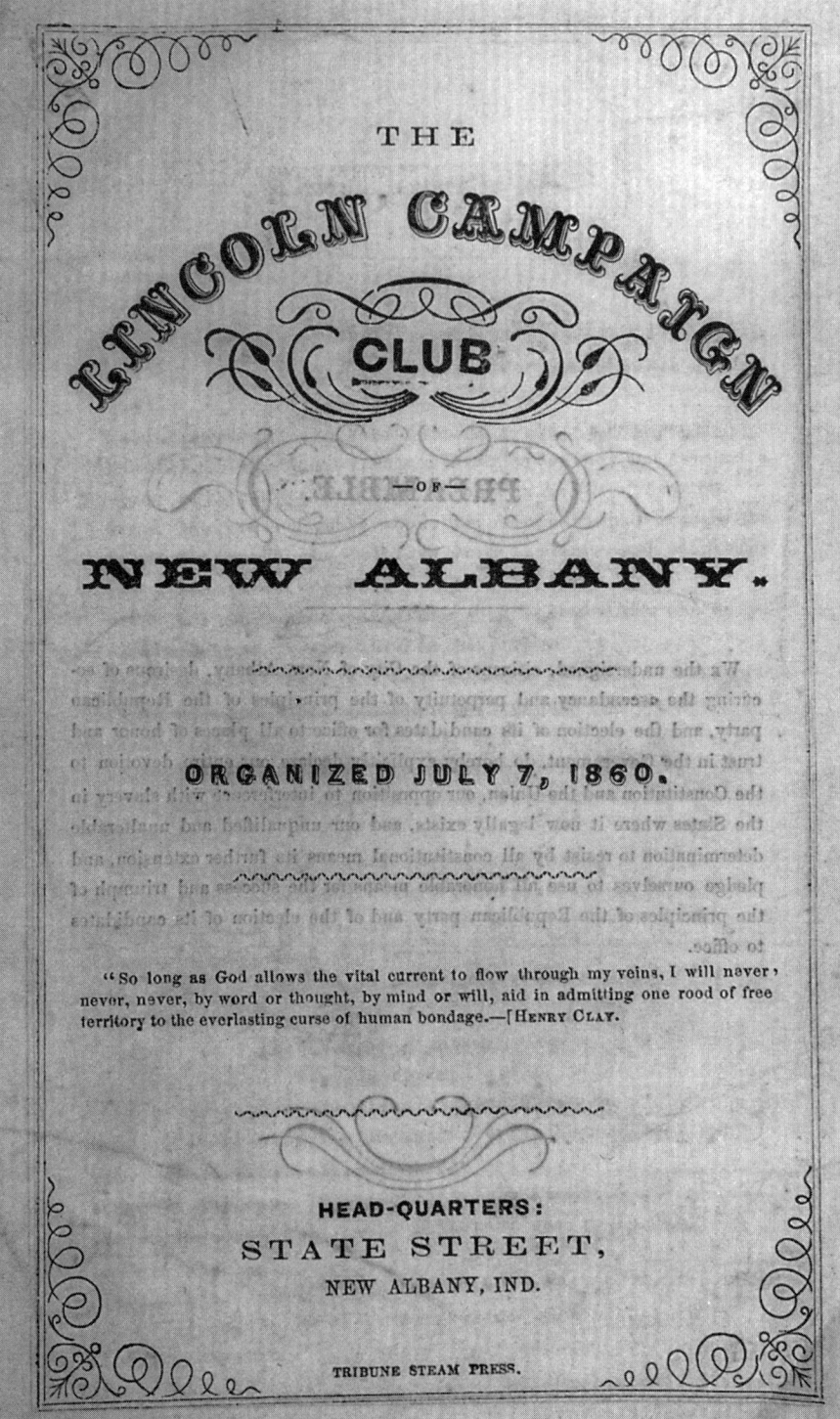

negotiated and made secret preparations for the march through Georgia.[47] Brooks was mustered out of service of the United States on March 20, 1866.

Brooks was known for helping the poor and often borrowed money for that purpose. "He never gave less, and often gave more, than a tenth part of his income to purposes of charity and religion,"[48] stated the preacher at his funeral. As president of the New Albany–Salem Railroad, Brooks was the only one who could issue free passes for rail travel.[49] And as assistant quartermaster he was one of the men in charge of signing passes enabling freed slaves to cross the Ohio River. For example, on January 4, 1865, he signed the following pass: "Andrew J. Murphy, Contraband, has been employed in the service of the United States as Cabin Boy on the U.S. Ram *Monarch* for the past twelve months, and under existing laws he is free and is entitled to pass as a free man."[50] Two weeks later Brooks signed another pass for Andrew J. Murphy, allowing him to take the rail cars to St. Louis and back again. In all of his capacities—as elder of Second Presbyterian Church, president of the New Albany–Salem Railroad and assistant quartermaster of volunteers under Secretary of War Stanton, it is likely he gave passes to fugitive slaves to ride the rails legitimately. As quartermaster he was in a position to assist African Americans in crossing the river or otherwise to befriend runaways as well as newly freed slaves.

John Loughmiller, one of the ruling elders at Second Presbyterian from 1837 through the Civil War, was privy to the majority of anti-slavery discussions held on the presbytery level. According to the Presbytery minutes, he was the elder who most often accompanied the pastors to those meetings. He was there, for example, in April of 1841, when the Salem Presbytery (N.S.) sent out its request to other presbyteries to answer the question, "Shall the sin of slavery be tolerated in the Presbyterian church?" And he always voted in the affirmative on the anti-slavery resolutions. Loughmiller left Shenandoah County, Virginia, because of slavery and settled first in the Ohio River town of Bethlehem, Indiana, before he transferred his membership from Bethlehem Presbyterian to Second Presbyterian church in New Albany. He was very civic minded, serving not only as councilman for the Second Ward in New Albany in 1847–48, but also as trustee of the public schools from 1855 to 1857. His name often appeared in the New Albany papers as one linked with helping the poor. A *New Albany Daily Ledger* article of November 16, 1857, published a request from Loughmiller asking for donations of clothing for the poor to be brought to his shop on Main Street.[51]

One can see that the position assumed by Second Presbyterian church under the leadership of the three major pastors—Reverends Sneed, Bishop and Atterbury, along with the support of the ruling elders, particularly Brooks and Loughmiller,

Opposite: Lincoln Campaign Club brochure, New Albany, Indiana. The cover reads "So long as God allows the vital current to flow through my veins, I will never, never, never, by word or thought, by mind or will, aid in admitting one road of free territory to the everlasting curse of human bondage." Henry Clay quotation. (Courtesy Isaac P. Smith Letters and Papers)

links it to being supportive of the African American community in Floyd County. Moreover, the fact that Levi Coffin knew that he could get help from Atterbury when he came to New Albany in search of support for former slaves shows Coffin had prior knowledge of Atterbury and Second Presbyterian church as a place friendly to blacks. The presence of African Americans within the membership, profiles of members showing them to be anti-slavery and Whig/Republican, the strong oral tradition linking Second Presbyterian to the Underground Railroad (Chapter 7), and not least of all, the position of the building on the banks of the Ohio River, supports this. While this study does not necessarily show the pastors and members to have been abolitionist or fanatical in their attitude, it does show they were anti-slavery with a spirit of benevolence toward free blacks and slaves alike. In their own way they were forthright in their denunciation of slavery and did not view anti-slavery expression to be outside the realm of the work of the church and its mission.

The New Albany Theological Seminary

The establishment of a Presbyterian Seminary in New Albany, and its relationship with Lane Seminary in Cincinnati, Ohio, is important for our present study. Lyman Beecher, the founding president of Lane Seminary and a key preacher in the revivalist movement, spoke at the Mt. Tabor camp meetings at the invitation of Rev. Sneed.[52] Lane Seminary was a symbol of abolitionist activism. One researcher openly calls the Lane Seminary students of 1834 "Underground Railroad operators."[53] The Lane students performed much benevolent work among blacks in Cincinnati, preaching and teaching, setting up Sunday school classes, and assisting them by raising money for food, clothing and education. Their work was set against the background of Cincinnati's pro–Southern personality and anti-black bias. This, combined with the students' missionary zeal to "convert the West," helped fuel the abolitionist attitude of the Lane student body. The students' activism was met by the Seminary board's ban on missing classes, forming student organizations, holding public meetings and giving addresses. This harsh reaction to their work on behalf of the black community forced the issue and created a student walkout. The protest was led by Theodore Weld and ultimately resulted in a nucleus of students who enrolled at Oberlin College in northern Ohio.[54]

In 1847, thirteen years after the Lane walkout, the New Albany Theological Seminary[55] was established. It was located at the corner of Elm and Seventh streets on the near east side of New Albany. The first Board of Trustees of the Seminary was composed of Old School men, that is, members of First Presbyterian Church and the New Albany Presbytery (O.S.): Charles Woodruff, William Plumer, John Bushnell, Henry B. Shields, Pleasant S. Shields, William A. Scribner, James Wood, Sylvester Scovel and Mason C. Fitch. New Albany Theological Seminary was established for the same purpose as that of Lane Seminary — to train young men for the conversion of the West and to supply the newly formed churches.[56]

Because of the Lane rebellion in 1834, the establishment of another "seminary in the West" was also suspect; the more conservative men were fearful that the New Albany Seminary would be transformed into another training ground for abolitionism. This was particularly worrisome since the very idea behind locating the Seminary on the Ohio River, within a stone's throw of a slave state, was to establish a middle ground regarding the church and the slavery issue. The hope was that young men from both camps would be attracted to New Albany. However, two of the newly hired professors, Erasmus Darwin MacMaster and Thomas E. Thomas, though both Old School men, were outspokenly opposed to slavery. Dr. N. L. Rice (O.S.), editor of the *Presbyterian of the West* and a bitter enemy of MacMaster, was extremely fearful that these men would use the seminary as a sounding board for their "abolitionist" views and destroy what peace still existed in the Presbyterian church. The physical closeness to a slave state, however, worked against men like Rice, and soon the Seminary in New Albany became a center of opposition to those in the church who did not want to "rock the boat" on the slavery issue. In the end the school could not attract enough students due to the ensuing controversy and was forced to close. The Seminary was eventually moved to Chicago and became McCormick Seminary (O.S.). Because of their position regarding the church and the slavery issue, neither MacMaster nor Thomas were initially invited to teach at McCormick.

Dr. Erasmus Darwin MacMaster, who lived in New Albany on East Main Street between Eighth and Ninth streets, was the first president of the Seminary in New Albany, 1849–1857. He had previously been president of Hanover College, 1838–1845, and of Miami University, Oxford, Ohio, 1845–1849. His father was a minister in the Reformed or Covenanter Presbyterian Church, which had gone so far as to exclude slaveholders from its membership. In his inaugural address at Miami, MacMaster had openly condemned slavery.[57] It was common knowledge that MacMaster was one of the strongest anti-slavery men in the Old School Presbyterian Church and, although no evidence has been found that he actively participated in an Underground Railroad system, his anti-slavery attitude would have helped to combat the pro-slavery, anti-black bias present in the community. In fact, just prior to MacMaster's coming to New Albany, Rev. N. L. Rice, editor of the *Presbyterian of the West*, in a series of articles accused MacMaster and Thomas E. Thomas of being abolitionists, unfit, therefore, to teach at the New Albany Seminary. MacMaster was formally charged with trying to "form a thoroughly abolitionist seminary in the northwest and there to train young men to become agitators and destroyers of the peace of the church."[58] MacMaster denied that was his intention, but he admitted considering slavery "intrinsically, essentially and necessarily immoral," and he further admitted that he frequently expressed that view on the New Albany campus.[59] Even though MacMaster was resolute in his stand against slavery, he could not be called an out-and-out abolitionist because he "looked the other way" regarding fellow Presbyterians who lived in the slave states.[60]

Thomas E. Thomas was an Englishman who supported MacMaster in his anti-slavery views. He graduated from Miami University, where he had studied under John Bishop's father, Robert. Thomas followed MacMaster as President of Hanover College and arrived in New Albany in 1854 to teach Biblical literature and exegesis at the Seminary.[61] He, along with MacMaster, would have provided an anti-slavery climate for the community and the young men enrolled at the Seminary. In his support of MacMaster's views, he "would follow his convictions of duty at all hazards. He was frank and fearless in the avowal of his opinion, and there was no difficulty in determining on which side of a question he stood."[62] He became actively engaged in anti-slavery efforts in an attempt to force the Old School into taking a stronger stand. In 1846 he had presented his views on slavery to the General Assembly, where he was identified by the *Princeton Review* as one of the *two* abolitionists at the meeting. Eventually, abolitionism became synonymous with the New Albany Seminary, and the directors of the school found themselves in a position where they had to deny rumors that the school was being converted into an institution to promote abolitionist sentiment.[63]

Parallels can be drawn between Lane Seminary in Cincinnati and the Theological Seminary in New Albany. (Rev. Rice, for one, attempted to draw those parallels by accusing Dr. MacMaster of being an abolitionist.) (1) Being a town along the Ohio River and bordering the slave state of Kentucky, New Albany had the same problem with bias against the black population that Cincinnati did. (2) New Albany had economic ties to the slave states just as did Cincinnati. (3) Both cities had newspapers that favored the Democratic political party, vocally supporting slavery and the exclusion of blacks from the state. (4) Both seminary student bodies came primarily from the Eastern seaboard, and the schools were not able to attract many students from the South as had been hoped. (5) Both schools broke new ground by admitting an African American student. The first class of nine young men at New Albany, for example, included James M. Priest, from New Jersey who, after finishing his theological studies, was sent as a missionary to Liberia, Africa. (6) The student body possessed the same missionary zeal as that of Lane. As has been stated, the American Home Missionary Society was very active in Indiana. More than half of the Lane graduates had been at one time or another Home Missionaries, and these New Albany Seminary students were destined for the same thing. Among the white graduates in the first class were two of John Finley Crowe's[64] sons, James and Thomas, from Madison, Indiana, Samuel John Baird from Ohio, Samuel Hart from Illinois, two men from Missouri and one from Pennsylvania.[65] The comparison between the two seminaries stops, however, when it comes to leadership. The New Albany Seminary did not apparently have a charismatic leader such as Theodore Weld to stage a protest and a walkout.

Although the New Albany Seminary was to have remained neutral regarding the slavery issue, it did not. In 1856 the *New Albany Daily Ledger* accused one of the seminary students, A. J. Yeager [Yeater], of being an agent of the Underground Railroad. Slavery was on the minds of these students. If a professor remained silent on the subject or refused to answer questions, his silence could easily have been interpreted as a disloyalty to God.[66] If fanaticism was present among any of the young seminarians, it is likely that John Dole, the American Anti-Slavery Society representative in Floyd County, recruited students from the Seminary for his work.

The Methodists

The Indiana Methodist Conference was organized in 1832 at a meeting in New Albany, but Methodism had already reached Floyd County much earlier. McMurtrie, in his *Sketches of Louisville* (1819), observed that the inhabitants were all either Methodist or Presbyterian. Wesley Chapel, the "Old Ship of Zion" as it was called, was organized on June 20, 1817. One of the earliest supporters of Methodism in Floyd County was John Shrader, a spiritualist.[67] After about a dozen years, a brick church was erected at the corner of First and Market streets. A frame addition was built to the front of the church by August Knoefel and used for "mercantile" purposes.[68] There is an oral tradition that Knoefel was part of an Underground Railroad system in New Albany.

The Methodists, like the Presbyterians, were touched by the spirit of abolitionism through revivalist preachers who called on members to repent of the sin of slaveholding. Anti-slavery sermons went hand in hand with revivals. William Cravens was a Methodist Episcopal pastor who preached openly in Southern Indiana against slavery. Peter Cartwright, a Methodist Episcopal clergyman who preached in Clark County and other Southern Indiana communities, was noted for his anti-slavery sentiments. The movement gradually spread westward through Indiana and into Illinois. By 1838 six out of the sixteen Northern Methodist Conferences had an anti-slavery majority.[69]

In 1838–39 Rev. John C. Smith, pastor of Wesley Chapel, became the instigator and leader of a number of huge and powerful revivals, which swept New Albany–Floyd County like nothing else had in its short history. Hundreds of citizens were converted through this man and his revivalist style of preaching. Wesley Chapel outgrew its space and in 1839 Centenary Church was formed.[70] The revivals continued into the 1850s. Particularly in 1852, both Wesley and Centenary saw continued growth as a direct result of revivals.[71] The new life of the Methodist convert, like that of the Presbyterian, involved "taming the West," improving society and making the world a better place in which to live.

In 1845 Methodism split over the issue of slavery into a Northern and a Southern group. By 1846 a splinter group from the Methodist Episcopal Church of Portland, Kentucky, requested annexation to Wesley Chapel in New Albany, which remained with the Northern branch. The other splinter group joined the Methodist Episcopal Church South at the time of the annexation request.[72] The split of this neighboring Kentucky congregation helped to swell the ranks of anti-slavery members at Wesley Chapel.

Late in the year 1856, the *New Albany Tribune* and the *New Albany Daily Ledger*, often antagonistic toward each other because of their different political views, started arguing through their editorial columns about abolitionists being invited to New Albany to lecture. The second topic of dissension was over the "political preachers" who were using their pulpits in New Albany to give political speeches against the evils of slavery.[73] Among the preachers named over a period of weeks, the Rev. Benjamin F. Crary of Wesley Chapel seemed to be the primary target of criticism and discussion.[74] Crary, born in Jennings County, Indiana, on December 12, 1821, and educated in Cincinnati, graduated from Pleasant Hill Academy (Belmont College) in 1842. He had at one time or another been a school teacher and a lawyer and finally an itinerant, revivalist Methodist preacher in the Indiana Conference. He served such places as Moorefield, Vienna, Brownstown, Bedford, Rushville, Indianapolis, Bloomington and New Albany. He, too, was an evangelist, known for his eloquent and forceful preaching. In 1856 he wrote an anti-slavery letter to the *Advocate* that turned the *New Albany Daily Ledger*, already critical, totally against him.[75]

At the General Conference at Indianapolis in 1856, Crary strongly recommended that the discipline be changed so as to exclude slaveholders from membership.[76] The *Ledger* complained that:

The Rev. Benjamin F. Crary, pastor of Wesley Chapel Methodist Church, 1855–1857. (Source: *Methodist Review*, March 1896, p. 176)

> Democrats found in one of the churches of this city are told by the pastor of that church that they ought to be scourged out of God's temple and driven beyond the light of civilization and refinement by small cords in the hands of runaway slaves.[77]

A week later the editor, when speaking about runaway slaves, jested that "If they crossed the river into New Albany, they would probably be supplied by brother Crary with small cords and set to lashing Democrats and Filmorites." In both cases, the *Ledger* was reacting to a sermon preached by Crary in which he warned the Buchanan and Fillmore supporters of New Albany, "Avaunt Villains! Leave Town! Pull out!"[78] Crary continued to be the object of scorn as the *Ledger* labeled him a "political preacher" who attempted to drag all the Protestant clergy down with him. It claimed that the whole body of Protestant clergy should not be held responsible for this atrocious conduct, that of "turning the house of God into a political arena."[79] The others who were labeled "political preachers" by the *Ledger* included J. V. R. Miller of Vincennes, William W. Hibben of Madison, Beecher Tyng, a lecturer from the East and Henry Ward Beecher of Indianapolis. Along with these men, the *New Albany Daily Ledger* denounced a well-known Congregationalist preacher from New York, Dr. George B. Cheever.[80] The newspaper continued,

> Political preachers are trying to make it appear as if the whole body of protestant clergy regard the Democratic party and its principles as wrong. [They should be advised to] render unto Caesar the things that are Caesar's and unto God the things that are God's ... instead of desecrating the pulpit with political harangues.[81]

The *New Albany Tribune* answered the *Ledger's* editorial of November 13, 1856, with a letter from an anonymous writer who signed with only the letter "A." In defense of Crary, "A" wrote, "He is new to our community and yet he is being assaulted and called an abolitionist. He is not but only takes the position on the slavery question that the entire Methodist Church North holds."[82]

In this same column, the *New Albany Tribune* claimed that the *Ledger* had also attacked Dr. Stevenson, pastor of First Presbyterian Church (O.S.) on Bank Street, by labeling him a member "of the Crary school." The next month the *Tribune* reported that Mr. Yeater, a "young friend of the Presbyterian Theological Seminary," was the one who carried "A's" letter to the newspaper. Yeater was the seminary student who "spilled the beans" and identified Dr. Stevenson as the writer "who has now shown his true colors regarding his views on slavery." "This betrayal of confidence makes the seminary student unfit for clerical honors," claimed the *Tribune*. The student, Yeater, who worked for the *Tribune,* was constantly stirring up trouble and getting into controversies with the "roller boys" over the subject of slavery. The editors claimed they "would much rather have the good will of Wash Carter, although a colored man, than the good will of Yeater." They continued, "The public will doubtless hear of him again some of these days as conductor of an Underground Railroad."[83]

The Indiana Methodist Conference met in New Albany in October, 1857. On the fourth day of the conference, Rev. John C. Smith, former pastor of Wesley Chapel Methodist in New Albany and chairman of the Committee on Slavery, presented the following resolution:

> Whereas, Slavery is an unmitigated evil, dissolving the marriage relation between its victims, separating parents and children, promoting adultery and cruelty, and is the sum of all villainies; therefore
>
> Resolved, 1st, That in the judgment of this Conference the time has fully come when all Christians, and especially all Christian Ministers, should fearlessly lift up their voices and unite in vigorous action for the extirpation of this great evil.
>
> Resolved, 2d, That we view with abhorrence all attempts, from whatever source coming, to suppress a full, free, and candid discussion and expression of opinion in regard to this subject.
>
> Resolved, 3d, That while we deny that the general rule of the discipline on slavery protects or guarantees slaveholding in any sense, yet we are in favor of so amending it as distinctly to prohibit the holding of human being as property, (except when it clearly and distinctly appears that the good of the slave is to be promoted thereby.) [This amendment was proposed by Rev. E. H. Sabin.]
>
> Resolved, 4th, That while we disavow any purpose or desire to interfere with slavery beyond our ecclesiastical jurisdiction, it is, nevertheless, our firm purpose and resolve, not only as ministers, but as citizens of this land of freedom, holding rights and suffrages in common with other freemen, to prevent, as far as in us lieth, by all righteous and honorable means, the extension of slavery into territory that is now, and of rights ought forever to remain, free.
>
> J. C. Smith, Chairman.[84]

One by one, the preachers stood and gave their reaction. Crary reported that he was all for the report as it stood. He believed that slavery had become a national issue and that all restraints had been broken down. He was aware that men in Indiana had become slave catchers and were hunting runaway slaves with hounds. "Now is the time for men to speak out clearly and distinctly," voiced Crary. Many of the men stood and professed their abhorrence of slavery, that they were, in fact, anti-slavery to the core, but that they could not approve of the resolutions as they stood. The body could not agree and finally disbursed for the day without coming to a consensus.[85]

The next day the resolutions were again raised for discussion. Crary spoke against those who refused to accept the resolutions. He criticized their reasoning, claiming they believed slavery "protected" the old, the sick and the lame and that without it slaves would be even more vulnerable. "Since yesterday men have threatened to leave the church if these resolutions are passed. If any such people wish to leave the church, let them go and joy go with them. Some have accused me of riding a hobby [horse]. That is a mistake; I am riding a living horse!" said Crary. That same day, the *Tribune* editor got involved and urged the Conference to "put through" the resolution declaring slavery

> to be the sum of all human villainies, ... and it being the duty of all Christians to unite in vigorous action for the extirpation [abolition] of the great evil and declaring in favor of so amending the Discipline of the church as distinctly to prohibit the holding of human beings as property.[86]

But the *Ledger* disagreed and claimed the *Tribune* editor was misreading his audience, mistakenly believing the majority of men at the Methodist Conference were anti-slavery in their views. To the chagrin of the *Ledger*, however, the anti-slavery resolutions passed on October 6, 1857, with a vote of forty-eight to twenty-two.

Crary was utterly opposed to slavery, politically a Whig and later a strong Republican, "an abolitionist at heart, and an uncompromising enemy of the fugitive slave laws."[87] During the Civil War (1863), General Asboth detailed him to take charge of the contraband soldiers on the Tennessee River. By order of General Grant, Crary organized these able-bodied men into the First Tennessee Heavy Artillery, assigning them to duty in the river forts. In 1864, he served in the General Conference as chairperson of the "Committee on Slavery," and immediately after the war he was one of the leaders in the organization of the Freedmen's Aid Society. "The advocates of slavery and intemperance often received vigorous shocks from his well-charged battery,"[88] as Democrats at Wesley Chapel witnessed more than once.

Just as at Second Presbyterian, there is evidence that the Methodist churches in antebellum New Albany had a relationship with the African American community. John Shrader, preacher, carpenter and undertaker, handled funerals and burials for the African American citizens of New Albany. Rev. Payne, an African Bishop, preached at the John Street Methodist Episcopal Church in 1857,[89] and again at Wesley Chapel the next month. Rev. E. H. Sabin spoke at Centenary Methodist Church January 27, 1858, and was highly criticized by the *Ledger* for being an abolitionist.[90] Henry Ward Beecher preached several times at the Methodist churches in New Albany in 1858.[91] And immediately after the Civil War, the Methodists, like the Presbyterians, became involved in assisting released slaves. The Methodists helped through the Freedmen's Aid Society of the Methodist Episcopal Church. Its object was to "labor for the relief and education of the Freedmen."[92] The greatest percent of the poor in the county during this time were blacks who had arrived from the South. The city newspapers in fact claimed nine-tenths of New Albany's poor were from the black population.

During the antebellum period, Methodists made up the largest religious segment of Floyd County. Lipin's study shows that many of New Albany's richest men and women were Methodists, and since Methodism was the largest denomination in New Albany, "they were more likely to come into contact with the lower orders. However, the extent to which wealthy Methodists were isolated from their plebeian coworshippers remains unknown."[93] Nonetheless, the influence of its members would have touched all levels of society to some degree. That, combined with the anti-slavery personality of the various Methodist churches in Floyd County, would have provided some counterbalance to the negative rhetoric of the *New Albany Ledger*. In fact, Dummer M. Hooper, the influential mayor of New Albany during the critical period of 1863 to 1865, was a Methodist.[94] His son, William S. Hooper, was a Methodist preacher in Southern Indiana during this period and wrote in his diary, "I believe that the Lord has raised him [Lincoln] up to rid the land of slavery and an attempted aristocratic Southern government."[95] There is no evidence to be found that Revs. Smith and Crary or other Methodist ministers helped runaway slaves as they fled through Floyd County, but their attitudes on the slavery issue certainly number them among those individuals in New Albany who were sympathetic toward slaves. A later chapter will address two Methodists, Louis Hartman and August Knoefel, who, according to oral tradition, gave assistance to runaway slaves.

Because of Floyd County's close proximity to the slave state of Kentucky, and the presence of a strong anti-black bias, anti-slavery sentiment remained extremely clandestine, and a written record of its presence is almost nonexistent. There were white churches other than the Presbyterians and Methodists in Floyd County during the antebellum years. It is likely they did not all share anti-slavery views. Nevertheless, there is no doubt that anti-slavery sentiment did exist. Many of the evangelical Christians who settled Floyd County from the East possessed a spirit of benevolence toward the slave. Likewise, many Germans who immigrated to America to escape oppressions of their own settled Floyd County and did not arrive with a pre-conceived bias toward blacks. Instead they identified with each other because they suffered from the same bias and indignation placed on them by society. The popular and legal idea of keeping a tight control on the influx of blacks coming into the county found support. The ideas of Hinton R. Helper and the colonization movement both worked toward ending slavery but also saw deportation as a way of removing people of color from American soil. The voices of African Americans in this Southern Indiana community, therefore, were suppressed. The suppression involved not only their political views but also their hopes, ideas and dreams of the future. Their very history in the early years of Floyd County development has been clothed in obscurity. The isolation imposed upon them during the early years of Indiana's existence makes that history especially interesting and important.

Chapter 5
The Free African American Community

The importance of the Floyd County African American community in assistance given to runaway slaves should not be underestimated. The idea that white citizens were the sole operators of a system called "The Underground Railroad" is a myth. That individuals in the white community gave assistance cannot be doubted. However, it was the African American community that was the backbone of the Underground Railroad in the New Albany–Floyd County area, and the white community would have found it difficult to function in that capacity without the help of the African Americans in their midst. Whether African Americans helped in a spontaneous way or from within an organization, they formed the link that ultimately made it possible for their brothers and sisters to cross the Ohio River and move safely through Floyd County. Because slaves began escaping from the upper South into Indiana at a very early date, it is important to study the first black settlers who arrived in Floyd County.

The Early Years

African Americans settled in Floyd County at its very beginning, and their history is a rich one indeed. In fact, the black presence on Floyd County soil is older than either the county seat of New Albany, which was incorporated in 1813, or Floyd County itself, which was established in 1819. In 1808 Colonel John Paul, a white who purchased the first tract at what would become New Albany, noted that white squatters occupied the site; these included Martin Trueblood, a sawmill operator who also ferried travelers across the Ohio River,[1] and John Aldrich, a hunter and trapper. A black known only as "Morrison" helped clear the land and lived with a Mr. McGrew at a place known as "McGrew's Point."[2] After McGrew moved on, Morrison remained to become a citizen of New Albany. In 1814 Patrick Shields, who was a Covenanter

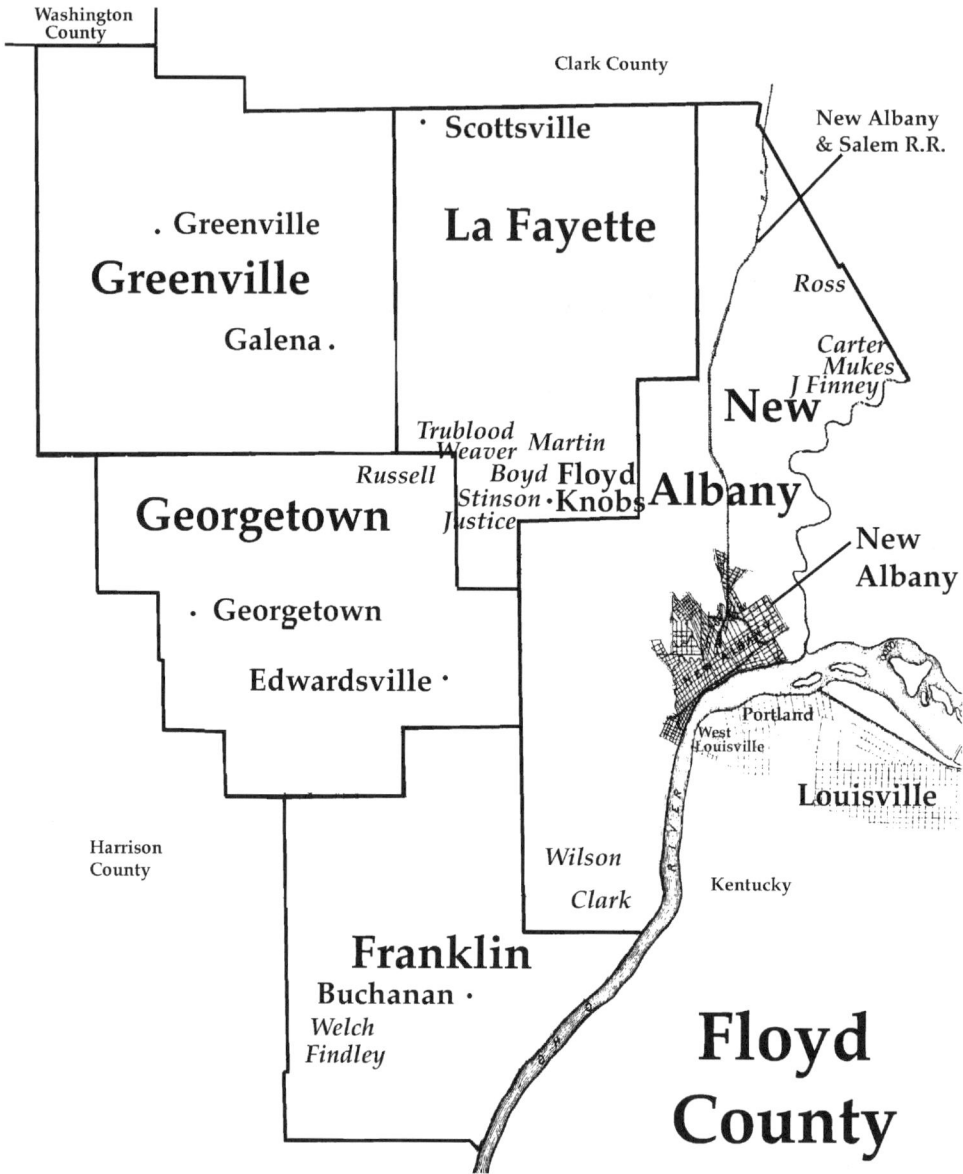

Map of Floyd County, Indiana, showing location of farms owned by African Americans during the antebellum and Civil War period.

Presbyterian, moved to Georgetown in Floyd County from Virginia and brought "Sam" along (no surname given), a black man who helped Shields clear his first two acres of ground. The Harrison County Sheriff's Tax Book of 1811 shows that Shields owned one slave for whom he was taxed $1.[3] African American brothers William and Jeremiah Clark[4] were early settlers from the South who purchased property in

Franklin Township near the Ohio River and became successful farmers. Jeremiah Clark, in fact, gave some of his land to the Methodists for a church building that was erected in the southeast part of Franklin Township. The log church was in a state of decay by 1881 and was pulled down. All that remained to mark the spot were tombstones in a small graveyard.[5]

Other blacks, Joshua and Jesse Wilson, possibly brothers, arrived in the Floyd County area as early as 1812. They lived on land they owned not far from Middle Creek along the Ohio River in Franklin Township. The first divorce granted by the courts in Floyd County involved Joshua, who was a pilot on the Ohio River, and his wife, Elizabeth. He was ordered to publish his application for divorce in the *Indianian*, a newspaper published in Jeffersonville before Floyd County had a newspaper. Additionally, on September 19, 1819, a grand jury returned a bill of indictment against him for assault and battery. Court records also mentioned the fact that Joshua, who was engaged in river transportation and owned and commanded his own fleet of steamers, had taken eight keelboats to New Orleans. In each instance he walked back to New Albany from New Orleans.[6] Joshua Wilson was a man of means and in 1817 was regarded as the wealthiest man in Indiana. Because of his wealth, his name appears in various other places of record. In 1816 and 1822, he purchased 67½ acres of George and John Oatman's farm through the Oatman Estate at a cost of $2,000. Jesse Wilson purchased Beverly Hurd's farm in Franklin Township. In 1817 Joshua and Jesse each built a brick house, one on the Stoy farm and the other on the Collins farm. Both buildings were completed in 1820 and were the first houses in Floyd County to be built of brick.[7] Joshua's mansion cost him $10,000. The handsomely carved woodwork was brought to New Albany from Philadelphia.[8]

Joshua was very light in complexion and was not mentioned as a "man of color" until the time of his death when his will was probated. It has been speculated that he was a highly regarded son of a wealthy white man. He was referred to as "Yellow Wilson" in Ohio River navigation directions that used his large brick home as a benchmark.[9] The 1820 census records count him as a white man, age between sixteen and twenty-eight (that early he was listed as living in what was then Harrison County). On September 10, 1822, Joshua married a white woman, Mrs. Dahman, whose husband had been accused of murder and subsequently hung. This was the first hanging that occurred after the formation of Floyd County.[10]

The 1830 Floyd County census again showed Joshua as being white with two black females under the age of ten, and two black males between the ages of ten and twenty-four living in his household. Joshua contributed on several occasions to the building fund for the first Floyd County courthouse—one sum of $30 was given outright and another contribution of $70 was to be donated at the time of the completion of the building. A relative, Samuel Wilson, contributed the sum of $25 to the same fund. The Floyd County court records also show that Wilson bought and sold cattle that bore his own brand, "JW."[11] On August 22, 1830, Joshua Wilson sold his land for $2,000 to his heirs, Ludson, Pendleton and Allen Wilson. He owned more than 130 acres of farmland in Franklin Township, plus a two-acre lot in New Albany's West Union area (in the Griffin Tract). The heirs' debt of $2,000 was to be forgiven if they promised him a number of things. The stipulations included furnishing Joshua with all of his necessities for the remainder of his life including meat and drink, board and lodging, clothing and laundries, in sickness and in health, along with the sum of $200 to be given to each of their sisters, Louisa and Cynthia, and $100 to their older sister, who was not named. Joshua lived seven more years after the agreement was signed, and on February 13, 1837, his will was probated and his estate opened. The administrator of his will was a neighbor, Samuel Angel, possibly mulatto. Given Wilson's mobility, his occupation as commander of a fleet of steamboats and the position of his house on a remote section of the Ohio River, it is likely he assisted fugitive slaves to cross the river from Kentucky into free territory.

Another early Franklin Township family was the Findleys, who traveled from Virginia and were a part of the great wave of African Americans who were searching for independence, autonomy and freedom from oppression by moving to the Old Northwest.[12] Many Findleys arrived in Southern Indiana during the early part of the

Descendants of Caesar Findley (Finley) (*left to right*): William Finley, Jr., Keith Ratliff, Anna Finley (seated), Linda Ratliff, William Finley, Sr. (Photograph courtesy of Jennifer Suzanne Vezner)

nineteenth century and settled primarily in Harrison and Floyd counties. They arrived at the same time as Paul and Susannah Mitchum, a white couple who felt it their God-given duty to give their slaves freedom. At that time government land cost approximately $1.25 an acre, and with the help of the Mitchums they were able to purchase land and begin farming on their own. Some who arrived with them were Bright Mitchem, Littleton Mitchem, Mace Mitchem, Mike Mitchem, Tom Mitchem, Harry Mitchem, George Cousins, James Finley, Lewis Finley, James Powell, Oswald Wright, John Welch, Joe Finley and Solon Carter along with their wives and children.[13] Floyd County Court records show that on September 11, 1828, Caesar Findley, whose descendants still reside in Floyd County, purchased property from Noah and Elizabeth Beauchamp.[14] On May 15, 1847, Josiah Findley, who may have been a brother to Caesar, purchased the property from the heirs of Joseph Findley, who was Caesar's sole heir.[15] Josiah Findley, who owned and farmed the "Caesar Findley home place" for many years, began purchasing land in Floyd County in 1845 and continued to expand his property until he sold the "home place" to Henry Prassler on February 28, 1866.[16] The 106⅔ acres of land which was sold at that time was not to include the Findley family graveyard. It was to be reserved by the Findley family with all the "appurtenances," which included the elaborately carved tombstones and stone wall surrounding the graveyard. The Findley house, barn and outbuildings, much of which were constructed of poplar logs, are still standing and used by the present owners. The Findley family cemetery is on a knoll not far from the house and contains at least nine legible, cut tombstones.[17] The stones of Josiah's wife, Malinda, and several of their children and grandchildren are visible. Malinda died on December 27, 1867. Her grave marker is a beautifully cut stone that depicts an angel and has a poem: "Remember as you pass by, as you are now so once was I. As I am now, so you will be. Prepare for death and follow me."[18] One tombstone also shows that a Findley daughter married Eli Welch, who was born in Harrison County in 1829.

Another Findley family owned approximately 160 acres of land in Taylor Township, Harrison County near Buena Vista. This farm was only a couple of miles south of the Caesar Findley farm. The present owner recently reported that the Findley cemetery is still visible on the property and contains at least two graves, both of them with cut headstones. The only legible stone, however, is that of Andrew J. Findley, age eighteen years, who was buried in 1863. The property was once owned by Thomas Findley who sold it to Elias Findley in the 1850s. Elias also purchased property in 1849 in New Albany Township, Floyd County. His name appears in the 1850 census of Floyd County. Thompson Mitchum, a boatman, lived with him. Census records show that this Findley family also came from Virginia. As in the case of Joshua Wilson, it is very likely that the Findley families aided runaway slaves due to their close proximity to the river, the remoteness of their farms and their ability to "network" with family members and other black farmers.

The Stinson family arrived in Floyd County early and settled in Lafayette

Descendants of Charles Stinson: *Front row (left to right):* Phyllis Thomas, Portia Thomas Wheeler, Blanche Talbott, Allison Rickman, Alice Louise Rickman, Lillian Peters, April Walker. *Back row:* Frances Talbott Rickman, Etropia Talbott Allen, Winzell Thomas, Beverly Talbott Hearn, Richard Posley. (Photograph courtesy of Jennifer Suzanne Vezner)

Township. Records show that Charles Stinson purchased his first property in 1830 in the West Union Griffin Tract within New Albany Township. By 1836 he had purchased the first of several parcels of farmland in Lafayette Township. The Justice family along with Weavers, Russells and Boyds, all black farmers, were their neighbors during the 1850s and 1860s. Stinsons continued to reside on the family farm until 1913 when the estate of George Stinson was filed. Members of the Stinson family are buried on the land they owned, which is located on East Luther Road in Floyd Knobs.[19] Descendants of the Charles Stinson family still reside in New Albany and the southern Indiana area today. Again, as in the cases of Wilsons and Findleys, the presence of black families living in a cluster in the remote hills of Lafayette Township northwest of New Albany points to a likely safe haven for runaway slaves.

African Americans purchased property very early within the town of New Albany as well. On July 16, 1824, John Finney bought a lot on Lower Market Street from an early white settler, George Silliman. Finney continued to purchase property in town in the years 1825, 1827 and 1829, and in 1837 he bought more than 200 acres within the Illinois Grant.[20]

Frank Lewis and his mother, "Grandmother Lewis," were also early Floyd County settlers who came from Virginia. In 1860 the New Albany newspapers reported that "an old negro" by the name of Frank died in the lower part of New Albany. This is probably the Frank Lewis who received a Deed of Manumission through the Floyd County courts in 1849.[21] The 1860 newspaper article said he was about ninety years of age, and his mother, said to be about 110 years of age, was still living.[22] Two years later, in November of 1862, it was reported that Grandmother Precilla Lewis died at her home on Lower Spring Street in New Albany. She was 112 years old and had been a resident of New Albany and its vicinity for nearly fifty years. She would, therefore, have been one of the first people to settle New Albany. She was highly esteemed by everyone, and she distinctly remembered incidents about the American Revolutionary War and the Indian wars. The newspaper account of her death said she had retained all of her faculties, almost wholly unimpaired, until the day of her death.[23] Another African American woman who died in Floyd County at a very old age was Sylvia Manly, who lived to be approximately 100 years old. She died in June of 1905 and had come to Floyd County from Virginia as a young woman with her husband, Burkett Manly.[24]

An early Floyd County court record of an African American living in New Albany was that of a free man, Arthur Brooks, who on May 13, 1820, took his former owner, William Letcher of Kentucky, to court. (Note that Brooks was still given the right to take his owner to court in Floyd County despite his "color" and the restrictions placed on African Americans.) Arthur Brooks, who was represented by an attorney, gave a statement in court that Mr. Letcher had brought him to New Albany. When Letcher decided to take Brooks back into the State of Kentucky to enslave him again, contrary to the laws of the State of Indiana, Arthur Brooks approached the court for an order protecting his rights as a citizen of Indiana. The court ruled that inasmuch as Letcher had voluntarily brought Brooks into the state and established him in business here, he could not, under the law, take his liberty away from him, and therefore, Brooks was a free man.[25]

Floyd County was only one year old when the 1820 census was taken. Though we know some of the names of Floyd County African American residents from other sources, this group of people remains a nonentity in that census with only white heads of households named. All African American residents, and there were at least sixty-nine, according to the U.S. Bureau of the Census for that year, were listed as being a part of the household of a white family. Some of them were no doubt slaves or indentured servants brought to the new territory by white owners, but not all. Census records for the surrounding counties, including Jefferson County, Kentucky, list "free black heads of households." This absence appears to be a deliberate error on the part of the census taker. As was previously stated, blacks were purchasing farmland as well as lots in New Albany by the time the first Floyd County census was taken.

The 1830 Floyd County census shows 265 free African Americans. This time black heads of households are listed (see Appendix C). It is, however, incomplete because it does not list blacks who are known from other sources to have lived in Floyd County at the time. Jerry and William Clark, Joshua Wilson and his family, the Stinsons, as well as others, owned property in the county. Also, it is not clear whether the names of African Americans listed in this census included those indentured servants who lived under the roof of a white family. By 1840 the Floyd County black population had nearly doubled, showing 402 African Americans. Furthermore, with the 1840 census more information about households became available and one can begin to know more about the people and their function within the county.

African American Society

It was often thought that the African Americans who were moving into Floyd County would become a financial burden, either because it was commonly believed they were lazy or had no training for "real" work. This was indeed a false notion and a myth. Even though their opportunities for advancement beyond certain occupations were limited, census records show that they not only owned property but practiced many trades. They were farmers, barbers, teachers and preachers, carpenters, blacksmiths, drivers of wagons and other vehicles, steamboat firemen and workers on the river, lumbermen, coopers, blacksmiths, brickmakers, rope makers, whitewashers, servants, laundresses, seamstresses and milliners. Rev. William Paul Quinn reported to the General Conference of the AME Church in 1844 that the black population of Indiana and Illinois as a body of rising farmers and craftsmen had "every constituent principle among them, when suitably composed, to make them a great and good people."[26] They frequently used their earnings, both from skilled and unskilled labor, to purchase family members out of slavery into freedom.[27]

Grace McKee, who was born in New Albany and has lived there at least fifty years of her life, possesses a diary written by her grandfather, Alexander Martin, a Civil War soldier. He wrote during the Civil War that Captain French of his regiment on board the *Brown* discharged all his white crew deckhands and firemen except a watchman and two leadmen and hired a full crew of freedmen. Martin wrote,

> They are more faithful, sober, honest and less trouble in every respect than the old crew of white men. The new order permitting him to rate them as firemen and common seamen [sic] wages accordingly, works with the increased pay and recognized position, stimulating the negro to unwonted zeal in the discharge of his duty.[28]

Martin also wrote that on October 20, 1863, his New Albany regiment took on board the *Monarch* at Cairo, Illinois, nine slaves fleeing Arkansas in order to avoid performing labor for the Rebel army. According to Martin's commentary, they had continued working in the cotton fields for planters and had been kept in ignorance of the Emancipation Proclamation. They were delighted with the prospect of working as free men for wages and comfortable clothing and food.

The census records of 1840 and 1850 show various African Americans living outside the city limits; they were purchasing and working the land as farmers or wood sawyers. In fact, the vast majority of them lived either around the edges of New Albany or in the northern suburbs. Roughly one-half lived on the fringes of town, one-fourth lived within the city and the remaining one-fourth lived in the surrounding countryside in outlying townships. Some of those living north of the Vincennes Turnpike and farming on their own land were: John Fulton, John Finney, William Nelson, Rueben Mukes, Peter Ross, Benjamin Cook, Martin Edwards and Adam Burch. Those farmers owning their own property in Lafayette Township were William Boyd, Alexander Melton, Mary Weaver, Charles Stinson, Hugh Justice, Jonas Carter and Asa Martin. The Weaver farm stayed in the family until Peter Weaver sold it in the mid–1900s to the Floyd County school system for the building of Floyd Central High School. New Albany Township included the following black farmers: John Hagan, Thomas Locklayer, Peter Whiten and Pampia Harper, a "Hewer of Wood." Franklin Township black farmers were: Jeremiah Clark, John Hankins and Josiah Findley. This area was known as the "Budd Road Frenchtown Settlement,"[29] which began at the river and went up the bluffs into the Knobs. Georgetown Township farmers included George Russell and Francie Grisney. By 1860 the number of black farmers in all of Floyd County had decreased with only sixteen farmers and six wood sawyers remaining. John Weaver, Peter Ross, George Russell and John Stinson were listed as farmers in Lafayette Township, and Josiah Finley, James Finley and Eli Welch remained in Franklin Township. Reasons for this decrease remain unknown, but it can be surmised that the land could no longer sustain the growing family units. Additionally, pressures from white land speculators who coveted the land, along with rising property values, may all have worked together to convince the black pioneers that their future no longer existed in the countryside, and that they would be better off to sell their homesteads and find employment in metropolitan areas.

Important to our present study is the fact that the Floyd County census records for 1850 and 1860 show that many African Americans had occupations related to river transportation and the steamboats. The 1850 census shows there were twenty-eight boatmen, several steamboat firemen and a steamboat cook. The 1860 census shows sixty-one blacks with occupations related to the riverboats: steamboat firemen, stewards, cabin boys, porters, engineers, chambermaids and cooks. A substantial number in both censuses listed "laborer" for occupation, some of whom could have worked on the river. Many of those who worked as laborers were also connected with the transportation industry as draymen and drivers of wagons, carts, omnibuses and other vehicles carrying produce back and forth to market. The idea of constructing a railroad between the Ohio River at New Albany and Salem, Indiana, was apparently conceived by a group of Salem citizens who thought the idea had merit in view of the rough dirt road that often became muddy and impassable. In an 1849 pamphlet written by James Brooks, president of the New Albany–Salem Railroad, for the purpose of raising funds to support the railroad, said that an average of 100 wagons per day each way passed on the road from Salem to New Albany and back again. "These wagons were estimated to carry an average of one ton of freight going in [to the river] and one-quarter of a ton going out [in the direction of Salem], which would make one hundred and twenty-five tons of freight passing over this road daily in wagons."[30] Many of the farmers did their own driving, but it was also an occupation covered heavily by hired drivers. The high number of African Americans occupying their time in river-related occupations and transportation was an important link for the slaves desperate to cross the Ohio River in the "Falls of the Ohio" area.

Both the 1850 and the 1860 censuses show that more than half of the black population in Floyd County were born in Indiana while the majority of the remainder were born in Kentucky and Virginia. African Americans moving into New Albany itself settled primarily in West Union, the tract of land shaped like a wedge and located north of the bridge at State and Cherry streets running along the west side of State Street north to West Street. German immigrants also settled in this area of New Albany. In part because of the close proximity of German immigrants and African Americans in West Union, the Germans undoubtedly lent a hand in helping runaway slaves. Pearl Grundy Kimbrough's grandfather settled in New Albany after being released from slavery during the Civil War. He stated it was the working-class German immigrants who helped in Underground Railroad work.[31] Smaller black settlements were located on West Fourth Street between Spring and Elm, in Mt. Isam at the top of Pearl Street Hill (colloquially known as "Vinegar Hill" or "Limerick Hill," named for the Irish immigrants who also settled there), in the area north of present-day Beechwood Avenue, in the "Near East End Neighborhood" below Fairview Cemetery, and in Providence, the area located near the K & I Bridge in southeast New Albany. During New Albany's heyday from the 1830s through the 1850s, when the steamboat industry was at its apex, many African Americans who worked as servants were also concentrated in sections of New Albany where the wealthy merchants and ship captains lived on the periphery of the commercial section of town.

As the Civil War drew to a close, others came and settled in isolated areas up in the Knobs and worked as laborers or farmers. Benjamin LaForce and his family came from Kentucky and purchased farmland in Franklin Township before the 1870 census was taken.[32] Willis Walker and his wife, Mary J. Walker, and their family, Olivia J., Shelby W., Samuel D. and Stephen M., came to Indiana immediately after the Civil War and purchased land located near Old Vincennes Road.[33] They had a grandson, William Bush, who also lived with them. Walkers purchased Floyd County land in 1873, 1874 and 1885; it included at least seventeen acres of ground and a roadway.³⁴ Willis died on March 17, 1901, at age seventy-seven.³⁵ Although it is known by the descendants of white neighbors that Mary died before her husband, her death was not recorded with the Floyd County coroner. Mary and Willis Walker were both buried on a knoll overlooking the valley off Quarry Road and Old Vincennes Road. Some of the neighbors, members of the Bezy and Didelot families, helped to prepare both of the Walkers for burial. They were laid out on ironing boards and buried on either side of a sassafras tree. An early white settler from Connecticut named Caleb C. Dayton had already been buried there and had a tombstone at one time.³⁶ However, neither of the Walkers had tombstones.³⁷

Churches

During the antebellum years, African Americans were struggling to better their situation and give moral fiber to their lives by establishing their own organizations, including churches, schools and lodges. It is believed that the early African American settlers came together and worshipped in their homes just as the white citizens did. Baptisms were held on the Ohio River bank or in Falling Run Creek. Many of the first services of The African Methodist Episcopal (AME) church were held in the home of Elijah and Nancy Campbell located on Naghel Street between Blair and Albany streets. All that remains of the Campbell property, now a vacant lot, is a stone well with the names "Campbell, Grundy and Morris" carved on the inside wall.

William Paul Quinn was a man who came to New Albany as a circuit preacher in conjunction with his work in establishing a church in Louisville called Quinn Chapel (AME), known as the "abolitionist church." Quinn's name has been linked with helping runaway slaves in Indianapolis as well as other areas of the state.³⁸ As a preacher in the AME Church, he was appointed by the general conference to be in charge of the missionary work in the West. This included Illinois, as well as the Indiana circuits of Blue River, Richmond, Indianapolis, Terre Haute and Salem. Quinn had boundless energy, and the New Albany black community benefited from his work. AME records for the Salem Circuit show that by 1841 the New Albany church had twenty-two members. The group had a church building by then because the newspaper reported that the structure was destroyed by fire in July of that year. The common belief at the time was that the fire was set by individuals who did not like the promotion of abolitionist ideas or anyone attempting to elevate the black population.³⁹ By 1844, the number of members had increased to forty-two.⁴⁰ In 1845 Quinn reported that New Albany had fifty-five members, Jeffersonville had fifty-two, and Salem had fifty-eight. Paoli had a larger number, sixty-five, because of the black rural settlement of Lick Creek nearby.⁴¹

Newspapers during the early history of New Albany were often vague in their description of the African American churches. This shows a lack of willingness on the part of some of the white society to understand formation of black organizations at the time. For example, terms like the "West Union Church," the "Colored Methodist Church," "African Church" or the "Christian Church in West Union" were all used as descriptive terms.

By 1845 at least two black churches existed, Bethel AME Church on West Main Street and the Baptist Church located on Lower First Street between Spring and Elm. In fact, Second Presbyterian church records show that some of their African American members transferred membership to the "Colored Baptist Church" in 1845, indicating that that is probably when it had its beginnings.[42] Four black preachers were working in New Albany during the 1860s: B. L. Brooks from the District of Columbia, William A. Dove[43] from Pennsylvania, Henry White, a missionary preacher who lived with Elijah and Nancy Campbell, and Thomas J. Brown, a "Laboring Methodist Episcopal Preacher" from Kentucky.

Schools

New Albany school board records show that on August 11, 1831, the board was asked to determine whether black children were to be admitted to the school system. After discussing the issue the board passed a resolution to the effect that they were not to be admitted.[44] Therefore, as soon as it was established, the AME Church, in its attempt to elevate the black population, began to expand its religious role to include educating black children. In this way Floyd County children were able to receive a basic education.[45] It is not known whether classes met in a one-room school building, a private home or in the AME Church building. Some of George Washington Carter's children received a "common school" education in New Albany as early as the 1850s, although several of the Carter sons also attended school for their early childhood education in Buxton and Chatham, Ontario, Canada.[46] The African American teachers in 1850 included William J. Greenly from Pennsylvania, and William Harding, Jr. (Harding was born in Kentucky but was living with his family in New Albany by 1848.) In 1850 there were at least thirty-six Floyd County black children in school. The 1860 census shows that William I. Grundy, born in Pennsylvania, and Julia Brent, born in Indiana, both mulatto, were teaching. In 1860 ninety-four Floyd County black children were in school. It was not until 1869 that the Indiana General Assembly passed a law requiring that schools be organized in the state for "negro children."[47] The New Albany School Board met on August 13, 1869, and appealed to the city council for the construction of a school building for "negro children" and for money with which to pay the teachers. On March 1, 1870, the board voted to purchase a lot on Olden Street for the purpose of building a "negro school."[48] Four years later the board rented the second floor of the Baptist Church on Upper Fourth Street for another school for black children.[49] According to the enumeration for 1873, there were 2,438 white students and 207 black students enrolled in the city school system.[50] Scribner High School for African American students was established in 1880 in an existing building on Spring Street, which stood at the site of the present City-County Building. By 1882 the enrollment of white students in the city schools was 5,830 and the number of black students had increased to 534. The Division Street School, in the east end of New Albany, was built in 1884, at a cost of $1,752 and is said to be one of the oldest black school buildings still in existence in the State of Indiana.[51]

POLITICAL ORGANIZATIONS

The AME Church also became involved in political endeavors. Black leaders from all over the nation began establishing their own political organizations and launching campaigns to achieve civil rights for blacks.[52] At least two New Albany men became involved in this effort. One was William J. Greenly and the other, Byrd Parker. Greenly, a member of Bethel AME Church in New Albany, became the delegate to a "Convention of the People of Color" held in Indianapolis on August 8, 1851. He was also the secretary of the convention.[53] He and his family of seven children resided in West Union. His oldest son was a boatman.

Byrd Parker, born in North Carolina, first appeared in the Louisville city directory in 1848. He lived at 110 Ninth Street between Grayson and Walnut streets. By 1850 he, being a missionary agent for the African Methodist Episcopal Indiana Conference, had moved to New Albany and had become the minister at Bethel AME. He continued to serve as a preacher at Quinn Chapel in Louisville and thereby had contact with black leaders of that community.[54] Parker lived in the West Union area of New Albany near William J. Greenly and Elijah Campbell. In July of 1853 he attended a "National Convention of Colored People" in Rochester, New York, organized by Frederick Douglass.[55] The purpose of the convention was to discuss ways in which to elevate and improve the general condition of people of color; Parker was a member of the committee formed to study the "importance of colored persons engaged in commercial pursuits."[56] In October of 1853 Parker resigned as pastor of the AME Church in Louisville (Quinn Chapel) and as missionary agent for the Indiana Conference. He moved to Chicago, Illinois, and became involved in African American politics there. He was elected to the state council, receiving 231 out of 245 votes cast. By December of that year, Parker began working as a traveling agent for the *Frederick Douglass' Paper*, covering the states of Illinois and Wisconsin.[57] During this time he became associated with several Underground Railroad operators in Chicago, including John Jones, James D. Bonner and Artemas Carter. Jones and Bonner owned and operated a business called the "Intelligence Office" located at No. 88 Dearborn Street. Through their business, which was probably used as a cover in their Underground Railroad work, they procured jobs for blacks until they could be safely transported to Canada.[58] Parker's network of contacts, which included Frederick Douglass and William Paul Quinn, as well as free African Americans in both slave and free states, should be looked upon as an important link to an organized effort in helping slaves reach free territory. His leadership abilities, his established friendships in both Louisville and New Albany, his friendship with Frederick Douglass, his contacts with acknowledged Underground Railroad operators in Chicago and his mobility should be viewed as important for runaway slaves seeking freedom.

Lodges

Another likely link of Byrd Parker to the Underground Railroad in Floyd County was his involvement with the African American lodge. Black Free Masonry was established in New Albany by the early 1850s. W. H. Gibson, Sr., a leader in the African American community in Louisville in the last half of the nineteenth century, wrote a book in 1897 titled *History of the United Brothers of Friendship and Sisters of the Mysterious Ten*. The book is a narrative about the founders and organizers of the African American Lodges and benevolent organizations during the mid–1800s in Louisville. Included is some information about the founding of a Masonic Lodge in New Albany.

Free Masonry

In the year 1850 Rev. Bird [Byrd] Parker, minister of the AME Church (now Quinn Chapel) met a number of gentlemen at the house of Jesse Merriweather. The object of the meeting was to consider the propriety of organizing a masonic lodge. Several meetings were held, and finally they concluded to organize.... A question arose in the meeting whether it would be advisable to establish a lodge in Louisville while the prejudice was so strong against free negroes.... This question caused a split, and the majority decided to locate the lodge at New Albany, Indiana, for a while at least. The necessary number for institution was secured and they went to Cincinnati, Ohio and received their warrant from the Grand Lodge of Ohio. Richard H. Gleaves, Grand Master of Ohio, granted the warrant for Mount Moriah Lodge No. 1 to begin on June 12, 1850.... For three years they remained at New Albany, Indiana. They labored under many disadvantages, such as crossing the river in skiffs at midnight, amid high water and heavy drifts, at the risk of their lives, and then walked five miles up to the city.[59]

The Louisville group had several ready-made contacts in New Albany that afforded them safe places to meet. One was the home of Rev. Byrd Parker. Parker's move to New Albany by 1850 was probably for his own safety since things may have gotten too risky for him living in Louisville. The Louisville group could also have met in the home of William Harding. Harding was a steward on the riverboats at the time that Gibson and Merriweather were also employed on the boats as musicians. Gibson and Merriweather had their subscriptions to *The North Star,* later called *Frederick Douglass' Paper,* mailed to Harding in New Albany, for safety's sake, and he in turn passed the paper on to them. William Harding was a friend and neighbor of George Washington Carter, whose barber shop on Lower Main could also have been

The grave monument of African American Henry Clay. The monument shows his membership in the Masonic Lodge. West Haven Cemetery, New Albany. (Photograph courtesy of Jennifer Suzanne Vezner)

used as a convenient meeting place. Carter's shop was on the west side of town and close to the river. In this way the group would have avoided the busier section of downtown.[60] It was also possible for the men to meet at the home of Henry Clay. We know from the obituary of Henry Clay,[61] a New Albany friend and neighbor of Harding, that he was a Mason. John Sanders, another friend and neighbor of Clay, Harding and Carter, was also a member.[62] Albert Butler, born in New Albany February 28, 1840, was another member of the Masons and Odd Fellows.

A reference to a black Masonic Lodge in Portland, Kentucky (directly across the river from New Albany, where blacks have lived since it was established), is found in the following narrative of Margaret Webb's father, 639 West 7th Street, New Albany, Indiana, as told to Iris Cook, the WPA interviewer:

> He says that his father was a slave, and told him that runaway negroes used to come across the Ohio river from Portland. Plans for the escapes were hatched in a colored Masonic lodge, located in Portland. They would cross the Ohio river in a skiff, manned by fishermen (supposedly) and if the coast was not clear on this side they would go up the river for a short distance. Some went all the way up the river, until they got past Louisville, and then crossed over, probably at about Utica.[63]

The establishment of a black Masonic Lodge during the early 1850s should be seen as an important connection to the assistance of slaves crossing the Ohio River from Louisville to New Albany. The lodge offered a ready-made link between the black communities in Louisville and New Albany, both a secret organization and a brotherhood.

The Civil War Years

The isolation African Americans experienced in antebellum Floyd County in the areas of housing, employment, education, membership in churches and lodges, burials and society in general continued as the country entered the Civil War. The reaction in Floyd County toward the idea of using blacks as soldiers was reserved, to be sure. The editor of the *Ledger* voiced doubts as to what caliber of soldiers they would make, and whether or not they would remain loyal to the Union or become spies for the Southern forces. The newspaper gave an example of blacks who came into the Federal army camp at Cairo, Illinois, to sell fresh produce but later communicated what they had seen in the camp to the Confederates.[64] Able-bodied blacks were barred from enlisting until May, 1863, when Lincoln declared that they were allowed to enter the service of the United States and to bear arms. On May 13, 1863, it was reported that Governor Andrews of Massachusetts had sent officers to New Albany to enlist recruits for the "colored regiments." A "colored war meeting" was held for all African American citizens at the "colored Methodist church in West

Union." Dr. Revels and Col. Robinson of Indianapolis addressed the group. Following an editorial on July 8, 1863, regarding the futility of attempting to carry on the war using black troops, the *Ledger* editor proposed that all "negroes" who were recruited by Andrews' sergeants to help fill up the Massachusetts units should, after the expiration of their term of service, be permanently excluded from Indiana. Believing the Exclusion Act would continue to be in effect, the editor stated, "It will be unconstitutional for them to return to Indiana."[65] But when Indiana Governor Morton enforced President Lincoln's declaration that blacks were to be recruited and allowed to bear arms, the *Ledger* became more conciliatory and made the following announcement:

> Mr. A. Huncilman has received authority from Governor Morton to recruit for the colored battalion ordered to be raised in this state. Recruits will receive liberal bounties, and can learn all particulars by calling upon Mr. Huncilman or Jessie J. Brown. All the colored men in this county have been enrolled, and are as liable to military duty as white men. They have a chance to volunteer, receive bounties and avoid the draft, the same as white men. It is with them to choose what they will do. It is certain they will have to enter the service, either as conscripts or as volunteers.[66]

The newspaper reported that only ten or fifteen African Americans from Floyd County volunteered for the three-year service. James Williams and Enos Mitchum were among the first Floyd County blacks to volunteer on November 30, 1863. By January, 1864, Huncilman had recruited thirty-seven men. By June, 1864, thirty-five more were reported to enlist from Floyd County.[67]

Gale and John Weaver, residents of Lafayette Township, were drafted in September of 1864 as part of the Second Congressional District.[68] Private William Frank Dawson, nineteen years old, enlisted with Company G 115th, State of Indiana, U.S.C.T., on September 9, 1864. He was discharged on February 10, 1866, in Indianola, Texas. Dawson died on July 24, 1933, and is buried in the National Cemetery in New Albany.[69] Dr. William A. Burney, who fought with the 28th Regiment, was the only African American physician in New Albany during the post–Civil War years. He was on the Board of Health and in the Floyd County Medical Society, and he assisted William O. Vance in the establishment of a newspaper called *The Weekly Review*, which was published in 1882 and 1883.[70] Some African American Civil War veterans are buried in West Haven Cemetery and they include: Allen White, Mr. Scott, John D. Dodson, Robert Gregg, Vance Williams, Franklin Carpenter and Sidney Knight. George Stinson and his wife, Nancy, who grew up in Floyd County, are both buried in the New Albany National Cemetery. Stinson was a private during the Civil War.[71]

The majority of the men in Terrell's list were not in the Floyd County census of 1860. Because the Exclusion Act barred blacks from moving into the state after 1851, where these men came from remains a puzzle. One possibility is that they lived in another Indiana county in the immediate area or that they were "contrabands of war" brought north with Union troops. "Contraband" was the term used to describe a slave who fled to the Union troops. Even though the contrabands remained with the troops, they were not allowed to join forces and bear arms with the Union army until late in the war. Not knowing how best to use contrabands, Union officers ordered them to perform menial tasks. In Louisville, for example, General J. T. Boyle, Commander of the Western District of Kentucky, employed them in filling up rifle pits that were dug in September of 1862. After that they were to dig sewers for drainage of the military prisons and hospitals in Louisville.[72] The West Union area in New Albany was referred to as "Contraband Quarters" where sometimes more than twenty people were crammed into two-room houses. On July 22, 1862, a long line of four-horse wagons conveyed a large number of contrabands through New Albany. "They were conducted to a new asylum provided for them in the northern suburbs of the city."[73]

African Americans in Floyd County served in the Civil War in various other ways. Because of its size and location on the Ohio River, New Albany became a medical center for sick and injured soldiers. Black volunteer societies that were connected with African American churches in Louisville and New Albany helped to relieve the suffering of soldiers on both sides of the river. They provided additional nursing services in order to supplement the inadequate services provided by the federal government. A controversy arose as to where to place the African American casualties brought to New Albany. For the most part they were kept at the wharf on the "floating hospital" (a damaged steamboat that was no longer seaworthy), in Anderson College on Lower Third Street, which was referred to as "Hospital No. 5," and in separate wards of the other ten hospitals located about town. However, late in the war Medical Headquarters in Louisville issued an order to convert the Public Square in New Albany into a hospital for African American soldiers because of the poor condition of the floating hospital. This idea caused an uproar among many in the community.[74]

As the war progressed, New Albany regiments also took some slaves under their protection who had fled to the Union army for safety, possibly hoping to reach freedom in the North. The regiments used them, not only as nurses, but also as barbers, cooks and laundresses. The names of several women who came to New Albany in this way and became permanent citizens are known, including Lucy Higgs Nichols, Polly Campbell and Patsy Lindsey. But remaining in New Albany, even if brought there under the umbrella of protection afforded by an officer of a New Albany regiment, was risky business. Lucy Higgs Nichols, Polly Campbell and Patsy Lindsey were examples of people who succeeded in this.

In 1862, Lucy Higgs fled to the 23rd Regiment of Indiana Volunteers at Bolivar, Tennessee. She remained with them as a war nurse and followed them back to New Albany, where she continued to nurse the wounded and sick in the New Albany war hospitals. She married John Nichols in 1870 and remained in New Albany until the end of her life.[75] Her last years were spent in the county poor house on Grant Line Road because she had no one to care for her. She was made an honorary member of the G.A.R. Sanderson Post because of the services she performed during the Civil War. According to the *New Albany Daily Ledger*, Lucy is buried next to her husband in the "colored cemetery." It is assumed this is a reference to West Haven Cemetery, but there is no record there of her burial.[76]

Polly Campbell, born under slavery in Meader County, Virginia, January, 1813, was sold several times and eventually became a house slave at a large cotton plantation near Vicksburg, Tennessee. She fled to the 53rd regiment of Indiana Volunteers on July 4, 1863, when General Grant captured Vicksburg. There she worked for General Walter Q. Gresham and General Rogers as a nurse, cook and laundress. She continued on to New Albany with the regiment on a steamboat loaded with sick and wounded soldiers who had been ordered to the military hospitals. "Aunt Polly" continued to nurse the wounded soldiers after her arrival, among them Gresham, who had been wounded in the battle of Peach Tree Creek below Atlanta. She remained in New Albany until her death in 1908. For all of her invaluable service to the Union army during the Civil War, she was never paid a pension from the government and was living in the county poor house at the time of her death.[77]

Patsy Lindsey fled to the Union Army in the Vicksburg, Tennessee, area, close to Grand Gulf at Sherman's Landing. She stayed with New Albany's 23rd Regiment, but during the siege of Vicksburg, Isaac P. Smith, quartermaster of the 23rd Regiment, wrote to his wife, Abby, that he was worried for Patsy's safety if she stayed with the regiment. Therefore, she was sent north to New Albany with James A. Doll, a member of Second Presbyterian Church and neighbor of the Smith family. Patsy was taken under the protection of the Smith household. She undoubtedly worked for them as a servant and lived in their home on Main Street for a time before moving to her own house in New Albany. Patsy died January 11, 1881, at age seventy-six of "dropsey."[78]

Hannibal Carter and Edward Carter

Two prominent New Albany African Americans deserve special attention for their contribution to the Civil War effort: Hannibal Carter and his brother Edward. Despite restrictions placed on African Americans, these men had a certain amount of mobility and were able to cross state lines. They were among some of the first blacks in the United States to muster into service during the Civil War. The two Carter brothers became a part of the Louisiana Native Guards formed in New Orleans initially to protect interests of native New Orleans citizens. Although the exact date is unclear, some time in the spring of 1861, George Washington Carter and sons Hannibal and Edward took the steamer *Vicksburgh*, which ran on the lower Mississippi, down to New Orleans. According to the *New Albany Ledger*, they were there on April 12, 1861, when Fort Sumter fell and the Civil War began.⁷⁹ *The Appeal*, which published a biography of Hannibal in 1891, also reported that the men were "on the Mississippi Steamer, 'Vicksburgh,' when the war broke out."⁸⁰ Their presence in New Orleans at the start of the war is also confirmed by the fact that the names of Hannibal and Edward Carter appear on the roster of the Louisiana Native Guards in 1861. Edward was a captain in the First Regiment of Louisiana Native Guards, and Hannibal was a captain in the Second Regiment of Louisiana Native Guards.⁸¹

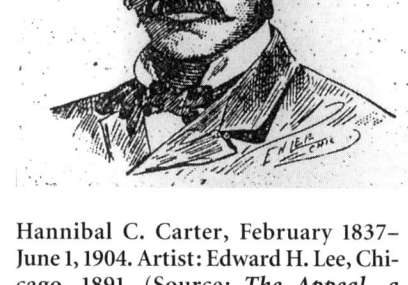

Hannibal C. Carter, February 1837–June 1, 1904. Artist: Edward H. Lee, Chicago, 1891. (Source: *The Appeal, a National African American Newspaper*, Boston, Massachusetts, July 25, 1892)

By March of 1862, Louisiana Governor Thomas O. Moore inducted the First and Second regiments into the state militia. "They were not enthused about serving the confederacy, and attended regimental musters only irregularly, showing only enough enthusiasm to allay Confederate suspicions."⁸² Even so, they approached the Confederate army with notification that they were ready to fight. They were, however, rebuffed when it actually came to joining forces with the Confederates against the Union. By April, New Orleans had fallen to the Union army and the Confederate troops were gone. The men of the Native Guard, therefore, never put on the uniform of the Southern army, and they never fired a gun for the Confederacy. By August, General Butler was in command there. The officers of the Native Guard approached General Butler about joining forces with the Federal troops. Initially he declined their offer on the grounds that the War Department did not permit black soldiers. However, when the Confederates recaptured Baton Rouge and threatened to attack New Orleans, Butler became desperate and invited the officers of the Native Guards to his office to talk. He needed assurance from them that they wanted to serve the Union. When Butler questioned the officers about why they served with the Confederates, they said, "We were ordered out and dared not refuse, for those who did so were killed and their property confiscated."⁸³ Butler eventually realized how useful these men who had been left behind could be for the cause of the Union. He had a change of heart, and on August 22, 1862, he issued an order requesting the Native Guard to enlist in the service of the United States.⁸⁴ He continued to recruit blacks during the fall of 1862. Edward Carter was mustered into service on September 27, 1862, and Hannibal Carter was mustered in on October 12, 1862, in what was eventually called the First and Second regiments of Infantry of the Corps d'Afrique of the Union army.⁸⁵

On October 25, 1862, Edward marched with the men of the First Regiment out of Camp Strong Station for Algiers, Louisiana. Hannibal remained with the Second Regiment in New Orleans until October 30, when they journeyed by foot and by rail to Opelousas. They remained at Ship Island and Fort Pike, on Lake Pontchartrain guarding prisoners and protecting the Opelousas Railroad until December 31, 1862.[86] This regiment was also assigned the duty of supervising the new plantation system in that region. They met with much hostility from the planters. Captain Hannibal Carter wrote to Col. N. W. Daniels in February of 1863 that slave owners had charged the Native Guard officers with causing unrest among their slaves and were demanding removal of the Native Guard from the countryside.[87] This was just one episode among many that the regiments of the Native Guard had to deal with because of prejudice.

In April of 1863, the Second Regiment marched up the Mississippi Sound to Pascagoula and finally took part in a skirmish, defeating the Confederates. Two Union soldiers were killed and seven were wounded.[88] Hannibal became ill from exposure due to the heavy drilling and marching while his regiment was at Ship Island.[89] Edward accompanied the First and Third regiments up the Mississippi River and commanded his company in the assault on Fort Hudson. He went into the battle with ninety-one of his men but only twenty survived; he himself was injured.[90] Edward resigned on October 21, 1863, due to ill health and moved to Busby, Tunica County, Mississippi, where he worked as a farmer. Hannibal resigned on May 30, 1863, and moved to Tennessee.[91]

During the Reconstruction period, many of the officers of the Native Guard became leaders in the Republican Party. Hannibal assisted in the reconstruction of Tennessee in 1867. In 1868 he was elected as representative from the Eighth Congressional District. In that same year he moved to Mississippi and became involved in the politics of reconstruction there, also. He represented Warren County, Mississippi, in the State Legislature three times and was twice appointed Secretary of State.[92] He was active in getting the Gray-Carter Civil Rights Bill passed in June of 1873 as a member of the Mississippi State Legislature.[93] This bill had to do with the rights of blacks in public places. He had been refused a seat in the white section of the Angelo Concert Hall in Jackson, Mississippi. As a result, he secured a warrant for the arrest of the doorkeeper, Mr. George Donnell, who had barred him from the white section. Hannibal won his case before Chancellor E. W. Cabaniss. Donnell appealed to the State Supreme Court for a writ of *habeas corpus,* arguing that the civil rights bill of 1873 was unconstitutional on the grounds that it interfered with property rights. He and his lawyer insisted that if forced to seat blacks in the white section, the proprietor would lose business, resulting in the depreciation of his property.[94] Carter argued that this was an issue of human rights, not property rights, and that the civil rights act was in accordance with the doctrine of equality of all men. He claimed that blacks, in the spirit of the Fourteenth Amendment, which had raised a suppressed class "to a plane of absolute legal equality with the hitherto dominant cast," had been invited and had accepted the invitation "to enter the race of life as competitors with the white man to attain new goals for themselves."[95] Carter won the case in the State Supreme Court. He was an unsuccessful candidate for Congress in the Second District against General J. R. Chalmers in 1882. After that he moved from Vicksburg to Chicago, explaining, "It [Vicksburg] ceased to be a healthy locality for a free man."[96] Hannibal died in Chicago on June 1, 1904.[97] He, like his father, George Washington Carter, was a remarkable man who did not let restrictions because of race get in the way of his ability to achieve. His mobility during a time when it was almost impossible for blacks to travel, as well as his ability to become politically active and achieve much for African Americans during reconstruction, show his exceptional skill.

During the Civil War period, there were other African Americans not so well known who became heroes in the truest sense of the word. These were the men and women who helped their brothers bound by the limitations of slavery to escape. Most of their names remain unknown but some have been recorded. We now look closer at the free black community in Floyd County and its involvement in the Underground Railroad.

African Americans and the Underground Railroad

The attempt made by the white community to bar African Americans from making economic and social progress was a way of perpetuating slavery on free soil. Because of this relationship between slavery and racism, free and enslaved alike shared a common burden, and active assistance in helping runaway slaves on the part of free blacks in Floyd County comes as no surprise. For example, according to a narrative told by Jacob Cummings in 1894, Charles Lacey, William Finney and Zeke Goins assisted Cummings in his escape from slavery in 1839. Cummings had fled from a farm near Chattanooga, Tennessee, where he had been enslaved and cruelly treated. He reached the Ohio River in the latter part of September, broke a lock fastened to a skiff and made his way across to Mt. Vernon, Indiana (located in the far southwest corner of the state). "Cummings turned up the Ohio River, and at New Albany, in Floyd County, Indiana, met his first abolitionists— Uncle Charles Lacey, William Finney and old Uncle Zeke Goins."[98] Cummings stayed and worked for them a couple of weeks before moving up the river to Charlestown. Two miles above Charlestown, Cummings was arrested and taken down to Jeffersonville, where he was brought before a Clark County judge who declared the law had no right to hold him. Several men hurried him out of the courtroom and left on horses. After other troubles along the way, he made his way to Cabin Creek, a black settlement in Randolph County, Indiana; eventually he reached Canada.

Fifty-five years had elapsed between the time Cummings met the New Albany men and his interview in Canada. Not only could his recollection of the names have been inaccurate, but the interviewer may have elaborated Cummings' story to fit his own needs. Nevertheless, the names of Lacey, Finney and Goins are common to both Floyd and Harrison counties. The relationship among these black families across county lines must be considered when examining Underground Railroad activity. The 1840 census shows that William Goins' household contained three adult males who lived in the city of New Albany. A John Finney owned land outside the city limits on Silver Creek in New Albany Township. Samuel Lacey lived near John Finney. Census records as well as the Black Register of 1853 show many Findleys, Finleys, Finneys and Goins, Goin or Goings. Details about the Finley farm in a remote part of Franklin Township not far from the river have already been mentioned. The 1850 census shows that Isaac Finley and his family lived in rural Harrison County close to the Floyd County line. Communication between the Finleys and runaway slaves coming up from the Ohio River would have been possible. Joseph Finley was even labeled by the *Ledger* in 1866 as a "colored republican radical."[99] In Messrs. Lacey, Finney and Goins we see clear evidence of African American citizens from New Albany assisting a runaway slave.

It is very likely that an organized effort to help runaway slaves existed among the African Americans in the "Near Northeast Neighborhood" of New Albany. Among the black people in that neighborhood one has a combination of relative affluence and mobility, occupations that were related to one of the transportation systems, membership in a Masonic lodge, and contact with the black community in Louisville. It has been established through census records and city directories that George Washington Carter, Edward Carter, Henry Clay, John Sanders and William Harding, as well as other blacks, lived there. In the case of three, Edward Carter, William Harding and George Washington Carter, their back doors faced each other. Many of the African Americans who lived in this neighborhood and away from the West Union area were property owners. This relative affluence afforded them some protection from the criticism often leveled against the West Union inhabitants for sheltering and protecting runaway slaves. It is known that the riverboat steward, William Harding, who lived on East Sixth Street, was sympathetic with the abolitionist movement. Henry Clay[100] resided on the west side of Pearl between Elm and Oak.[101] Clay, born in Bourbon County, Kentucky, June 4, 1806, moved to New Albany in 1827 and was a blacksmith who worked for the New Albany–Salem Railroad. Before that he had been employed as a blacksmith on the steamer *New York* and worked on the river for a number of years. Other blacks lived near him in the Third Ward around the railroad station and included not only other railroad workers but also a man by the name of Washington Johnson, a riverboat steward who was born in Ohio. A Methodist minister from the District of Columbia, the Rev. B. L. Brook, lived there in the 1860s. Close by in the Upper Second Ward resided the barber, James Carter, a relative of George Washington Carter; James Porter, a riverboat steward; and Peter Findley, a steamboatman. A little farther east in the Upper First Ward was John W. Sanders, also a riverboat steward who lived on the south side of Sycamore between Upper Sixth and Seventh streets. Next door to Sanders was abolitionist Henson McIntosh, a ropemaker, of whom we will hear more in a later chapter, and David Lewis, an African American who lived on the other side of McIntosh. John Hill, George Washington Carter's brother-in-law, was a barber.[102] He lived on Shelby Street just below the Northern Cemetery. George Washington Carter lived on the west side of Eighth Street above Sycamore Street and owned several acres there bordering the New Albany–Salem Railroad.[103] This placed many households of black families who had a working relationship with the river and rail transportation systems not only near each other but also close to the New Albany-Salem Railroad depot and tracks, a confirmed route of the runaway slaves. In fact, since George Washington Carter educated several of his sons in Canada between 1846 and 1856, he could have worked out a plan to take slaves north with him using a legitimate ticket to ride the rails. Given his bold character, he could have carried that out.[104]

Throughout the Civil War years, the newspaper continued to fault free blacks for helping runaways.[105] After the war started, the *Ledger* criticized the free black community for assisting contrabands and other escaped slaves: "If the colored residents of this community [New Albany] who are lawfully so, were to discourage the immigration of negroes unlawfully, we believe they would get along peaceably and without trouble."[106] Without mentioning any names, the newspaper accused an African American resident of West Union of aiding runaways and hiding them in his home. The newspaper warned, "The keeper of the house should be taught a lesson which would make him more careful in the future how he violates the laws."[107]

We find many examples of runaway slaves attempting to hide within the free African American community in New Albany. For instance, Jane, a slave belonging to a man living thirty miles "back of Louisville," ran away from her owner during the summer of 1856. She managed to get across the river into New Albany where she "hid" in West Union among the free black residents. She represented herself as a free woman, at least to outsiders, and after residing there for several months married an African American man living there. One Sunday afternoon the woman's former master happened to be passing the home of an African American family in New Albany and by chance saw his former slave. The next day he came back to New Albany and reclaimed her. This caused considerable excitement among the residents of West Union because the owner reclaimed her without a warrant or any other authority and was allowed quietly to take her back to Kentucky.[108]

Not all blacks, however, could be considered friends of the runaway slave. Some valued their own freedom too much to risk being arrested. Others saw turning in runaways as a way of making money. In an unpublished WPA report written by Iris L. Cook, there is a narrative told by Sarah Merrill (whose mother had been a slave in Kentucky) of 1710 Monon Ave., New Albany, dated May 19, 1936:

5. The Free African American Community

> I have heard my mother and father tell this story more times than I can remember. My great-uncle, Lewis Barnett (was a slave) and was brought to Louisville from the south, to be sold at auction. He escaped, and crossed the river, at about Portland, and with 12 other negroes came through New Albany. He came out State street and down where Cherry street is now and went west on Cherry til he hit the knobs west of the town. The slaves were covered up in a wagon full of corn.[109]

The WPA report goes on to say that an African American family in the Knobs took the fugitives in and kept them for two days. The runaway slaves, thinking that the family was protecting them and attempting to send them farther north, trusted them explicitly. However, the family betrayed the fugitives, probably to collect a reward, and notified authorities in Louisville. All twelve of the runaways were then arrested and taken back to Louisville to be punished and sold. Sarah Merrill continued,

> In Louisville, my uncle Lewis denied his master. "I never seen you before in all my life," he says. Therefore, he was compelled to be sold again, and was sold on the block for $1,500.00 and he was taken to New Orleans. He came back three times to see us after that, when the war was over, and we children have heard him tell this story many times, and point down Cherry Street, and tell us *that* was the way I went when I was trying to get away. (We lived on State street near Cherry.) We came from near Munfordville, Kentucky. My father and mother were slaves.[110]

There is no doubt that the early presence of a substantial African American community in Floyd County was a contributing factor in the assistance of slaves who attempted to reach freedom through its borders. The fact that African Americans worked in a variety of occupations that gave them access to the river, the city, the countryside and the transportation systems helped in their ability to support those people running away from slavery. The account of the Carter brothers traveling by steamboat to New Orleans in 1861 also shows that, despite the rules and restrictions placed on them, some blacks possessed a certain amount of mobility and were able to move around the country. The same was true for their father, George Washington Carter, who traveled back and forth from New Albany to Canada in the 1850s to educate his children. In contrast to the mobility of some, the fact that many African Americans in Floyd County lived in relative isolation — either outside of New Albany on farmland or within the city in "confined" districts — gave runaway slaves a temporary place to hide. Just how did runaway slaves leave Floyd County and were did they go from there? We turn our attention now to the general routes used by runaway slaves in their flight through the central part of Southern Indiana.

Chapter 6

Underground Railroad Escape Routes

It appears that most of the slaves who came through Floyd County came from Tennessee or Kentucky and not from the deep South. Exodus from the border state of Kentucky picked up speed at the approach of the Civil War and reached a peak during the war years. It is apparent that this buildup came as the institution of slavery grew weaker and slave owners lost the ability to cope with events as they occurred. In 1862 a slaveowner from Tennessee, bringing his family and slaves with him, was asked when he reached New Albany if he wasn't afraid of bringing his slaves into a free state. He responded that "as a property of value, they are about played out."[1] Even though the January 1, 1863, Emancipation Proclamation was not meant to apply to the Kentucky slave, it became the means by which many began simply to walk away. Whites in authority on both sides of the river simply "lost it," provoking a New Albany man to report in a letter to his brother in 1863 that runaways were coming through Indiana, but no one was stopping them.[2] In fact, on the eve of Lincoln's Emancipation Proclamation, a general fear swept Kentucky communities as slave owners believed a slave insurrection would surely take place during the holiday season as a direct result of abolitionist teachings and in anticipation of Lincoln's Emancipation Proclamation. Kentucky counties along the Ohio River border and those counties directly below Louisville were particularly gripped by fear.[3]

There were three major corridors, or flight paths, through Indiana; each route had lines and branches off and around it.[4] "Stations" were generally ten to twenty miles apart. The western route started at or near Evansville, went north through Princeton, Rockport, Petersburg, Vincennes, Terre Haute, Lafayette, Rensselaer and South Bend and converged with the middle route at Battle Creek, Michigan.[5] The eastern route started at Cincinnati, Ohio, crossed over into Indiana and went north to Hamilton, Richmond, Fountain City, Winchester, Portland, Decatur, Ft. Wayne, Auburn, and on to Coldwater and Battle Creek, Michigan. Levi Coffin (reputed to be the head of the Underground Railroad system), operated from his house, known

6. *Underground Railroad Escape Routes* 85

Map of the state of Indiana showing locations of Underground Railroad activity mentioned in the text.

as "Grand Central Station," along this eastern route. He was a Quaker and lived at different times in Cincinnati, Ohio, and in Fountain City, Indiana, nine miles north of Richmond. It is believed that with his help more than 3,000 slaves passed through those areas on their way to Canada. Coffin had a garret off an upstairs bedroom reached by a secret stairs, along with other hiding places on his property.[6]

The present concern is with the central corridor, which passed through the Indiana border counties of Crawford, Harrison, Floyd and Clark. This central area along the southern border of Indiana was a corridor of many routes since slaves attempted to move away from the river in many places and in many ways. Floyd County itself borders only approximately thirteen miles of riverfront, but the central corridor included much more territory. Places in Harrison County known to be crossing points at the Ohio River were New Amsterdam, Mauckport and Morvins Landing, all leading up through Corydon, Paoli and Walnut Ridge near Salem in Washington County and through Bloomington in Monroe County. Salem has been called a "main Underground Railroad line" because it contained Covenanter Presbyterians who lived on the northwest side of town, Quakers whose settlement was located to the east side of Salem, and some blacks who lived in the countryside. If runaway slaves could get as far as Salem without being caught, they had a good chance of making it through the state. Many names of those who assisted fugitive slaves in Monroe County are known, and Underground Railroad routes were familiar enough to have been given names. One was called the "Isaiah Reid Line" and another the "Thompson Line."[7] African Americans who helped in the Bloomington area were William Hawkins and Knolly Baker, a Bloomington barber. Other names of people who may have been involved were Thomas Smith, James Clark, Rev. J. B. Faris, T. N. Faris, John Blair, Samuel Gordon, Samuel and William Curry, Robert Ewing, John Russell, D. S. Irvin, W. C. Smith, Austin Seward and John Hite. "If they didn't all take an active part, they were in sympathy with those who were helping and thus encouraged and supported the cause," claimed Henry Lester Smith.[8]

Much Underground Railroad activity occurred in Harrison County opposite Brandenburg, Kentucky, and one of many accounts of citizens helping slaves escape involved the David Bell family. In the 1850s David Bell and his family were owners and operators of the ferry at Mauckport, Indiana. It was common knowledge that Bell was a conductor on the Underground Railroad. In 1860 he and his son, Charles, were jailed in Brandenburg, Kentucky, for helping a fugitive escape to Indiana. Another son, Horace, rescued his father from jail. Shortly thereafter, armed Kentuckians kidnapped Horace at a stage stop in New Albany. A group of armed men from New Albany got a river posse together, boarded a ferryboat and set off down river to rescue him. That rescue attempt failed, but Kentucky authorities eventually released Bell. Later New Albany's Woodward Hall was the stage for a new drama titled "Horace Bell, Champion of Freedom."[9]

An often overlooked fact is that there was a substantial community of free men and women living southeast of Paoli near Chambersburg in Orange County. Because this was not far from the main buffalo trace and the New Albany–Salem Railroad tracks, it was undoubtedly one of the places fugitives moving through Floyd County went. During the period 1820 to 1850, there were up to fifteen or more established settlements of free African Americans in Indiana, and many of them had never been slaves. Mention has already been made of the fact that free blacks moved into Indiana along with the other pioneers of that period during the time when some Southern states had passed laws prohibiting free men and women from living within their borders. Quakers moving westward often invited blacks to join them. An examination of black settlements in Indiana shows that in nearly every case, they were located on one of the flight paths and near Quaker settlements.[10] Those blacks who settled in the isolated knobs of Floyd County, though not necessarily near Quakers, were definitely on a flight path leading away from the river. Their relative isolation along with the fact that they settled in clusters would have given fugitive slaves the temporary protection they needed.

The central route also included Clark County, directly to the east of New Albany. Here escape routes led through Clarksville, Jeffersonville, Utica and Charlestown and up to Madison in Jefferson County.[11] Various accounts have emerged that point to the existence of an abolitionist organization in Clark County. For example, at 11:00 p.m. one night five blacks were seen crossing over to Jeffersonville in a skiff. Two white men had been seen lurking in the vicinity of C. Q. Armstrong's residence and it was believed that they "stole" the slaves. Armstrong offered a reward of $500 for their return or the arrest of the kidnappers.[12] The white men probably lived in Jeffersonville or had contacts there. An African American by the name of John Knight was arrested in Jeffersonville in the fall of 1857 on a charge of helping two slaves of Mr. Thompson in Jefferson County, Kentucky, to escape.[13] Another African American, Hannah Talbott, was also arrested in Jeffersonville for her involvement in helping fugitive slaves in Clark County.[14]

Dr. Nathaniel Field of Jeffersonville, a physician and Protestant minister, was an agent for William Lloyd Garrison's newspaper, *The Liberator*.[15] Jonathan Shaw of Nettle Creek in Randolph County, which is east of Indianapolis and just north of Fountain City, helped him in this endeavor and was a possible link in helping runaway slaves coming through Clark County reach the northern part of the state. When that became known, the local newspaper criticized Field for circulating "the Pope's bull against slavery among the Catholics of Jeffersonville."[16] Field, born in Kentucky, was a strong abolitionist. He edited the *Christian Review*, the *Journal of Christianity* and the *Israelite*. For a short period of time in the late 1830s, Field also edited a weekly political journal called *The Jeffersonville Republican*.[17] He was an Adventist who announced that the second coming of Christ was to occur in September of 1843 (the date of April 14, 1843, was also used). His church in Jeffersonville became divided over the issues of slavery as well as Field's teaching about Christ's second coming, and he eventually left the church.[18] Field was president of the first anti-slavery convention ever held in Indiana and was appointed vice-president of the national American Anti-slavery Society.[19] He presided over a Free Soil Convention in Indianapolis, October 21–22, 1852; its purpose was to foster a stronger and better organization. Out of this meeting was formed a state Free Democratic Association.[20] Early in 1863, Levi Coffin, who was at that time living in Cincinnati, visited his friend, Dr. Field, to plead the cause of the contraband soldiers and their families. Coffin spent the night with Field and the next day collected $30 toward his cause.[21] The most telling evidence regarding Dr. Field's "hands on" work with the African American community, however, involves the Claysburg Settlement in Jeffersonville. Field owned eight acres of land located on the north side of town and had it platted; it became known as the Claysburg Settlement. From very early on, the "Claysburg Settlement" consisted of a large African American population. Claysburg was named in honor of Cassius M. Clay, a militant anti-slavery Kentuckian.[22] In 1842, an African Methodist Episcopal church was established there.

In addition to Dr. Field, three other preachers in Clark County need to be mentioned for their strong anti-slavery views. They are Rev. Calvin Fairbank, Peter Cartwright and John M. Dickey. Rev. Calvin Fairbank, a Methodist minister, was arrested in Jeffersonville, Indiana, in November, 1851, and then imprisoned for assisting a slave named Tamar to escape from Louisville through Jeffersonville and on to Salem.[23] A Methodist Episcopal preacher who traveled through Clark County and preached there on a regular basis by the name of Peter Cartwright was noted for his anti-slavery sentiments, but he was not as radical as Dr. Field and Rev. Fairbank. Rev. John M. Dickey, a Presbyterian minister who was also a traveling bishop and preached in Kentucky and Southern Indiana, convinced some Clark County men to give up the lucrative business of slave catching. Though he was reared in a slave state, he looked upon slavery as a curse and ultimately won over nearly all his people to anti-slavery sentiments.[24] He was the only person in Southern Indiana who voted for the Liberty party ticket, which stood for free soil principles.[25] Many called Dickey "the old Abolitionist," a name which he accepted with much pride. He was well known in the Southern Indiana area for hosting discussions and debates on the slavery issue.[26]

Wilbur H. Siebert wrote that with a length of frontier running along a great river, the states of Indiana and Ohio were the most favorably situated of all the Northern states to receive fleeing slaves.[27] Not only the river itself, but also its numerous tributaries, became channels of escape into free territory. In Floyd and Clark counties, Falling Run Creek and Silver Creek[28] were probably used to cover human scent, particularly if the bounty hunters were using dogs. Siebert's material, stored in the archives of the Ohio Historical Society Library, includes a letter from John Thomas in Azalia, Indiana, written April 5, 1896. He wrote that he was connected with an escape route that started at New Albany, went from there to Canton in Washington County where a "Friend," James L. Thompson, helped runaway slaves to the Seymour area in Jackson County. Willis Parks, an African American, brought them about fifteen miles to John Thomas, who took them from Azalia to Raysville (southwest corner of Henry County), a distance of approximately seventy miles. From there the runaway slaves went to Fountain City. John Thomas thought thirty to forty escaped slaves passed through Azalia.[29] Another letter, written by D. J. Leeper from Selma, Indiana, on December 13, 1895, said that the route he was involved with started at New Albany and went through Farmland in Randolph County and Camden in Jay County.[30]

From a brief examination of the central corridor in Southern Indiana, it is clear that Floyd County was part of a greater corridor of escape that ran north from the Ohio River through Orange and Washington counties and included the counties of Harrison to its west and Clark to its east. This central Indiana route was important for one who was trying to free himself from the shackles of slavery. Existing infrastructures acted as guides—the New Albany–Salem Railroad tracks that eventually lead all the way to Lake Michigan, creeks that emptied into the Ohio River and the old buffalo trail, which led up and out of the Ohio River Valley, were all used as the starting point for some escaping slaves as they began their search for freedom. We now turn to the corridor in more detail, looking first at escape across the Ohio River itself and then at the specific routes, places and people who supported slaves as they made their way toward freedom.

The Ohio River: Ferry Transportation System, Steamboats and River Labor

At various times there were several ferries crossing the river from Louisville, Kentucky, to locations in Floyd County. Landings were located near the eastern border between Floyd and Clark counties at Silver Creek, at Providence (where the K & I Bridge is now located in New Albany), at the foot of Bank Street in downtown New Albany, and at Falling Run Creek (also referred to as Black Creek) on the west side of downtown New Albany. The earliest known ferry to operate on a regular basis was the Joseph Oatman Ferry, which ran from 1805 to 1811, located near Falling Run Creek.[31] In 1819 a Mr. Stroud was operating a ferry from 36th Street in Portland, Kentucky, to the foot of Bank Street in New Albany. And the 1821 New Albany tax records mention five ferries crossing the Ohio River.[32] There are many accounts, both in oral and written form, about how fugitives used the ferry system to escape during the 1850s and 1860s when ferries were larger and no longer privately owned. Cases heard in the Louisville Chancery Court show that at times the ferrymen, either by design or error, permitted slaves to cross to the Indiana shore from Louisville without legitimate passes and thereby became a link in their passage to freedom.[33] When winters were so cold that the Ohio River froze, the ferries were prevented from running, and slaves used the ice as a bridge. Slaveholders in northern Kentucky were said to have moved their slaves inland at such times to prevent them from attempting to cross over the ice bridge.[34] The extent of the passenger travel between New Albany and Portland during New Albany's time of booming industry was huge. During the first four months of 1857, the Louisville and Portland Railroad Company transported more than 140,000 people to the ferry, an average of 1,200 per day.[35] It would have been a difficult task to monitor adequately passengers using the ferry system.

An example of a certificate that each free African American had to present before he or she could legally go on board a ferry reads as follows:

> Headquarters Military Commission, Louisville, Kentucky, September 22, 1864. This certifies that the Commission appointed by orders from headquarters, Western District of Kentucky, to investigate the case of contraband and captive negroes coming to the City of Louisville, State of Kentucky, do find that Rachel Wells, 18 years old, 5 feet, 5 inches high, copper complexioned and "fair" in general appearances. Free born [sic] in State of Ohio and by the President's Proclamation is entitled to her freedom, wherefore she is entitled to pass North of the Ohio River into free territory. Also her three children, Horrace, Sarah and Evline.
> Signed by W. B. Dunn, Capt. and ProMarshal.[36]

It has been mentioned previously that a large number of free African Americans had river-related occupations during the 1850s and 1860s — nearly a quarter of the black, working population. This does not include the number of blacks who worked as draymen, drivers of omnibuses, wagons and carts who used the ferry system on a daily basis. A New Albany newspaper brought to the attention of "all Negroes and Mulattoes" the fact that J. A. Moffett, mayor of New Albany, had published an ordinance requiring all draymen, hackmen, wagoners, cartmen and all those driving or using vehicles to procure a license before the first Monday in June, 1853, or receive penalties of the law.[37] The wagon traffic going north out of New Albany was very heavy as was evidenced by the need for a railroad in the late 1840s.

The following is found in an unpublished WPA report written by Tyler Veasey and is based on an interview with Miss Nettie Irwin, 42 E. 5th Street, New Albany. Although no date is given, it is reasonable to assume that the report was written in the mid or late 1930s.

> According to one story told by an old negro slave, some of the fugitives were secreted in loads of merchandise and brought across on the ferry, although these boats were watched and guarded carefully to prevent any escaped negro from crossing the river on them.[38]

Vehicles most used in hiding slaves were two-horse, covered carriages or open wagons, in which they hid under hay, straw or produce. Under especially hazardous conditions, tradition says, slaves were sewn up in feather beds. According to one researcher, a veteran vehicle in this service acquired the name of "The Liberator."[39]

6. Underground Railroad Escape Routes

A man by the name of Milton Clark from Portland, who was a friend of James R. Cunningham, drove a wagon with merchandise back and forth across the river and often carried fugitives over as well.[40]

According to Veasey, another former slave said that slaves came over on a flatboat to Providence in New Albany. They were also aided by men posing as fishermen who were stationed up and down the river, always prepared to take escaping parties across. Their signal fires could be seen on the banks for miles.[41]

George Morrison, a former Kentucky slave who was interviewed in New Albany in 1937, told of slaves taking wagonloads of corn to the Louisville market and bringing back to the farm large quantities of groceries and supplies. A slave who knew George and who frequently made the trip to the Louisville market with his master told him the following story. He was unloading corn when a white man approached him, showed him money and asked him if he wanted to be free. The slave stopped what he was doing and immediately went with the man, who hid him in his wagon under provisions. They crossed the Ohio River on the ferry. "That's the way lots of 'em got across here," said Morrison.[42] It is impossible to know who the "white man" was. He could have been a paid employee of an anti-slavery organization, a "Helperite" or simply an individual acting on his own. One wonders where the money he had came from and why he offered it, almost as if it were a bribe. It is possible that this "story" was "abolitionized" at some point.

Another account is that of Isaac Throgmorton, who used his own ingenuity in order to get across the Ohio River. Throgmorton was born in 1809 in Kentucky. While a slave in Louisville, he was first a gardener, then a barber, and later worked on a steamboat on the Ohio River. His owner was a peddler who treated his slaves quite well. Sometimes Throgmorton almost felt he was free because he lived and worked with free people. His owner, however, would occasionally send for him and remind him that he was not a free man. Later he was turned over to a new owner in Louisiana. His life became difficult after having lived and worked with free people. He also witnessed many cruelties perpetrated on slaves. Even though his new owner treated him fairly well, when he married a new wife, she and her relatives were not kind to Throgmorton. His master was old and Isaac knew that if left in the hands of the master's wife and family, his life would become unbearable. Throgmorton, therefore, made the decision in 1853 to flee to Canada. Getting away was not particularly difficult. At the time, his owner was a heavy planter in New Orleans who spent a lot of time traveling in the summer. He wanted Isaac to accompany him as his personal barber. Throgmorton saw his chance to run away when the man brought him up to Louisville for the summer. Throgmorton described it this way:

> I had been seeking a chance for all those eleven years, and the first chance that I saw clear, I started off fishing. I had all my arrangements made to go down to New Albany, and carried my fishing tackle in my pocket. The ferryman at New Albany asked me if I was a freeman, and I said "Yes." Said he, "Where are your

free papers? You must show your free papers, or have somebody that knows you are free." I said, "Your son knows me." (I went over the day before with a freeman, and the son saw me.) He asked his son if he knew me, and he said, "Yes, he went over the other day." From New Albany I went to Jeffersonville, and there took the cars and came right along to Canada. When I got to Cleveland, I hadn't eaten anything for two days and as soon as I got off the cars, I rushed to the lake, and found what was called the "May Queen," that was going to sail for Detroit. There I got something to eat. When she drew in her plank and rang the bell, I felt as if the shackles were broken off, I felt free. It was a beautiful night, and I sat up until 12 o'clock, watching the lake, and thinking of my freedom, and of the scenes I had seen in Louisiana. I felt like a new man.[43]

Yet another story is that of Tom Bishop, owned by Isaac T. Miller, who lived five miles south of Louisville on the plank road. Bishop left his master in early April, 1860, and hired out on the steamboat *Peytona* as a deck hand and fireman. Miller sent his two farm superintendents, Conn and White, to apprehend him when the *Peytona* docked in New Albany. With the help of New Albany's Marshal Akers, they were able to find and arrest Bishop by searching a different vessel, the *Baltic*, which had just landed at the wharf in New Albany on its way to New Orleans. Bishop had been hired by the captain of the *Baltic* by stating he was a free man who resided in New Albany.[44]

The following three newspaper accounts attest to the drama involved in fugitives crossing the Ohio River on the ferries.

> **Runaway and Arrest.** Yesterday a negro woman, the property of Mr. J. W. Newland, of Louisville, came to this city [New Albany] in company with a white man named Elisha Reynolds. According to the woman's story the man had made an appointment to meet her at the cars of the Portland railroad. Upon arriving there she met her companion, and the interesting couple proceeded to the ferry landing together. Being dressed in the height of the fashion, in silks and furs, and having a thick veil over her face, the officers of the ferry boat did not suspect the woman of being a negro when she came on board. It is said, however, that the impatient swain could not restrain his ardor, and just as the boat was landing on the Indiana shore, he lifted the veil and kissed the lips of his inamorata. This spoiled the whole of the scheme, for some impertinent looker on discovered the color of the lady, and just as she was stepping on to the dock Mr. Conner demanded to see her free papers. She protested that she was free but had lost her papers, but subsequently confessed all the circumstances. The man proceeded up the bank, and when he saw that his dear companion was nabbed, proceeded to a coffee house to drown his sorrows in the bowl. The woman having been conveyed across the river, she was taken to the Louisville jail before Mr. Newland or his family were aware of her absence. Subsequently, two of the Louisville officers came to this city, and, assisted by one of our own police, arrested the man Reynolds, and conveyed him to the Louisville jail. The man is a large, burly looking fellow, well dressed, and is said to be a black-leg by profession, which may account for his partiality to black women. While on the ferry boat he boasted largely of the money he had won in Louisville. He will most probably be sent to Frankfort to keep company with brother [Rev. Calvin] Fairbank. We do not

approve of the practice of Louisville officers coming to this city after persons charged with offenses on the Kentucky side, and taking them off without due process of law. Even a negro thief has a right to be heard in self-defense, and if arrested here he should not be carried off till his case is heard and the proper requisitions made.[45]

Negroes Not to Cross the River. A guard is now stationed at the ferry dock on each side of the river to prevent all negroes not having passes from crossing on the ferry boats. Lately there has been a perfect exodus of slaves from Kentucky, in this direction most of them from the neighborhood of Louisville. It has therefore been determined to arrest all negroes without passes, who may attempt to cross the river at the ferries either at this city or at Jeffersonville.[46]

Runaway Negroes. The placing of the guard at the ferries has already resulted in the stopping of a large number of runaway slaves who were making their way into this State. Nearly all of these runaways are furnished with passes by some Federal officer — generally Captains and Lieutenants, and most of them have belonged to men of unquestioned loyalty, and have left good homes, where they had plenty, on the representations of Abolition officers that in the free States they would have liberty, which, with these negroes, means "nothing to do" and plenty to eat. Those who have tried this experiment of Abolition freedom are now seeing how woefully they have been deceived.[47]

Any African American, slave or free, employed in the river transportation system, whether on steamboats, ferries or skiffs, was subject to close scrutiny by slave owners, employers of free blacks and "slave catchers." Two of Captain Gilchrist's slaves employed on the steamer *Interchange* ran away while docked in New Albany and got as far as Seymour before being caught. An off-duty Louisville policeman, Dick Moore, arrested them and received $500 from Gilchrist for his trouble. The escape route from New Albany to Seymour was obviously a well-used one since Captain Gilchrist knew to pursue in that direction.[48]

Though many slaves who attempted to use their employment on the steamboats as their means of escape were eventually captured, it will never be known just how many of the enslaved actually reached freedom in this way. Kentucky Court of Appeals cases show only the tip of the iceberg but do attest to the fact that steamboat transportation was used to escape to freedom.[49]

Crossing the Ohio River presented a challenge for fleeing slaves. They could hide for a short time among others of their race in Louisville until a plan could be worked out for escape, which apparently involved contact between people on both sides of the river. Other slaves took the chance alone and devised a plan to cross the river by using their own ingenuity. Once on Indiana soil, they had to rely on the good will of others or think quickly on their own. More than likely, owners had set in motion a plan to catch them before they were able to get far from the river.

One of the ways some slaves attempted to leave the Ohio River valley was by using the railroad. Although they were not always successful in their escape, the New Albany–Salem Railroad offered an alternative and possibly a quicker and safer way to get to Canada.

The New Albany–Salem Railroad

One of the oldest railroads in Indiana was the New Albany–Salem Railroad, later known as the Louisville, New Albany, Chicago line and still later as the Monon. The New Albany–Salem Railroad was organized July 8, 1847. It eventually became an important economic link because it connected two waterways—the Ohio River and Lake Michigan. For the same reason, it was important for the slave trying to reach free territory in Canada. Buckmaster calls such railroad lines "surface lines to freedom."[50] It was said trainmen became as zealous abolitionists as the Quaker farmers. In the beginning, the line reached only as far as Borden (then called New Providence), where it was met on a daily basis by a stage coming from the north. On January 15, 1851, the first train reached Salem.[51] Gradually the line extended to Bedford, Bloomington, Greencastle, Crawfordsville and, finally, Chicago and Lake Michigan. It is shown as an escape route on a map devised by Wilbur Siebert. If a building could tell stories, the old railroad depot, which stood behind the present-day New Albany post office and was torn down in November 1996, could tell us much about fugitive passengers who used the railroad line as an "over the ground" escape route.

Several elders and other influential members of Second Presbyterian church were in one way or another involved with this railroad line. Elder James Brooks was the first president of the railroad, and elder James Haines was the New Albany conductor for many years during the antebellum period. John R. Nunemacher, also a member, printed the railroad tickets. As president, James Brooks was the only person with the power to issue free passes. Hargrave, who wrote a history of the New Albany and Salem Railroad, claims this issuance of free passes became an "outstanding evil" that accounted for a huge loss in revenue to the railroad.[52] Brooks was pressed into giving passes to such people as farmers whose land had been used in the building of the rails or whose livestock had been damaged and landowners who felt their family should receive passes in exchange for the railroad company stacking supplies on their property. It is possible that Brooks also gave free passes to runaway slaves, either independently or as part of an organized effort. He could have done it out of his Christian conviction as a Presbyterian, from his hatred of slavery, or from pressure applied by an Anti-Slavery Society member or a friend in the African American community.

A story unfolds in both the *Louisville Daily Courier* and the *New Albany Daily Ledger* of a conspiracy of African Americans, abolitionists and railroad employees to help a runaway slave safely on board the train and out of New Albany. The *Louisville Daily Courier* reported having heard from one of Louisville's police officers that the conductor of the New Albany railroad refused to give permission to New Albany police officers to search the railroad cars for a runaway slave who was on board. In fact, the runaway succeeded in getting away. The next day the *Courier* printed a reply from Agent Stevens in which he refuted the accusation and claimed that the employees of the New Albany Railroad were not in the practice of harboring fugitive slaves. Mr. Stevens did admit, however, that there was a runaway slave on the car that day but claimed that the conductor did not attempt to protect the runaway. Stevens explained it away by saying that the conductor tried to stop the row that was going on at the platform with the watchman who had the runaway in hand. In the ensuing disturbance, the runaway managed to escape onto the cars again before the train pulled away. Under the fear of losing Kentucky patronage, Agent Stevens asked that the *Courier* correct their accusation so that the community would not get a false impression.

Several days later the *Courier* retaliated by printing Louisville Police Officer Kirkpatrick's side of the story. Officer Kirkpatrick stated that the conductor's name was Mr. Haines and that Officer Meeker along with another New Albany officer had arrested the fugitive at the cars. The fugitive acknowledged he was a runaway slave. At the same time two abolitionists (one of them black), attempted to rescue him. They succeeded in getting him safely on the cars and when the officers attempted to re-arrest him, Conductor Haines and the abolitionists got on the platform and declared that the cars were theirs and that the police officers could not enter them. Then the officers heard the black abolitionist give the runaway directions as to how he should proceed in order to complete his escape farther north, and the cars moved off.

Furthermore, the *Courier* wrote that it had it on good authority that the man who was in charge of the scales in the depot at New Albany had been constantly giving aid and comfort to runaway "negroes" and that he hid them under the scales until the very moment the cars were ready to start. According to a pre-arrangement with those on board, the fugitives were then brought out from the hiding place under the scales, safely placed on board and "sent on their way rejoicing." "We are advised that, on an average, at least one slave for every day effects his escape on the cars of the New Albany and Salem road," the newspaper reported. But this figure is probably inflated. With a rate of frequency involving on the average one escape a day, more fugitives would have been caught and reported in the local newspaper. The established pattern of their escape would sooner or later have been noticed. Obviously, the *Courier* was trying to make the city of New Albany and its railroad look bad since this was an incident in which Kentucky "property" had been "stolen." The competitive nature of the two large river communities was always an issue. In the same article, the *Courier* warned New Albany that because their railroad was largely patronized by Kentuckians, they had better put an immediate stop to such proceedings. The Jeffersonville railroad, the paper claimed, did not permit "negro stealers" among its employees, and the same policy should prevail on the New Albany–Salem Railroad.[53]

Other suspected links to this "system" of escape for slaves involve men in the black community who lived in the area around the railroad, such as Henry Clay who lived across the street and also worked for the railroad as a blacksmith, William

Harding, Edward Carter, George Washington Carter and others. George Carter, in fact, owned land bordering the tracks and later sold the property to the city for use as the northern cemetery, today the Fairview Cemetery. As the earliest trains left the New Albany terminal and moved along Carter's property, they moved at a very slow pace; the average speed did not exceed 17 mph.[54] It would not have been difficult for a runaway slave to hop onto the moving train.

Another story about the railroad line being used as an escape route involved a slave known only by the name of "Toney." Toney escaped from his owner in Kentucky and made his way north along the New Albany and Chicago Railroad as far as Monroe County, where he was caught. As his captors were heading south with him, he saw an opportunity to escape near Salem, Indiana. Here he slipped away, hid in a cornfield until night and again turned north. This time he fell into friendlier hands. He hid near Bloomington until the hunters lost his trail. He then hid under some sacks of wheat in a farmer's wagon and left for Mooresville.[55]

That there was a definite escape route along the New Albany, Chicago Railroad line from New Albany to Borden was also brought out in William Wallace Borden's *Reminiscences*:

> Many incidents of this period of my life (boyhood) recur to me, but none which appeals so strongly as the return of fugitive slaves. We were on the direct line of the Underground Railroad. Escaping negroes were often seen stealing through the woods on either side of our valley and making for the station in the adjoining county [Washington County]. Frequently the slave hunters who found it a lucrative pursuit would rest at our inn while handcuffed slaves in the last stages of wretchedness or destitution shared the entertainment with their guardians.[56]

Early in December 1856, the *New Albany Daily Ledger* reported the capture of two runaway slaves at Salem, Indiana, who had fled Louisville, "traveling on the New Albany and Salem Railroad track all Sunday night." It appears they crossed the river on Sunday and arrived within five miles of Salem on Monday morning, where they gave a boy $3 to take them into Salem. On reaching Salem, they went to a public house and called for their breakfast, at the same time asking for a private room in which to eat. This, of course, excited suspicion, and a man named "McKinney" demanded of one of them his free papers. The "negro" immediately drew a pistol and pointed it at McKinney's breast, but the cap exploded and no damage was done. The bystanders then seized the man, and his companion started to run. The second person was, however, pursued and arrested, and both were brought back to Louisville on the train. The authorities knew they belonged in Louisville but had no knowledge of the name of the owner. One of them had a certificate stating that the bearer was a free man, signed with the name of Capt. James Montgomery. This, however, was declared a forgery by those acquainted with Capt. Montgomery's handwriting. The *Ledger* continued, "Both had through-tickets purchased at the Louisville office.

It is quite evident that there is a gang of scoundrels in Louisville who are engaged in running off negroes. We hope they may be captured and punished."[57]

It appears that the railroad station in New Albany was often the scene of much excitement over the fugitive slave issue. As tension began to heighten over slavery and rumbles of war were in the air, everyone of African descent was suspect. African Americans were thoroughly checked when they attempted to ride the public transportation system and were sometimes denied the privilege of riding "over the road" because of fear on the part of whites that the freedom papers they exhibited were counterfeit.[58] When runaways were captured north of New Albany, they would pass through the train station with their captors on their way south.[59] After the Civil War started, the *Ledger* reported another instance of "Negro Excitement" at the train depot:

> **Excitement.** An effort was made at the depot this morning to get up another negro excitement. Several negroes belonging to the crew of the Silver Moon were at the depot to take the cars for Cincinnati, where they reside. A report began to circulate that they were runaways. After some little commotion, however, the matter was quieted, and the negroes proceeded on their way undisturbed.[60]

From this example, it is evident that the railroad depot and the cars were being watched.

In April of 1860 a slave owned by Mr. Newton McClure was shipped by rail in a box from Nashville, Tennessee, by a free man named "James." The slave passed through Louisville to Jeffersonville on the railroad cars and made it as far as Seymour, where he was found out because of damage to the box, was arrested and taken back to Louisville. The box was to have been shipped to Mrs. Margaret M. Thompson in care of Levi Coffin in Cincinnati, Ohio, on the rails leading through Madison.[61] In 1862, Indiana Regiment 44, in wanting to help a slave to freedom, hid a slave in a box of clothing, nailed the box shut and shipped him across the river. A few days later, after the box had been unloaded from the boat on the Indiana side of the Ohio River, he kicked his way out.[62] Additionally, a black woman was shipped as freight out of New Albany early in the history of that road.[63]

The New Albany freight commissioner, R. H. Campbell, resided at 476 East Main Street near Rev. John G. Atterbury, who lived at 472 East Main, and a block from Second Presbyterian Church. Campbell's advertisement read, "Storage, forwarding, commission merchant and railroad agent." He would have been privy to information regarding shipments of goods out of New Albany. As a major railroad station in Southern Indiana, New Albany would have handled a huge volume of merchandise shipped on a weekly basis to points north. Isaac Smith's wife, Abbey, had a brother, J. O. Campbell (Uncle Obe), who was a merchant in Louisville. James, his nephew, wrote an interesting and cryptic letter to his brother Sam, and made reference to R. H. Campbell and a shipment of goods. He wrote,

When I was in Louisville, I spoke to Uncle Obe concerning the "goods" Grand Ma wishes sent East. No one would wish to take them as they would be *compelled* to pay for them as extra baggage. I had better forward them with the Western Freight Line as it would not cost as much as by Express. They charge "three dollars" a hundred [pound]. I think they will not weigh as much as that. I will send them as soon as Ma [Abbey Smith] tends to getting them ready. When you, or any of "Grand Ma's family" write, let us know what you think of it. If you are satisfied, on they *will* come. They can be shipped with responsible parties here. R. H. Campbell & Co. are the agents. [64]

Railroads played an important part in assisting slaves in their trip north to freedom. They used the tracks as a guide if they were traveling by foot; they rode the rails hidden in some manner; they were able to procure a legitimate ticket from railroad personnel, free blacks or members of an anti-slavery group; or they purchased a ticket with falsified papers or a disguise. The New Albany–Salem Railroad played an important role in helping slaves attain their goal. But if a slave needed protection in Floyd County before it was safe to venture further north, where would he or she have gone for help, food or shelter? The next chapter deals with that issue.

Chapter 7
Specific Underground Railroad Sites

Second Presbyterian Church (Now Second Baptist Church)

The oral tradition that connects the former Second Presbyterian church building in New Albany, located at the corner of Third and Main Streets, with the Underground Railroad is deeply imbedded in the community. It is interesting that an African American congregation, that is Second Baptist church, purchased the building from Second Presbyterian church on December 10, 1889, when First, Second and Third Presbyterian churches united to become Hutchinson Memorial. The African American community must already have had a relationship with, and an emotional and physical tie to, that church building and, therefore, the purchase was no surprise. Margaret Webb, a lifelong member of the church, stated that the membership of Second Baptist was made up primarily of former slaves who found a home in New Albany during and after the Civil War.[1] One of these men, Alex Woodson, a former slave, was interviewed in 1937 by Iris Cook through the WPA Program. He stated that he had been a member and officer of Second Baptist Church for forty-one years.[2]

It seems suitable that the oral tradition should be presented without any judgment made about its reliability. Furthermore, it is necessary, whether verifiable or not, to make the oral history available so that others could arrive at their own conclusions. Taken by itself, the oral history may not seem to be reliable because, for obvious reasons, there are too many gaps in the information that has come down to us. However, when it is taken together with other information that we have about the church, such as the anti-slavery personality of Second Presbyterian and its pastors and members, the inclination is to believe much of the oral tradition; it fits with facts that are verifiable. This consistency of historical facts, along with the strong oral tradition, counts in its favor. The following oral tradition regarding the church and the Underground Railroad is emphasized by the African American members of

Second Baptist Church who have continuously occupied the building for more than one hundred years. Of primary importance is the section regarding the sub-basement of the building which, according to the tradition, offered a temporary sanctuary for slaves before they went further north. There are several claims that are central to the oral tradition:

"This church, along with churches at Charlestown, Madison and Blue River, served as a station on the Underground Railroad."[3]

One Underground Railroad route led from Floyd County upriver through Jeffersonville and Utica townships in Clark County toward Charlestown, all of which had black populations.[4] Furthermore, a cluster of African Americans traditionally existed in the settlement of Watson, which lies halfway between Jeffersonville and Charlestown.[5] Many of these Clark County blacks were farmers and boatman. First Presbyterian Church (N.S.) in Charlestown had at least one black member in 1821 by the name of Nancy Johnson, and there could have been others. She joined the church on May 20, 1821, and was baptized there on May 27 of that year.[6] The town of Blue River in Washington County is between New Albany and Salem near a main line of the Underground Railroad. The towns that are mentioned above, that is Charlestown, Madison and Blue River, along with Hanover, had at least one thing in common with New Albany and with each other. They all had Presbyterian churches—New School. This meant that the pastors, elders and, of course, some of the church members had steady contact with each other.

Family oral history for Pearl Grundy Kimbrough includes Second Baptist Church as part of the Underground Railroad. Pearl's grandfather had been a slave and settled in New Albany with his family after the Civil War. Pearl discovered a piece of paper among old West Haven Cemetery papers that records family recollections of Underground Railroad activity in New Albany. That the oral tradition linking the church to the Underground Railroad rests primarily in the black community is understandable. The African American community living freely in New Albany during the antebellum and Civil War years was the most important link in the assistance of the fugitives, and if and when help from Second Presbyterian Church occurred, members would have needed assistance from their black members or other free African Americans in New Albany.

"The church women brought baskets of food to the church hidden under their shawls."[7]

Second Presbyterian church session records show that Rev. Bishop's wife, Lucy, transferred to Second Presbyterian on August 29, 1847, from Second Presbyterian Church in Oxford, Ohio. The session met on a weekly basis in the pastor's office, at which time church business was discussed: day-to-day routine, special needs of the

Opposite: Second Presbyterian Church. Purchased by a black Baptist congregation in 1889, this building is still being used by Second Baptist Church today. (Courtesy Stuart B. Wrege Indiana History Room, New Albany–Floyd County Public Library)

members, the religious life of the church and the various problems of misconduct involving members of the church. The elder appointed to record the session always listed the names of those present; normally only the pastor and elders attended. It is interesting to note that in 1847 and 1848 the pastor's wife, Lucy Bishop, was sometimes listed as attending their meetings. The presence of a woman at session meetings probably shows a progressive attitude on the part of Rev. and Mrs. Bishop as well as the elders. It may also indicate that the women of the congregation were active in helping the poor and needy and that Lucy Bishop acted as their spokesperson. Session records also refer to the establishment of a women's group within the church, possibly for the purpose of assisting the huge influx of refugees from slavery that came into Floyd County during the Civil War period.

"Evidence of fugitive slaves having found temporary sanctuary in the sub-basement of Second Presbyterian Church could still be seen before the devastating flood of 1937. Slaves would stay in the church basement until there was safe passage to go northward. The Underground Railroad activity at this church was an "open secret" and not likely known by all the church members."[8]

The *New Albany Tribune* of July 30, 1852, gives a thorough description of the church at its dedication. It calls the ground floor, entered by a descent of four steps down, "the basement," which contained the pastor's study, a lecture room and another room used for social meetings of the church. It continues,

> These rooms are thirteen feet high, entirely above ground, and well aired and lighted. Indeed we do not remember to have seen a church basement so pleasant. This result has been attained by the slope of the lot on which the building stands.[9]

The main room of the building can still be reached today by a flight of stairs ascending from the vestibule. It is a very elegant and airy room seating 600 worshippers on the main floor and another 100 in the gallery above.

> The room is located above the noise and dust of the streets and commands a view of the river both up and down.... The entire building in all its parts will be warmed by two furnaces built in the cellar below the basement.[10]

Today one can enter the sub-basement or cellar and see that the space is broken up into rooms that are divided by floor-to-ceiling walls on either side of an open middle section. These walls have several openings which, before the flood, were above eye level and measured approximately 2' × 3'. The openings appear to be windows looking out into the mid-section. It would have been possible for a person of normal size to enter the rooms through these "windows." Other than housing the two furnaces, one wonders for what purpose these cellar rooms were originally constructed. Several members of this church were involved in construction of the building. Isaac Smith was the chief architect and builder. The carpentry and joinery work was done by John Loughmiller, and the establishment of Hurlbut & Mann provided the carpets. What plan did the builder, Smith, have in mind when he designed them? It is possible that, as a member of this church, a Republican and an anti-slavery man, Smith's original intent was that the rooms be used as a place of concealment and refuge.

The Rev. H. A. King, pastor of Second Baptist church from 1937 to 1963, reported to his daughter, Ruth Bledsoe, that there had been discarded chains or leg irons and the marks of many footprints on the clay and cobblestone floor of the sub-basement. This oral history cannot be validated, however, because the 1937 flood left six feet of dirt and silt in the sub-basement, which has never been removed due to the possibility of structural damage to the building. No study by a licensed archeologist has ever been done there. There has also been considerable speculation over the issue of how runaway slaves reached the church without detection due to the busy nature of the dock, a mere block away at the foot of Bank Street. Moreover, the area between the church and the river was built up with houses and businesses. An answer may be found in the fact that, as we now know, the ferry did not run after midnight. Moreover, the *Tribune* occasionally gave the schedule of the New Albany night watch. For example, on May 20, 1852, the *Tribune* reported that "The night watch is suspended and will probably 'go the rounds' again in a week or two." Again on December 8, 1852, it reported, "The watch will be discontinued in future." It is also possible that if the sub-basement was being used as a place of refuge, the runaway slaves came in from another direction, such as the street, and not directly from the river. This sub-basement has been preserved intact as it was left after the flood of 1937 and can be visited today by appointment.[11]

It must have seemed to former slaves stepping onto Indiana soil as if nothing had changed. They arrived often in poor health, had nowhere to go, no place to sleep, no food or clothing and few, if any, earthly possessions. Additionally, they were thrust "overnight" into new relationships, new situations. It is a possibility that the Second Presbyterian Church building was used to give temporary lodging, not only during the Civil War, but also after the war when freed slaves headed north in large numbers. By July of 1865, virtually every basement and every available space in New Albany was being used by the recently freed men, women and children. The newspaper reported that many of them were in terrible shape. Their suffering invoked the sympathy of the people.[12] Space such as that in the sub-basement of Second Presbyterian was probably utilized, as well as that of stables and other such spaces.

"*A tunnel under the road allowed doctors from the Civil War hospital across the street to take care of the sick and injured.*"[13]

The tunnel under Main Street leading from the cellar of the church to the buildings across the street to the north is factual, although no written record of doctors having assisted runaway slaves at the church by using the tunnel has been found. However, Elizabeth Nunemacher, a New Albany historian from the first half of the twentieth century who frequently wrote about Floyd County history in a newspaper column, said that Dr. Sloan and Rev. John G. Atterbury were among those who met the boat that brought to New Albany the sick and wounded from the Battle of Shiloh. According to Nunemacher, some churches, empty stores and hundreds of tents on Main Street as far as Upper Eleventh Street were used, with the Main Street School serving as medical headquarters.[14] Oral history maintains that the tunnel was also used as an additional place of refuge for runaways if there was danger of them being found in the church cellar. The tunnel is now filled in and bricked shut on both sides of the street. From early New Albany records it is clearly seen that the buildings on the north side of Main Street (350 and 354 Main) facing the church housed a hotel with a barbershop and restaurant from at least 1853 to 1889 and possibly earlier. It was first called the "Warren House" (J. Alexander was the proprietor); by 1856 the name had changed to the DePauw Hotel. Next to the DePauw Hotel at the corner, 348 Main, was the *Tribune* newspaper office — the Republican paper.[15] During the Civil War, New Albany became a medical center for sick and wounded soldiers because of its strategic place along the Ohio River, and most public buildings, including schools and hotels, were temporarily turned into hospitals. The DePauw Hotel could have been used for that purpose, although it is not listed among the major buildings used as Civil War hospitals.[16] There is evidence, however, that the hotel, described as having been at the "Northeast corner of Upper Third and Main was used as a prison and guard house for captured Confederate soldiers."[17]

A man who was employed in 1962–64 in the building that today occupies the former DePauw Hotel site reported that in the early 1960s he had walked into the tunnel. He entered it from below the building on the northeast corner, and described the tunnel in the following manner. The entrance to the tunnel was closed off by a heavy wooden door approximately seven feet high by three-and-a-half feet in width. The tunnel ran in a north to south direction under Main Street between 301 East Main and Second Baptist Church. The passageway itself measured approximately six feet, three to four inches high with red brick walls and an arched ceiling that was reinforced by wooden beams and concrete. He testified that because of its shape and size, this tunnel was designed for human passage and would not have been used as a storm sewer as some have conjectured.[18]

Given the presence of a Southern and anti-black biased element present in the community, and given the anti-slavery and benevolent nature of the Presbyterians in New Albany, this church most likely became a symbol to blacks as a place where assistance could be obtained. The aid to those in need probably included contraband soldiers and their families who came across the river after the war started, and continued into the next decade as waves of former slaves moved north of the river. Moreover, the steeple would have been very visible as a destination for people crossing the river. Perhaps some of the oral tradition sprang up after the Civil War as a way of attempting to fill in missing gaps of information. However, it is evident that a relationship between Second Presbyterian Church and the black community was present before, during and after the Civil War. And due to the danger involved in showing benevolent activity of any kind to runaway slaves (and this feeling spilled over into giving aid to contraband families), there existed an utmost need to suppress that truth.

The 1865 Livery Stable and Sweet Gum Stable

The stable, which was located at the southeast corner of West Seventh and Main streets, has been known in the community as Sweet Gum Stable[19] and more recently as Farmers Feed and Supply Store. The stable was situated on land only a block away from the Ohio River. In the fall of 1998, the building was sold at public auction and torn down on May 22, 1999. Oral tradition in the African American community, as recorded in "The Underground Railroad and Church History," states that the original stable was used as a place to hide slaves in their search for freedom.[20]

In 1834 Thomas Riddle, a steamboat captain from Pennsylvania, purchased the property, and by 1836 he had constructed a small, one-room house; he added a second room around 1850.[21] In 1865, his heirs sold the greater portion of the corner lot

Sweet Gum Stable on the corner of Main and West Seventh streets. (Photograph courtesy of Janel J. Harris)

to James Payton and William Robison for the construction of a livery stable adjacent to Riddle's house.[22] Payton owned and operated a hotel next door called the Payton House Hotel. Because of their close proximity, the hotel probably used the sleeping rooms located on the second floor of the stable as overflow space or for cheaper lodging. Horses were kept in the basement level, and the only outside entrance to that level (the building was constructed on a hill), was on the south side of the building. A narrow city street or alley passed immediately behind the stable between it and Lower Water Street at the river; the City of New Albany eventually closed the alley. Carriages were kept on the main floor of the building at the street level. The livery stable remained intact from 1865 until 1873 when it was destroyed by fire.[23] It wasn't until 1877 that the property was purchased by Frank Howard, who built what is known as Sweet Gum Stable on the foundation stones of the first stable. Sweet Gum Stable was dedicated on April 24, 1877.[24]

It is common knowledge that as the Civil War progressed, a mass influx of slaves from the South occurred. This migration left New Albany flooded with refugees. The waves of "freed" men and women crossing the Ohio River into Indiana started growing with the advent of the Civil War and reached a peak in the spring and summer of 1865. Sometimes 200 to 300 passes a day were issued by the provost in Louisville for entry into New Albany via the ferries.[25] The newspaper reported:

> **Still They Come.** Negroes who leave good homes, where they are well provided for, are daily thronging into this city from Kentucky. They come in search of liberty. Their ideas of this blessing, as a general rule, being a banjo, government rations, and nothing to do. Poor creatures! It will not be long until poverty and suffering will teach them that such liberty is worse, by far, then all they ever suffered with their masters.[26]

Any and all available spaces in New Albany were used to temporarily house these people. Besides the second floor sleeping rooms, the livery stable, which was of a balloon frame structure, would have been one of the places in New Albany that could have provided a large sheltered area. During this time New Albany was a large and bustling river town and the livery would have served as not only a place to shelter and feed horses, but also as a community meeting point. It would have rented horses and carriages, bought and sold livestock, provided fresh horses for stagecoaches and, as in this case, would have given some travelers a place to stay. "Frank Howard's stable at the corner of Lower Main and 7th Street will be ready for occupancy for man, beast and wagons within ten days," announced the newspaper in 1877.[27]

Besides the possibility of former slaves finding a refuge in the livery stable, there is another factor that probably figured into the stable's use as a sanctuary somewhat later, and the oral tradition preserved in the African American community could be influenced by the following occurrence. In the 1870s, particularly in 1876–1878, former slaves were again left defenseless. They had gained their freedom from slavery, but much of the white population still thought of them as chattel. Not only were they barred from the polls, but they became objects of brutality and other unspeakable crimes. Many former slaves who had drifted north before and during the Civil War had returned to the South after the war's end, hoping to make a life for themselves in familiar territory. However,

> The light of freedom first cast at the end of the civil war was going out, and many once again turned their minds toward flight. Many who had felt the lash of the slave driver now felt the lash of the klansman and the white politicians and they thought naturally of escape. Circulars were being distributed showing land was available in Kansas, for example, and by the thousands Blacks began deserting the south and heading north. Nothing could stop the exodus.[28]

Abolitionists who had helped in the Underground Railroad took charge and set up relief agencies. It was during this time that Hannibal Carter found it unsafe to remain in Mississippi and he moved to Chicago. Laura Haviland, a Quaker from northern Michigan, recorded statements of those fleeing to the north, statements such as the following: "I saw 100 men killed during 1878 and 1879, my brother among them. His crime was his persistence in voting the Republican ticket…. They gave me (a colored preacher) 200 lashes because I preached that God had given us freedom of body, soul and spirit."[29] Many who had thought their work was finished with the Emancipation Proclamation of January 1, 1863, and the passage of the 13th Amendment lent a hand. It seems likely that members of the Freedmen's Association, as well as other civic-minded citizens and evangelical Christians of New Albany, would have helped at this time. It is entirely possible that the livery stable at the corner of Lower Main and Seventh Streets, by that time known as Sweet Gum Stable, continued to harbor blacks who were once again on their way north a decade after the Civil War ended. Within the context of the times and from the perspective of African Americans, an "Underground Railroad" had to continue to function in Floyd County after the war.

"Sweet Gum Stable is significant in the area of transportation for its role in the movement of local residents and transients from place to place," stated Dieber in her historical analysis of the site when it was placed on the Historical Register.[30] Thus both the earlier livery stable and the later Sweet Gum Stable built on the same site were in all likelihood important for African Americans leaving the South for a freer life.

State and Cherry Streets

State and Cherry streets, while important roads in New Albany today, were already major arteries leading north and northwest in the earlier days of New Albany's history. State Street began at the Ohio River, went north through the main part of downtown, and followed the buffalo trace up into the "Knobs," eventually leading to Vincennes. Cherry Street branched west off of State Street at Falling Run Creek and hooked up with the Old Vincennes Road. While today Cherry Street leads primarily to residential areas, it was an important link to farm communities in the Knobs earlier in Floyd County history.[31] These major arteries were also used as escape routes for runaway slaves who crossed over the Ohio River at Louisville. Sarah Merrill, interviewed as part of a Works Progress Administration project in 1936, recalled that her uncle, Lewis Barnett, used Cherry Street as an escape route out of New Albany. However, he was apprehended and taken back to Louisville.[32]

A historical society publication from neighboring Washington County contains information that has applied to Cherry and State streets:

> Freighters and hucksters were often the means by which numbers of fugitives were enabled to cross the Ohio River at New Albany and Jeffersonville. These men hauled their produce to the city markets in wagons, and when they went to the Louisville market, the only means of crossing the river was on the ferry boats, and they usually had a load of merchandise engaged to haul on the return journey. Not infrequently there was some live freight concealed under the merchandise. These fugitives would remain concealed until night came on, when the teamsters would camp by the road side. Then coming from their hiding place, and being supplied with provisions and maps of the roads and route of the Underground Railroad, and such other information as was deemed necessary to enable the fugitive to reach the main line and the first station on the Underground Railroad, they proceeded on their way.[33]

Lon McCoy wrote in *Homespun Magazine*, "Most used, perhaps, in the Southern part [of Indiana] was the route which began at Louisville and crossed to Jeffersonville or New Albany. The Knobs behind New Albany became a famous haunt of the 'hounded' sojourners."[34] Often, of course, fugitive slaves were arrested, as was the case in February of 1851, when two runaways slaves were apprehended in the Knobs adjoining New Albany and returned to Kentucky.[35] Logan Esarey adds that they hid with friends in the hill country behind New Albany and then made their way north to Paoli and Salem.[36] Census and courthouse records establish that African American farmers lived on the outskirts of New Albany.[37] Quakers who had settled in and around Paoli were very helpful. North of Chambersburg (southeast of Paoli) in Orange County lived a Quaker couple by the name of Eli and Elizabeth Lindley, who had dug a secret pit in front of the fireplace of their 1818 cabin and covered it with a rug. Lick Creek, two miles south of Chambersburg, was an established rural black community, but before the Civil War, many of the residents of Lick Creek scattered to Kokomo, Chicago and Gary. According to tradition, a runner came to the settlement warning the group that slave catchers were moving toward their village.[38]

Pearl Grundy Kimbrough, manager of the West Haven Cemetery on West Street in New Albany, has an oral history in her family that was passed down to her through her grandfather and her father. Pearl was born in New Albany in 1918. Her father,

Charles Meredith Grundy, was born in New Albany in 1890 and died there in 1984, and for years he was manager of West Haven Cemetery. Charles' father, Burrell Stapleton Grundy, was born under slavery in Grundy, West Virginia, and was a young boy at the end of the Civil War. Burrell's father, William Grundy, worked as a slave on the Grundy plantation in Grundy, West Virginia, and Burrell's mother, Sarah Rochester, worked on a neighboring plantation. At the close of the Civil War Pearl's great grandparents, her grandfather, (Burrell), and his brothers[39] were given their freedom. Mr. Grundy, their white owner and father to William, gave each of his slave families a wagon, a cow and enough money to purchase a plot of land. They traveled west and crossed at a low point in the Ohio River at Mauckport, Indiana, eventually settling in New Albany. Pearl's father, Charles Meredith, and grandfather, Burrell, talked to Pearl about the Underground Railroad in Floyd County and this general vicinity. Her grandfather distinctly remembered the buffalo trace before it was paved as the extension of State Street. He said it was one of the trails used by the slaves as they headed away from the river, following its meanderings into the hills. The buffalo trace ran south of Freedomland, the large, historical African American cemetery off Paoli Pike.[40]

Burrell Grundy also told Pearl that the slaves crossed over the river from Rudd Street in Portland, which lies on the west side of Louisville and is now a part of that city. Many came into Portland on foot and crossed in fishermen's boats, he said. If the coast was clear, someone would wave a coal lantern on the Indiana side as a signal to the Portland side. He said there were many tragedies connected with these crossings. He also said it was "the Germans" who helped in the Underground Railroad in Floyd County. The slaves would be moved at night from one "third basement" house to another. ("Third basement" was a phrase coined to mean an extra basement or place of concealment below the regular basement.)

Pearl was told by her grandfather of at least four locations in New Albany that had "third basements" or that had harbored fugitive slaves along the State Street route:

(1) The location at 911 State Street, formerly the home of Louis Hartman, a prominent citizen and benefactor of New Albany. The house, which was located at the present site of Baitey's Funeral Home, was near the corner of State Street and Cherry Street. Hartman's first house on the property was torn down when the present one was built in the 1880s.[41] Any home or building at this particular corner of State and Cherry Street would have been an important stop for runaway slaves since it is a verified Underground Railroad route from other oral accounts as well. Charles Meredith Grundy, born in New Albany in 1890, lived in the West Union area and knew Hartman well. He reported to his daughter, Pearl, that Hartman helped fugitive slaves and later, after the Civil War, gave talks at Scribner, the "colored" high school, telling the students of the hardships the "negroes" had to endure.[42]

(2) The location at 1401 State Street, also known as the "Niemeier House" located

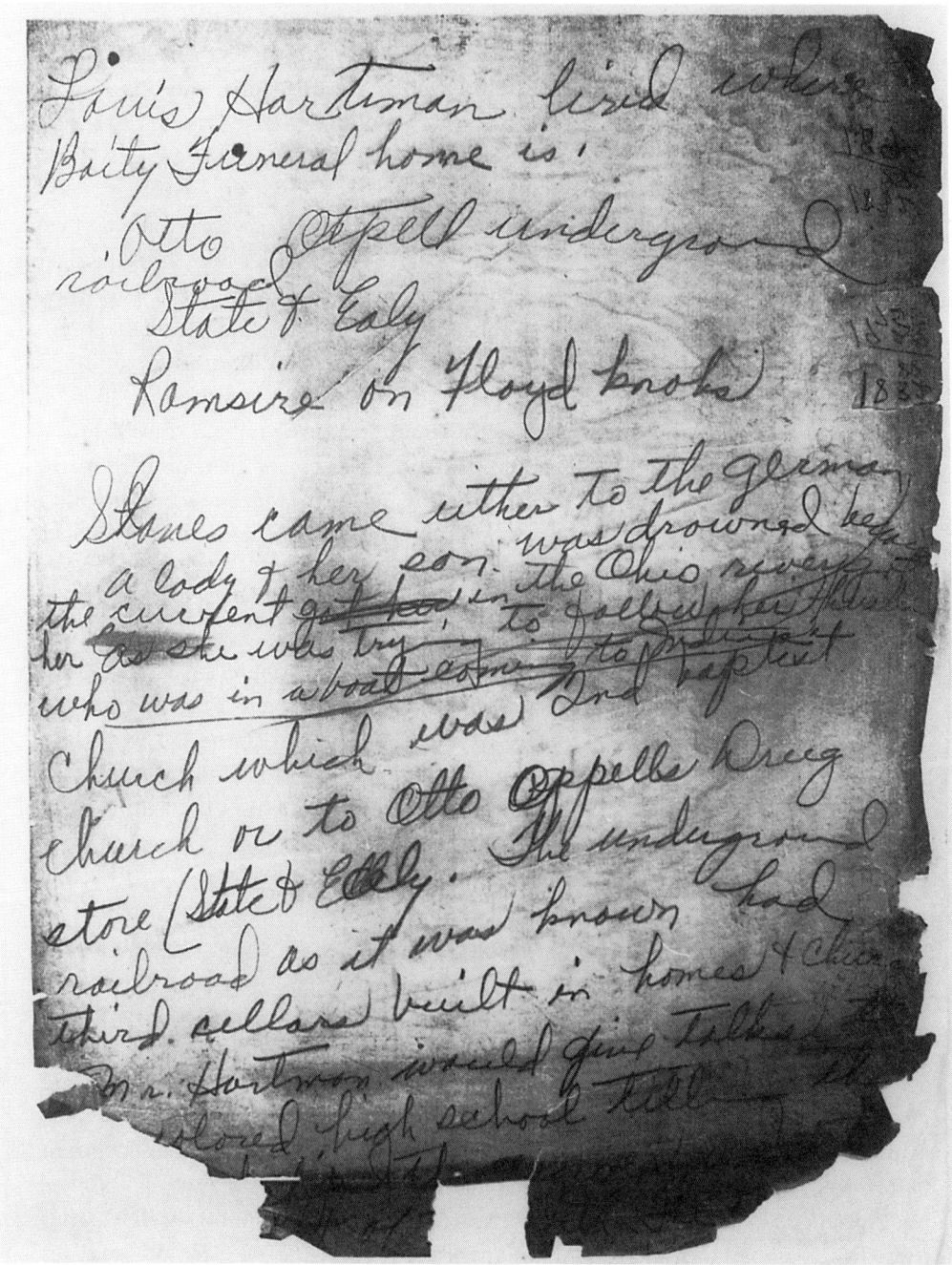

Old document passed down in the family of Burrell Stapleton Grundy recording aspects of the Underground Railroad in Floyd County. (Source: In the possession of the author)

Pearl Grundy Kimbrough telling the author her family's oral tradition of the Underground Railroad in Floyd County. (Photograph courtesy of Jennifer Suzanne Vezner)

on State across from Green Street.[43] It is a brick and stucco house with an "alley" on the north side, formerly a city street that cut through to Griffin Street. Although the front level of the house sits on State Street, the entrance to the basement is much lower than the front door due to the slope of the land. Hence the layout of the land and building is similar to that of Second Baptist Church and Sweet Gum Stable. Pearl knew that the basement had a wooden floor with a trap door that was always covered with a rug. The present owner verifies that the house has a wooden floor in the basement. Formerly a pond was located behind the house that provided water used in the production of beer at a brewery once located at the back of the property. The house was built in 1853 by Isaac N. Eastham and his wife, Eliza, who were from Knox County, Indiana.[44]

(3) The 1900 block of State Street at State and Green Valley. This was the site of a "third basement" house that no longer exists. Part of the stone wall that delineated the property line is still there and can be seen running along State Street.

(4) The site of August Knoefel's summer hotel in the present day Grandview

Estates area. The hotel, built in 1849, was torn down some years ago, but Grandview Estates can be seen from below on State Street as one looks up toward the "Knobs."[45] Oral history states that Knoefel harbored runaways as they headed out of the valley into the Knobs onto the plateau.[46] Knoefel, also known as Otto, was a druggist. He employed blacks at his hotel. Below the hotel a ledge or buffalo trace runs along the cliff leading up and out of the Ohio River valley. Runaway slaves following this ledge on their way up the Knobs would have been in a position to contact Knoefel or the blacks who worked for him.

The Grundy oral tradition document states that "Slaves went to Otto Otpel [Knoefel] druggist at State and Ealy."[47] Knoefel had his first drugstore in the front part of Wesley Chapel Methodist church, or "The Old Ship of Zion" as it was called, when it was located on the corner of First and Market streets. Knoefel must have had close ties to the church. Hartman and Knoefel, both being German immigrants as well as Methodists, could have worked together to help slaves safely out of town.

Fred Ramsier was also named in the Grundy oral history as a person who assisted runaway slaves. However, Ramsier was an immigrant who came to Floyd County from Switzerland in 1881—too late to have participated in what we traditionally think of as the Underground Railroad. Nonetheless, the fact that Ramsier is specifically named in oral history probably indicates that during his own time he was a friend to the African American community. Ramsier and his family settled on property located at the top of present day Daisy Lane. He was a stone mason who helped build the courthouse at Salem, Indiana. His grandson, Henry Ramsier, recalls that his grandfather had a good relationship with the African Americans who lived in settlements on either side of their farm. Henry's father, Fred Jr., was twelve years old when the Ramsier family came to America and later on had a dairy farm on Daisy Lane. Henry, born in 1907, recalls that they had a well on the main road that ran past the farm. A runoff from the well kept a trough supplied with water for the horses of those who passed by. It was a place where both blacks and whites met each day and socialized. When he was a small boy, black families from the neighborhood would come to their farm and pick dandelion greens and blackberries.

River Road and Five Mile Lane, Franklin Township

There has for decades been a strong rumor in the neighborhood around the River Road (Highway 111) and Five Mile Lane corner that the house there played a part in the Underground Railroad. The only evidence of which the present owner knows is to be found in a building behind the house. It was built the same time as

Opposite: The summer hotel built by August Knoefel, said to have been a refuge for runaway slaves. (Courtesy Stuart B. Wrege Indiana History Room, New Albany–Floyd County Public Library)

House at River Road and Five Mile Lane. (Photograph courtesy of Jennifer Suzanne Vezner)

the house and was probably used as a kitchen (c. 1850s). It has a room concealed under the floorboards. The owners had not been aware that a room existed beneath the building until at one point the floor gave way. The basement room may have been constructed for cold storage of food and beverages. The house was built in the Italianate style, popular in New Albany during the antebellum years.

Reference has been made earlier to the fact that a group of free African American Masons residing in Louisville secretly came across the river to the Indiana shore in order to meet as a group on free soil. These clandestine meetings took place in New Albany over a period of three years. Gibson specifically stated that the group disembarked on the Indiana shore five miles down river from New Albany. It is believed that that area was a "safe place" in part because African American farmers owned land in that part of the county, having purchased land there as early as 1812 and as late as the 1870s.

Cave and Spring Off Old Vincennes Road

Webster Lee Harraway, Jr. ("Webbie"), is the grandson of Charles Meredith Grundy. As a young boy he spent many hours with his grandfather as they main-

Outbuilding at River Road and Five Mile Lane. A hidden room is on the right side of the lowest level. (Photograph courtesy of Jennifer Suzanne Vezner)

tained and cared for West Haven Cemetery. His grandfather was a great storyteller and historian in his own right. He passed many stories down to Webbie about the history of New Albany. The following is a narrative as told by Webbie to the author on January 28, 1997:

> According to my grandfather there is a cave with a spring located in a gully as you go up into the Knobs to the left side of Old Vincennes Road after passing a pond and power lines. My grandfather, Charles Meredith Grundy, told me that slaves used to hide in the cave on their way out of New Albany and up the Knobs. There used to be a trail leading to it and as a young man I visited it. But Old Vincennes Road has changed. It used to go straight at the top, head toward Knoefel's hotel and then turn. Long ago a lot of New Albany's west end was swamp. In times of high water, boats used to go up and dock near where Scribner Junior High is now at the foot of Old Vincennes. A lot of Germans and blacks used to live up on Silver Hills and along the edge just above the swamp. The course of the Ohio River changed after the dam and the flood wall went in. All that is left now is Falling Run Creek, which starts at the Ohio River down below the I-64, Sherman Minton Bridge. The Germans and the blacks were neighbors, had a good relationship and used to help each other.

Harraway's grandfather may have been referring to Boiling Spring, which was discovered by early pioneers. It was located on the Knobs above New Albany on a buffalo trace. The trace was later given the name "Boiling Springs Road." The spring has long since disappeared, in part due to the construction of Interstate 64 as well as the development of housing. The large German and African American settlement Harraway is referring to is West Union and its west edge along the foot of the Knobs. The New Albany city directories from the Civil War period verify that immigrants and blacks were living in the same areas. At one time that part of New Albany had many slaughterhouses, tanneries and tallow works run by German immigrants, as well as a park where they had picnics and songfests.

St. John Lutheran Church, Greenville Township

St. John Lutheran Church, dating from 1820, was one of the oldest churches in Greenville Township, Floyd County, Indiana. It was located on Richland Creek, near the southern line of the township. The story unfolds in the following manner. On July 8, 1863, John Hunt Morgan led a group of Confederate soldiers across the Ohio River at Brandenburg, Kentucky, en route to a raid on Southern Indiana. Rev. Peter Glenn, the first pastor of St. John Lutheran Church and a man who served there for many years, was an anti-slavery man and a strong Union supporter known for his courage. When Morgan's Raiders left Corydon and fanned out over the countryside, some of the raiders rode past Rev. Glenn's home and St. John Lutheran Church. Glenn became incensed at the raiders "upon some slight provocation,"[48] and his passion got the better of him. He took down his gun and shot one of the Confederates. No sooner had he shot the soldier than he was himself shot in his doorway and instantly killed. His son was also wounded.[49] Morgan's raiders also burned his house and barn, and destroyed or carried off all that was of value. The church, however, was left standing and is still there. It has undoubtedly been somewhat altered, and new siding that replaced the old frame siding has been added, but the church remains in the midst of a graveyard with stones clearly bearing the names of the early members: Mordecai Collins, Jacob Summers, Jacob Engleman, Jacob Yenawine, John Engleman, Jacob Buckhart, Phelix Blankbeker, Phillip Bierley and several Martins and Zimmermans, among others.

The above account is taken from the *New Albany Ledger* report written immediately after it happened as well as from a paraphrase of the story as it was recorded for the 1882 publication of L. A. Williams' history, titled *History of the Ohio Falls Cities and Their Counties*. The *Ledger*, however, claims that the first shot fired, which killed one of Morgan's men, was fired, not by Glenn, but by someone behind a fence near Glenn's home. In revenge, therefore, the rebels set fire to Glenn's house. Glenn provoked the rebels to shoot him when he refused to desist from putting the fire out. The Confederates also shot Glenn's son in both thighs.[50]

A 1937 WPA report on the subject tells a much different story. James Brewster, a former state representative and senator from Harrison County and grandson of Harrison County Judge Porter, reported that the Home Guard, consisting of 300 men led by Col. Jorden, marched as far as Rev. Peter Glenn's house which, he said, was located four miles south of Corydon on the Mauckport Road. About the same time a body of Confederate Cavalry dismounted at Glenn's house and shot his son, John, who had appeared on the front porch with a gun. Glenn, who was outspoken on the subject of slavery, traveled into Kentucky to preach at times and bitterly denounced slavery from the pulpit. In so doing, he incurred the displeasure of many slave owners. "It was reported that some of these men were with Morgan and that they had Rev. Glenn marked and had decided to kill him."[51] Brewster continues with the story that as the Home Guard rode up, the Rebels rushed for their horses and that Glenn, seeing his son lying wounded and his barn burning, shot one of them. He in turn was killed and his farm house also burned.

None of the above stories tells of yet another "legend" that seemed to spring up in the neighborhood of St. John's Lutheran Church. This story gives a different explanation of why Rev. Glenn was provoked to shoot. The oral tradition in Greenville says that Glenn was sympathetic to the cause and plight of the slave. At the time Morgan's Raiders rode through, Glenn was protecting runaway slaves who were hiding in the building. The legend continues by saying that Morgan's men not only killed Glenn but also the slaves.

The oldest of these accounts is, of course, the newspaper report written at the time the incident occurred. There seem to be no first hand written accounts of

St. John Church being used as a hiding place or of any of the pastors there having assisted runaway slaves as they headed north.

Tunnels

Some of the Underground Railroad folklore that has developed in communities, and New Albany is no exception, involves the existence of tunnels and their possible use by runaway slaves. There have for decades been "rumors" regarding tunnels leading up from the Ohio River, going under streets and connecting some buildings and homes in New Albany. Research involving tunnels has resulted in information about storm sewers, dry cisterns, dugouts left over from prohibition days and below-the-ground food and beverage storage areas. The 1853 *Charter and Ordinances of the City of New Albany* gave John Lockwood and his associates permission to construct pipes under the city streets for the conveyance of gas lines to light city street lights, "provided that the said gas pipes shall not interfere with the drainage of said city through its sewers or other underground fixtures for the conveyance of water."[52] It is supposed that the underground sewer conveyances were approximately four feet in diameter, but the openings closer to the river could have been larger to accommodate the buildup of water underground as it reached its outlet—the river.

The Phineas M. Kent house has a separate small room under the front porch. Built in 1857, it is located at 1015 Main Street and is now the Episcopalian Parish House. Marks on the wall of this room indicate there was once an opening leading south toward Main Street in the direction of the river. The opening appears to have been approximately four feet in diameter. Phineas Kent joined John B. Norman as publisher of the *New Albany Daily Ledger* in 1849 for a short time. A Democrat, he was very involved in politics on the city, state and national levels. In view of his connection with the *New Albany Daily Ledger,* which spoke out against African Americans during that period, it is doubtful Kent was of anti-slavery sentiment. We have no evidence he would have assisted in the Underground Railroad and, therefore, it is reasonable to believe that the signs of an opening in the small basement room had to do with the drainage system.

Webster Lee Harraway related a story from his grandfather, Charles Meredith Grundy, that there was a tunnel under Spring Street leading from the old jail to the old courthouse. Grundy said that before the Civil War, runaway slaves, if caught, would often be held in the tunnel until the "slavers," as he put it, would come from Louisville to pick them up. Both the jail and the courthouse have been torn down, so there is no way to verify the presence of a tunnel linking those two buildings. In any case it would have played no role in the Underground Railroad.

Very clear evidence of tunnels built for human passage and not for the conveyance of water exists in at least three places in New Albany. One is at the Sloan/Bicknell house on East Main Street, built in 1852. This tunnel leads from the basement into the back yard in the direction of the Ohio River. It probably led to the carriage house and was used by the owners in times of bad weather. There is testimony of the tunnel's existence, not only from the present owners, but also from those who grew up in the neighborhood and who played in the area as children. Another tunnel used for human passage was under the "Ben Jackson House," which was torn down in the late 1970s. It was located on the south side of Dewey Street west of the Kentucky & Indiana Railroad tracks. The tunnel there led from the root cellar in a southerly direction. Testimony given by those who knew of the tunnel say that it was beginning to collapse by the 1960s.

The only other tunnel worthy of mention is the one that runs in a northerly direction from the basement of Second Baptist Church under East Main Street. Reference has already been made to it in the section titled "Second Baptist Church." Signs of the tunnel's entrance exist on the northern wall of the sub-basement. Testimony exists from a man still living in Southern Indiana regarding his having been in this tunnel in the early 1960s. His personal knowledge of the tunnel's size, the location of Second Baptist Church on the river, the strong oral history of the Underground Railroad connection with the church, and evidence of the church having an antislavery personality do lead one to believe that this tunnel might have been used by runaway slaves.

There is one factor that links many of these buildings together, and that is that Isaac P. Smith was the architect and builder of several of them. Smith was responsible for designing Second Presbyterian Church, the Sloan/Bicknell house, the city jail built at the northeast corner of State and Spring streets, as well as his own home on Main Street, which has a hidden room under the eaves on the third floor.[53] We are left with more questions than answers. However, the fact remains that with the possible exception of the tunnel under Main Street leading north from Second Baptist Church, there is no reliable evidence that spaces under the ground in New Albany were used by runaway slaves.

Chapter 8
Key Individuals

The most difficult task in a study such as this is to find and identify individuals who helped slaves in their escape across the Ohio River and through the Southern Indiana area. Unless an arrest was made and thus a written record created linking an individual to assisting slaves to escape, there is generally only oral tradition connecting individuals with Underground Railroad activity.

In 1839, for example, a white farmer, Milton Burford (Buford), who lived a short distance west of Georgetown, Indiana, was arrested in Louisville for attempting to help a slave owned by Attorney Francis Johnson to escape. Burford was taken before the Jefferson County police court for examination on November 5, 1839, along with John Clement and William Whalan, both of Clark County, Indiana. The three men were sent to the county jail to await their trial in the Circuit Court.[1] Burford, who had a distillery, owned nearly 400 acres of farmland near the Harrison County line that he purchased in parcels between 1817 and 1835.[2] His arrest gives us hard evidence that he participated in the Underground Railroad — if only in this one instance.

Another case is that involving Dr. Yocum and his nephew from New Albany. Even though no court records of the case have been found, the two men were arrested for "secreting the negro girl belonging to Wilkerson of Chaplin, Kentucky."[3] New Albany officers Wash Ragans and Weatherford delivered them to the Bardstown jailer in Nelson County, Kentucky, after their arrest.

The following individuals have a connection with Underground Railroad work, either through written record or oral tradition. All of them had a relationship with the free African American community in Louisville or Floyd County. In addition, they had occupations related to river transportation as well as lifestyles that revealed the presence of a spirit of benevolence toward their fellow human beings.

Henson McIntosh (alias Fremont)

From time to time citizens of New Albany were arrested on suspicion of "running off slaves," such as the examples of William Hosea and the DeVore brothers mentioned previously. In Henson McIntosh, however, we have an example of a citizen who was actually arrested, convicted and sentenced to the Kentucky penitentiary for helping slaves escape. McIntosh was an African American who resided in New Albany. Prior to the Civil War he moved to Kentucky where he was actively engaged in running off slaves. He used various aliases such as "Henson Fremont" and "Henry" McIntosh. The name "Henson McIntosh" began to show up in Floyd County court records in 1850. The Floyd County Recorder registered the fact that on July 9, 1850, McIntosh went to the Overseers of the Poor to contract for an apprentice in the person of Ann Dungen, "a poor colored girl," as his housekeeper.[4] This record probably indicates when he and his family arrived in Floyd County. The "Register of Negroes and Mulattoes in Floyd County" shows that he and his family registered on August 11, 1853; the register describes McIntosh as being "dark brown." His wife, Elizabeth McIntosh, and four children, Anna, Mary F., Janie and William, were registered also.[5] Isaac N. Akin of the Floyd Circuit Court vouched for him and his family. Elizabeth was born in Kentucky, Henson in Maryland, and the children in Indiana.

McIntosh lived for a time near the river in the first ward, on the north side of upper Main Street between East Sixth and East Seventh streets.[6] The city directory shows him as a "laborer." The 1860 census describes him as a "rope maker." Henson may have lived for a time in a small house on the property of one of the wealthy Main Street residents. During the antebellum period, a number of New Albany's elite built homes along upper Main Street. "The extent to which Main Street had become an enclave of the rich is illustrated by the large number of servants, over one-third of the total number in the city, who found employment on Main Street in the wards above the central business district."[7] A number of blacks who worked on the river also lived on the side streets between Upper Main Street and the river. Obviously, McIntosh, with his rope making skills, would have been involved in New Albany's ship building industry. In 1860 he and his family had moved to the upper part of the first ward next door to John Sanders, a black riverboat steward, on Sycamore. The neighborhood was made up of craftsmen and people who were connected with river and rail transportation systems. Many African American homeowners lived in the area.

Some time during the year 1859–1860, McIntosh left his family and moved to Louisville. Because McIntosh was still listed in the 1860 census for Floyd County, he may have maintained two addresses. On July 3, 1859, he was seen in the company of two slaves, "Frank" and "Betty," who belonged to Samuel K. Richardson of Louisville. The three were aboard the Ohio and Mississippi Railroad train in Indiana on their way to Cincinnati when the two runaways were apprehended.[8] Apparently McIntosh, Frank and Betty had taken the ferry from Portland to New Albany where they procured a horse and buggy from either a stable or a private source and rode north to Salem. At Salem the three caught the New Albany & Salem train to Mitchell where they transferred to the Ohio and Mississippi line, which would take them through

Seymour on to Madison and Cincinnati.⁹ They were only a short distance beyond Mitchell when they were apprehended by Louisville police officer R. M. Moore and James Chambers, who were heading west out of Seymour on that line. Moore and Chambers had the east bound train stopped and with the help of the conductors and others on the train were able to carry out the arrest. McIntosh was not arrested with the slaves at that time as it was "not practicable"¹⁰ nor expedient then to do so. However, McIntosh, having been suspected, was watched and followed until an appropriate time came to arrest him. On February 12, 1861, he was arrested by officer R. M. Moore of Louisville and Mitchell Lapalle of Portland and jailed in default of $900 bail.¹¹ He was charged with two offenses—that of migrating into the state of Kentucky illegally and, secondly, aiding two slaves of Samuel K. Richardson to escape from Kentucky on July 3, 1859. The witness against him was Mrs. Penny's slave, "Walker." McIntosh was sentenced to prison in Frankfort, Kentucky, for five years.¹² After serving less than one year McIntosh "escaped over the walls," on April 15, 1862, but was found and arrested six days later. He was sentenced to serve an additional two years and was released on May 20, 1868.¹³

In 1868 an article about him appeared in the *New Albany Commercial* describing him as a young "negro" man from New Albany who nine or ten years earlier was caught "panting with the spirit of liberty." There had been no contact between him and his wife during those years and his wife concluded, therefore, that he was dead. Eventually she married again and had four or five children by her second husband. She was shocked one day in June, 1868, when Henson, shortly after his release from prison, stepped into the door of her house. It was agreed between all parties involved that she must bear the burden of deciding which man was to be her husband—the first one, McIntosh, or the second, who was then legally so. The judge gave her three days in which to make up her mind. She decided in favor of the second husband and Henson quietly departed for Louisville, "giving his more fortunate rival peaceable possession."¹⁴

Having been a resident in New Albany for some years, McIntosh would have known the African American community as well as white citizens there. One could speculate that he may have been working within a "system" that included some of these residents. It is evident that he had a way of producing counterfeit freedom papers for Frank and Betsy to show proof of freedom when crossing on the ferry and getting on the train. The Register of Prisoners describes him as having a poor education. This indicates that he was most likely working with someone else who was able to forge the papers. We also know that McIntosh had money with which to purchase the false papers and ferry and railroad tickets. His arrest for helping slaves leave Kentucky and cross the river into Indiana is also a signal for us that there were others in the immediate area who helped slaves escape and who may have been part of that system. Who were these people and where did the money come from to carry out this scheme? Those questions remain unanswered, but it is likely McIntosh's abolitionist efforts were financed by an anti-slavery organization that had its roots and received its money from eastern abolitionist sources. Having lived in New Albany, McIntosh would have used his knowledge of places and relationships with people to further his work. He would have, for example, known George Washington Carter and William Harding who both lived in his New Albany neighborhood.

William Harding

William Harding (also known as "Harden"), an African American, worked as a steward on the riverboats. He resided in Louisville before moving to New Albany in 1848, where he lived for a time on Main Street between East Fifth and Sixth streets. He may have been employed by one of the riverboat captains who resided there; later two of his teenage sons also worked on the riverboats in the cabin crew.[15] During the 1850s he moved to the east side of East Sixth Street north of Sycamore (now Culbertson Avenue). Here he lived in a neighborhood of other African American residents suspected of helping runaways, namely, George Washington Carter, who lived on the west side of East Eighth north of Sycamore, and George's brother, Edward Carter, who lived on Shelby Street (locally called "Short Shelby") north of Sycamore.[16] Their back doors would have faced each other. It is also significant that all three houses are located very near the depot and rails of the New Albany–Salem Railroad, a verified route of runaway slaves. Just across the street from George Washington Carter lived William Hosea, the omnibus driver who was charged with consorting with Ralph, a slave of Bishop Spaulding of Louisville, to run off slaves.

Either from living in Louisville or through his occupation on the river, Harding was acquainted with three Louisville men, namely, James R. Cunningham, William H. Gibson and Jesse Merriweather, already named as leaders in establishing black Free Masonry in Louisville and New Albany. It is known that Cunningham helped Rev. Calvin Fairbank with the escape of the slave, Tamar, from Louisville. He was also arrested by the Louisville police on suspicion of helping slaves escape from Kentucky, but he was never convicted.[17] Cunningham and Gibson were musicians who performed on the riverboats. They, along with Merriweather, secretly went by steamer to Pittsburgh in 1852 to attend a Freesoil Convention organized by Frederick Douglass, William H. Garrett, Dr. Martin R. Delany and other leaders in the abolitionist movement.[18] While they were at the convention, they each subscribed to *The North Star* (later named *Frederick Douglass' Paper*), an abolitionist newspaper published by Douglass at Rochester, New York.

Because it was illegal for these Louisville men to have copies of an anti-slavery publication in Kentucky, they had the subscriptions mailed to William Harding in New Albany.[19] Harding secreted the subversive newspapers with him onto the boat. His friends would read the newspaper, discuss the subject matter and then hide them back on the boat in with the sheet music on top of the piano. "If the authorities had known of that seditious sheet, our peace and happiness would have been disturbed,"[20] Gibson later wrote. Harding, sympathetic to the cause of abolitionism and occupied as a steward on the riverboats, could have assisted the enslaved as well as newly freed people.

George Washington Carter

"George Washington Carter and his family were free African Americans who were active in the Underground Railroad and made many trips back and forth to black communities established in Ontario, Canada."[21] Two of the Carter children, Edward and Harriett, were born in "Lower Canada" in 1838 and 1839.[22] Several of his sons, including Hannibal, attended school from 1846 to 1856 in Buxton and Chatham, Ontario. This afforded the Carter family reason to travel back and forth to Canada and could have provided a front for assisting slaves to reach British territory.

The Carters originally came from a large plantation in Virginia. Many of the slaves from that plantation were very light-skinned and took the name "Carter" after their white owners and relatives. Carter settled in New Albany in the mid–1820s and purchased his first property on Upper High Street in 1829. He spent some time in the Scioto River Valley in Scioto County, Ohio, which also borders the Ohio River, and there met his wife, Rose Anne Wallace, who was born at Chilacothe, Scioto County, Ohio, in 1811. They were married in New Albany on September 27, 1836. (In 1844 the Carters named one of their daughters "Scioto.") It is possible that George and Rose Anne were caught up in the "Black Friday" racial violence of January 1, 1830, in the Portsmouth, Ohio, area. If so, they were forced out and would have fled for safety to Houston Hollow, a black settlement six miles north of Portsmouth. By 1832 they had returned to New Albany.[23]

The Carters were known in the communities in which they settled as people who were outspokenly abolitionist.[24] The boldness of George Washington Carter, for instance, is borne out through many instances in his life. Carter was a "man for all seasons." He was remarkable given the time in which he lived. Not only did he educate some of his children in Canada, but, as a barber and tobacconist, he owned his own business and various other pieces of property. For example, he owned the large livery stable run by John Shrader, a furniture craftsman and funeral director who handled burials for blacks in Floyd County. The stable was located on Main between State and West First streets.[25] Carter owned New Albany properties on East Market, West and East High streets, West Fifth, West First and Second streets, East Elm Street, and his house and lot on East Eighth Street with the attached "Humboldt Vineyard."[26] His estate at one time was valued at $50,000. He eventually sold some of this property to the City of New Albany for use as a cemetery (now Fairview Cemetery). In

8. Key Individuals 125

Top: Descendants of the Carter family (*left to right*): James A. Robinson, Lisa McIntyre, Jackie Brown, Darlene McIntyre, Adam Baity, Monica Baity, Kathryn Hickerson, Shannon Baity. *Bottom:* Descendants of the Carter family, first row (*left to right*): Paige Williams, Mariah Tolbert, Marisa Tolbert, John Tolbert, Jr., Angela Tolbert. Second row: Linda Ratliff, Mary Jane Carter Tolbert, Sharon Wilkerson, Diana Williams, Stephanie Tolbert, Ryan Williams. Third row: Phyllis Wilkerson, Donald Norris, Keith Ratliff, Pam Tolbert, John Tolbert, Pam Bowman, Gerald Bowman. (Photographs courtesy of Jennifer Suzanne Vezner)

1850 Carter traveled to Sacramento, California, to mine gold. His presence there is verified by the 1850 California census, which shows his property value at that time to be $6,000. When he returned from California, he established a bath house in addition to his other businesses. It was described as being a "delightful place to visit" with an elegant style — kept neat and clean.

On August 1, 1860, an incident occurred in New Albany that showed a link connecting Carter and his neighbors with the Underground Railroad. The African American population of New Albany had gathered at Hedden's Grove on Charlestown Road to celebrate the anniversary of West India's emancipation. One of the speakers, Rev. Kelly, an African American from Louisville (he may have been part Indian), was already known to the New Albany community for preaching abolitionist sermons in some of the area churches. Kelly gave two speeches that day. The newspaper described Kelly's first speech as "a full blooded abolition one" in which Kelly described the Underground Railroad. He told them he knew of sixteen passengers who had started on the route the week before. The *Ledger* reporter had no doubt that Kelly was one of the superintendents on the Underground Railroad and "while the Kentucky Christians are embracing this reverend blacksnake, he is furnishing their slaves with through tickets to Canada." The second speech was published in the *Ledger* and reads in part:

> I know we are told we should not agitate this [slavery] question, but I say it is our duty to agitate.... The great American people will agitate this slavery question until not a vistage [sic] of it remains as a foul curse upon our great country. The Democrats will permit every ignorant Irish and Dutchman to vote who do not even know who is President of the United States, while we native born citizens are denied the right, and they are even trying to bind our fetters the tighter about us. I say that you have a duty to perform, if you want freedom you must battle for it. I do not counsel you to open rebellion, but to use every lawful means to abolish slavery from our land.[27]

Two days later a letter to the editor appeared in the *Ledger* from none other than George Washington Carter. The letter reads as follows, in its entirety:

> To the Editors of the *Ledger*:
>   There have been several articles in your paper concerning a pic nic [sic] held on the first, and a speech that was made by one Rev. Kelly. Now this man is a stranger, and hails from a slave State, and a great portion of the colored people here know nothing about him or his principles; and I do not think that persons who know nothing of the man or his speech should be classed with him. For my part I know nothing of the pic nic, the speech, or the man that made it, until I saw it in the paper, and I think it was uncalled for, and detrimental to the best interests of all. I wish it distinctly understood that myself and many others in our city do not endorse but repudiate the remarks that were made. I do not know this man, never saw him in my life, nor do I ever care to see him. He calls himself an Indian.

John Fowles, Henry Clay, John Sanders, Edward Carter, John Hill, and William Harding concur in the above.

G. W. Carter

It is obvious that in order to help maintain peace in New Albany, leaders in the African American community would not have endorsed Kelly's speech given his rhetoric against immigrants. However, there is another point to be made here. George Washington Carter and the other men who signed with him attempted with this letter to distance themselves from the abolitionist speaker, who not only spoke openly and strongly against slavery but who publicly acknowledged having personal contact with the Underground Railroad. As for the men who signed this letter along with Carter, we know they lived in the same neighborhood and in the case of three of them, their back doors faced each other. William Harding, sympathetic with the abolitionist movement, was a steward on the riverboats. Henry Clay was a blacksmith who worked for the New Albany–Salem Railroad. John W. Sanders was a riverboat steward. John Hill, George's brother-in-law, was a barber who worked in George's shop. Edward Carter, also a barber, later became a "riverman." This places at least five households of black families not only near each other but close to the New Albany–Salem Railroad depot and its tracks. They were also men who had involvement in some way with the transportation industry.

Because Kelly aligned himself with activities on the Underground Railroad, Carter and his friends needed to distance themselves from him. Carter, in particular, had a lot to lose. He was well thought of in the community, he and his family were educated and he was the owner of considerable property. Possibly Kelly said too much when he spoke of having knowledge of "sixteen passengers who had started on the Underground Railroad route last week." These New Albany men did not trust Kelly. Therefore, Carter stated in his letter, "I do not know this man, never saw him in my life," and may have believed he would give out information about the Southern Indiana Underground Railroad operation that could have led directly to them.

Still another factor to consider regarding the Carter family and the Underground Railroad is that they may have had relatives living in Louisville. A Louisville barber, James Carter, was arrested there on January 21, 1861, for aiding runaway slaves. He helped the slaves of Dr. Keller and Dr. Medcaff escape.[28] He may be the same James who from time to time lived in New Albany and worked with George in his barber shop, but no proof has been found of this. The Floyd County "Negro Register" of July 1853 to February 13, 1865, listed a James E. Carter, "Age 21, yellow skin with a scar on his left cheek, sometimes a barber." Another James Carter is also listed there and is described as follows: "Age 24, yellow in color, mark on left arm near the elbow in the shape of a fish." Two "James Carters" are listed in the 1860 census for Floyd County.

In 1878, just after his death, the editor of the *New Albany Daily Ledger* wrote about George Washington Carter:

> He was a man of strong prejudices, and long before the emancipation of the slaves of the country was extremely anxious to secure social equality for himself and family, and for this purpose removed to Canada, but soon returned, fully convinced that the colored men of the states had better opportunities and advantages then [sic] those in British possessions. Social ostracism in Canada at that time was more excessive than in the United States.[29]

It is interesting that the *New Albany Daily Ledger* with its anti-black bias described George Washington Carter as "a man of strong prejudices ... extremely anxious to secure social equality for himself and family." George's shop was near the *Ledger* office. He regularly offered the *Ledger* office grapes from his vineyard and homemade wine.[30] If George was indeed, as the *Ledger* proposed, "anxious to secure social equality for himself and his family," any attempts at ingratiating himself to the white community did nothing to prevent the violence to his home and property during the riots of the summer of 1862. It was necessary for him and his family to barricade themselves inside their home on Eighth Street for safety from the white mob. Even so, the mob destroyed his vineyards and garden. The 1878 *Ledger* article continues:

> Upon his return from Canada, he again settled down to business, opening a fine barber shop, a business he followed for years, to which he added quite an extensive bath house.... In addition, he built him an excellent residence on Upper Eighth Street and planted quite an extensive vineyard. Had he been contented and closely applied himself to business, there is little doubt that he would have left his family quite a handsome fortune. His erratic character frequently led him into trouble, but none questioned his honesty and integrity.[31]

One can only speculate as to what the *Ledger* editor meant by referring to Carter's "erratic character frequently leading him into trouble." Available evidence shows he did not have an erratic character but instead led a stable life, had a good business, a fine house and children who were educated and industrious. Carter, known to many in New Albany as "Uncle Wash," died on May 4, 1878, at age seventy-seven. He was found in Silver Creek lying on his face in about eighteen inches of water. He had last been seen at the Fourteenth Street Depot in Louisville. The newspaper account of his death said that although he may have committed suicide "as for years he had occasional spells of insanity yet it is not improbable he was seized with apoplexy."[32] Carter is buried in Fairview Cemetery.[33] His plot is located on land he formerly owned on Eighth Street near the place where his house once stood.

Louis Hartman

Louis Hartman, a German immigrant, was a man whose heart was touched during the "Second Great Awakening" by the spirit of evangelism and the social consciousness evoked in the revivals that were sweeping the country and that also took place in New Albany. As an immigrant, he might have suffered some of the same indignation as those in the African American community living around him in the West Union area. He owned property and had buildings near the corner of Cherry and State streets, a verified route of runaway slaves. Later he owned a farm in the Knobs. Before the Civil War he was involved in a partnership with Mr. E. Beckman. They had a butcher stall in the Upper Market House at East Market and Eleventh Street. After that he ran his own meat stall in the Market House where the Plaza stood on Market Street.

Louis Hartman. (Courtesy Stuart B. Wrege Indiana History Room, New Albany–Floyd County Public Library)

Mr. Hartman came to New Albany from Germany in 1854 as a boy of fifteen years. He died on July 23, 1917, and the New Albany newspapers praised him for his business, civic, religious and philanthropic contributions to the community. After the Civil War he established "Louis Hartman and Sons," a wholesale flour, grain, feed and cereal business. He was a member of the Board of Directors of the Chamber of Commerce and an active member of the German Methodist Church. A stained glass window exists as a memorial to him in the old German Methodist Church (now the Seventh Day Adventist Church at 418 Spring). He helped secure the K & I Bridge, was in charge of the New Albany Street Railway system under a receivership of the United States court, aided in building the Belt Line Railway that enabled the Southern Railway to cross the Ohio River and to connect with other rail lines, helped establish a manual training school for New Albany youth, and as a member of the school board is due much of the credit for building the high school and public library at the turn of the century.

Having lived in New Albany for more than sixty years, Hartman was well-known not only locally but also in the surrounding area for his generosity and works of charity. His obituary stated, "He recognized the poor man as well as the man of affairs." He was deeply interested in the mission work of the church and also with assistance given to orphans. Eight pastors were involved in his funeral service at the German Methodist Church and the family received flowers, letters and telegrams of condolence from all over the country. It is noteworthy that one of the letters received and read at the funeral was from Rev. G. M. Noble, pastor of the African Methodist Episcopal Church in Louisville, Kentucky, paying him a high tribute.[34] Whatever Hartman's connection was to Rev. Noble and the AME Church in Louisville, it was undoubtedly one that contributed to making life better for the African American and could indeed have involved Underground Railroad work during the Civil War era as oral tradition suggests.

Information about individuals both black and white who assisted runaway slaves in Floyd County is buried so deep that it surfaces only occasionally, such as if arrest records of their activity come to light as in the cases of Milton Burford or Henson McIntosh. Furthermore, that written record only shows the tip of the iceberg. We have no way of knowing what part these people, along with others, may have played in successful attempts to either transport slaves across the river or otherwise assist them.

Chapter 9
Final Comments

Because of the secrecy and the hazardous nature involved in the giving of aid and assistance to runaway slaves as they came through Floyd County, folklore developed around the subject. It has, therefore, become important to try to document Underground Railroad activity and to separate folklore from fact.[1] Most of the written accounts of Underground Railroad activity were recorded after the Civil War, and many of them may contain embellishments. One of the earliest authorities, Wilbur H. Siebert, attempted to show that the Underground Railroad was one of the forces that helped to destroy slavery. Siebert and his students probably "pushed" the point they wanted to make when interviewing former slaves and individuals who had helped runaways escape. It has been said that after the Civil War it was popular to "get on the Underground Railroad bandwagon." However, in Floyd County, as well as other places in the country, it would never have been popular to associate oneself with the Underground Railroad movement. Particularly for the African American community, it did not pay to broadcast involvement because of the severe bias that continued to be leveled against them in this and other regions. This is undoubtedly one of the reasons some information has been lost.

However, it is now possible to reach several important conclusions about the Underground Railroad in Floyd County and the region. And in the process, it is revealed that several prevailing views about the Underground Railroad in this area are really myths that need to be exposed. Unfortunately, some of these myths are widely believed yet today.

Myth: *All information about the Underground Railroad in Floyd County has been lost and is no longer available.*

This myth is indeed false. The phrase "the absence of evidence is not evidence of absence"[2] is useful here. In part, it appears that if a "system" worked, no one heard about it. If the system did not work, the slave was arrested and the community heard about it, mostly through the newspaper. This is especially true of Floyd County and its peculiar place on the border of a slave state and the metropolitan area of Louisville. One would not expect to find African American citizens boasting of their work for the cause of freedom when help came from them in such a quiet, spontaneous and unassuming way. Likewise, in researching Second Presbyterian Church records, one would not expect to find a definitive statement linking members to active, vocal roles in an Underground Railroad system. This absence of a recorded "link" does not detract from or cheapen the other pieces of existing evidence showing that church members would have provided assistance for slaves coming through Floyd County if the opportunity presented itself. By studying subjects distinct from the Underground Railroad such as the historical context and the groups of people who were anti-slavery, including the African American population, one can discover much about the Underground Railroad itself. The information gleaned from court documents, newspaper accounts, census records, oral histories and other sources provides evidence of Underground Railroad activity in Floyd County.

Myth: *White people played a more prominent role in the Underground Railroad in Floyd County than did African Americans.*

There is little doubt that some of the people most responsible for assisting runaway slaves were the members of the free African American community in Floyd County. Several names of black citizens have been cited, such as Henson McIntosh and Messrs. Finney, Goins and Lacey. McIntosh was actively engaged in seeking out, possibly encouraging, slaves to run, while the three New Albany men who helped Cummings were simply reacting spontaneously to a brother in need. There are many others, however, whose names will never be known who sheltered, fed and clothed those who were searching for freedom. Newspaper articles, particularly from the period after passage of the Exclusion Act of 1851, refer to runaways being hidden in West Union or other rural areas of the county where African Americans resided. It is also possible that through the work of leaders in the black community, such as William Paul Quinn and Byrd Parker, a link was established between the free black communities in Louisville, Floyd County and Chicago through churches, lodges and the new black political scene of the 1850s.

Myth: *The Underground Railroad in Floyd County was highly organized and tunnels were a major factor in the escape routes.*

It appears that for the most part assistance in Floyd County was spontaneous, casual and not well organized. Free African Americans lived in areas throughout the city and county. It was possible, therefore, for runaway slaves to locate help within that community if they needed it. There are no signs that Floyd County had an Underground Railroad agent such as Levi Coffin who operated in Fountain City, Indiana, to orchestrate escapes.

The myth regarding the use of tunnels as an escape mechanism is a difficult myth to disprove because there are signs that tunnels did exist in various places in New Albany. On the other hand, one cannot show that most of these tunnels were used for hiding runaway slaves. The one exception, however, involves the tunnel that connects Second Baptist Church on East Main Street with the building across the street.

9. Final Comments

Myth: *Runaway slaves were free and safe as soon as they crossed the Ohio River and reached Indiana soil.*

Because of the system of slave-catching prevalent along the Ohio River border states, Southern Indiana was not a safe place for runaway slaves to stay. With the passage of the federal Fugitive Slave Law of 1850 and the state Exclusion Act of 1851, it became even more dangerous for runaways to remain in Indiana. They could be free only by leaving the state and the country.

Myth: *In identifying information about the Underground Railroad in Floyd County, sites and buildings used by runaway slaves are more important than the people who assisted them.*

Recent national attention that has been given to the Underground Railroad in this country has placed considerable emphasis on routes and sites. These are important, but no more important than the people who escaped and who assisted them. We are able to uncover the stories of some but not all of these people, and those stories give life to the narrative of the Underground Railroad.

Myth: *Runaway slaves could not safely make it through Floyd County without help.*

It is apparent that some runaway slaves came through Floyd County without assistance. In some of these cases they used their own ingenuity in getting across the river on the ferry either by purchasing their own ticket or by having a good disguise or a believable story to back up their claim of being free. Those Kentucky slave owners who were in the habit of sending a trusted slave across the river on errands during the day occasionally lost one to freedom. Slaves often used employment on the steamboats as a way of breaking free while being docked on the Indiana shore. Or, by being familiar with the river, they used skiffs found tied up on the bank to reach free soil. Slaves were often characterized as being passive, meek and docile. However, research has brought out the point that the will of the slave was not broken, and they often put much at risk to gain freedom.

In the beginning of this book the points were made that New Albany–Floyd County was not necessarily a good place for runaway slaves to come and that for several reasons much information about the Underground Railroad has been lost. Despite those facts, research has shown that considerable runaway slave activity did occur in New Albany and Floyd County and that much information is available after all. Floyd County deserves a permanent niche in the history of the Underground Railroad, both for what the residents did on behalf of runaway slaves and for what the slaves themselves did in overcoming the greatest of obstacles in order to reach freedom.

Epilogue

On August 25 in the year 1857, a young lawyer in New Albany, who did not further identify himself, wrote an editorial to the *New Albany Daily Ledger* questioning the failure of the Floyd County court system to abide by the state law in regard to blacks coming into the state illegally. He accused the Court of Common Pleas Judge, Jared Jocelyn, of asserting that the Exclusion Act of 1851 was unconstitutional.[1] The lawyer backed up his accusation by referring to the case of *Barkshire vs. The State,* which sustained the Exclusion Act. The case involved a Mr. Barkshire, an African American from Rising Sun, Indiana, who had brought a black woman from Ohio to Rising Sun in 1854 to marry her. Barkshire was fined $10 by the Common Pleas Court of Ohio County, Indiana, for "harboring a negress." Barkshire appealed his case to the Supreme Court of Indiana, which affirmed the Ohio County court's decision, claimed he had no wife and asserted that his marriage was null and void. The young New Albany lawyer asserted that the Indiana Supreme Court supported the Ohio County decision to uphold the Exclusion Act, but that the Floyd County court continued to do as it pleased in regard to the Act. "The Supreme Court sustains the law, but the Floyd Common Pleas [Court] will not," argued the young lawyer.[2]

I had discovered this "Letter to the Editor" in 1997 and wondered about the meaning behind it. What grounds did this lawyer have to accuse Judge Jocelyn of breaking the law? The answer to my question came like a "bolt out of the blue" when, with the help of the staff in the Floyd County Recorder's office, we discovered the "Freedom Papers, Bills of Sale and Manumission Papers" gathering dust in the City-County Building. Actually, I had been in the Recorder's office looking for something else at the time. I had discovered through Probate Records, as well as other sources, that there had been slaves in Floyd County. I thought I would check the early Miscellaneous Indexes to see if I could find any record of people being bought or sold. As I searched the Index I began seeing the words "Freedom" and "Manumission" after certain transactions. I made a list of all of these entries, but when I looked for the corresponding book, it was nowhere to be found. After much searching on my part, and finding nothing, I was resigned to the fact that an important part of Floyd

County history had been lost. The next week, however, I was rewarded with a telephone call from Janet Kay Mason in the recorder's office, who informed me she thought that the book I had been looking for had been found. I immediately went to check and discovered that the records of those blacks who applied for freedom and manumission papers through the Floyd County Court system were indeed there. They had been recorded in with the indentured servant records—a book not used for 100 years and, therefore, forgotten. I was ecstatic! Over the span of the next month I stood at the office counter and copied by hand the records of people who came through the Floyd County court system in order to insure with the authorities that they and their family members were free people and no longer slaves. A summary of these records can be found in Appendix E. The question that I had regarding the young New Albany lawyer's accusation against Judge Jocelyn was answered. In many cases the Judge and his staff were allowing blacks to come into the State of Indiana after passage of the 1851 Exclusion Act. By so doing, they were in fact breaking the law.

What are the meanings of the terms "Proof of Freedom" (often called "Freedom Papers"), "Deeds of Manumission," "Emancipation" and "Bills of Sale?" Free black settlers who were being forced out of some of the Southern states, primarily Virginia, South Carolina and Maryland, traveled West and had to carry proof of their freedom with them. When they arrived at their destination, they were to register their freedom papers with the local authorities. To "manumit" means to "set free." Sometimes the clerks in Floyd County used the terms "manumission" and "emancipation" interchangeably. Manumission was often granted a slave through the owner's last will and testament. A "Bill of Sale" was just that—a record of a person being bought or sold. In the Floyd County records these transactions were always that of a family member purchasing a slave in order to set him or her free. Though on the page itself each document appears to be flat and unemotional, the depth of each recorded document, whether it be a freedom paper, a manumission paper or a bill of sale showing the transaction of a free person purchasing family members out of slavery, is indeed deep and filled with emotion. The experience of copying and reading these papers has been one of the most meaningful experiences in my life. Elizabeth Buford's act of setting her husband, Richard, free shows the depth of feeling involved in such a transaction. Elizabeth was a free woman who purchased her husband in order to give him his freedom. The Manumission paper reads as follows:

Richard Buford, Manumission

> Know all men by these presents that I Elizabeth Cozzens alias Buford a free woman of colour of the County of Jefferson and State of Kentucky for divers and good causes and considerations me thereunto moving have manumitted set free *set free* and discharged from all manner of servitude my husband Richard Buford whom I purchased of James P. Rucker of Shelby County, Kentucky the said Richard Buford is 37 years of age dark brown complexion 5'11" high large size and has a [wisa] on his forehead between his eyebrows and weighs about 210.

And I do hereby declare the said Richard to be free and clear from all claims of all persons whomever as fully and completely as he could be made free by the laws of the land.
Witness my hand and seal this 22 day of October, 1853.

"X" Elizabeth Buford

Attest: Jared C. Jocelyn
      Augustus Jocelyn

State of Indiana County of Floyd: On the 22 October 1853 before me Justice of the Peace in and for said County personally appeared Elizabeth Buford a free woman of colour and acknowledged the foregoing instrument of writing to be her act and deed for the purposes therein contained. In testimony whereof I have hereunto set my hand and seal.

Jared C. Jocelyn

Filed in Floyd County, Indiana by Sam H. Owen, Recorder[3]

It is evident from these freedom papers that New Albany, as the county seat of Floyd County, was used by many blacks as a "gateway" into free territory. Between Cincinnati, Ohio, and Cairo, Illinois, New Albany was the largest community along the Ohio River considered to be "free" territory. Over forty-eight records of "Proof of Freedom" and thirty-seven "Deeds of Manumission" have survived. The cases were heard in the Court of Common Pleas and recorded by James G. Harrison, Samuel H. Owen, Samuel G. Wilson or Josiah Gwin between 1847 and 1864. Freedom and manumission papers were often recorded in out-of-the-way places. Not only was the issue of slavery an embarrassment, but at the time recorders may not have had a working guideline as to where to file them. Recording and storing them became an individual matter.

When reading through the Floyd County freedom papers, one is struck by two things. The first is that the majority of the freedom papers were recorded close to the time of the passage of the Fugitive Slave Act. After the passage of this law in 1850, the position of many blacks living in free territory became precarious, whether they were at one time runaway slaves or had always been free. Those slaves who had taken up residence in free territory were no longer safe due to the retroactive nature of the law, the presence of slavecatchers on both sides of the river and the fact that this law took away blacks' ability to speak for themselves. It stripped them of any voice to plead their case before a court of law. With the slave market close by in Louisville, both the capture and the selling of human beings could take place in a matter of hours before anyone could comprehend what had taken place.

The second striking thing is that for all of the anti-black bias present in Floyd County, several city and county government officials acted against the state law when they processed freedom papers for former slaves. In actuality they became "Underground Railroad agents" by assisting slaves or former slaves to gain freedom through the Indiana court system. Many freedom papers issued in Floyd County were granted to people moving into or through the State of Indiana after the state passed the Exclusion Act in 1851, when it was no longer legal for blacks to enter the state as new residents. The primary purpose of this law was to restrict African Americans from settling in the state and to keep the black population at a minimum. In June of 1853, the *New Albany Tribune* published a reminder to all blacks in Floyd County that by law they were required to register so that it could be determined who had the right to remain in the community and who was to leave.[4] The requirement to register had actually been in effect since 1831, but it was being emphasized at this time to determine who could legally reside in Indiana. In addition, the Exclusion Act stated that anyone who hired a "person of color" without the proper certificate was subject to a fine of $10 or more. In the end, however, the Exclusion Act was a futile one, for it was very difficult to enforce. It is important to note that by the very act of acquiring their "freedom," those blacks who registered at the courthouse and applied for freedom papers made themselves vulnerable by exposing themselves to an official written record. They could no longer remain obscure.

Motivations for making application with the court system for proof of freedom varied from person to person. In some cases a person's occupation placed him in a precarious position. Emanuel Moore Carter, for example, worked as a "boatman." His job would have taken him into ports of slave states where he could have been picked up by slave catchers, taken to a slave market such as that in Louisville and sold. Or if his steamboat docked in another state, he could have been prosecuted for breaking the law, that is, crossing over a state line as a nonresident "negro." His Freedom Paper reads as follows:

> Emanuel Moore Carter, Proof of Freedom
>
> State of Indiana, County of Floyd: The undersigned being duly sworn depose and say that they have known Emanuel Moore commonly called Emanuel Carter (after his maternal kindred) who is 5'11½" high (in height) has a scar on the right side of his under jaw, one scar on the big toe joint of his left foot, and one on the outside of the right foot extending from the second toe to the edge of the foot (the two last from cuts with an axe) is a light mulatto rather well made (reports himself to be about 28 years old) for ____ years last past that said Emanuel has been for that time reputed to be a free man of color and that they verily believe said Carter is a free man and a citizen of the State of Indiana.
>
> W. A. Clapp, Isham Key, Isaac Brooks, E. R. Day
>
> I have known the said Emanuel from his childhood. I have not examined the scars on his feet. Signed and sealed before me this 17 Nov. 1847. William A. Scribner, Clerk.
>
> Signatures: Mason C. Fitch, John E. Meyers, W. C. Conner
>
> I have known the above negro Emanuel Carter from his childhood and know that he grew up in this county of Floyd and State of Indiana. William A. Scribner, City of New Albany.[5]

Others registered as the result of their freedom being granted through the last will and testament of their owner. An example is the case of William Morris.

> William Morris, Emancipation Papers
> State of Virginia, Louisa County Court
>
> William, son of Susan, emancipated by the will of Miss Martha Morris, deceased, this day applied to the court to be registered, where upon the court does certify to all to whom it may concern that the said Will is a very bright Mullato, six years old, 3' 6" high, has straight hair is very likely and has no apparent mark or scar. In testimony that the affore said is truly copied from the records in my office. I, John Hunter, clerk of said court do hereby affix my seal in the 51st year of our foundation.
> April 10, 1827, Louisa County Court of Virginia[6]

Some slaves were released out of gratitude for meritorious service, as in the case of Maria Davis and her children. Maria's manumission paper reads as follows:

> Maria Davis and children, Jesse, William, Mary and Adeline
> Deed of Manumission
> State of Mississippi, County of Jefferson
>
> This indenture made and entered into this 26 day of April, 1847, witnesseth: That Squire Davis the party herein conveying of the children and slaves aforesaid — for and in consideration of certain meritorious acts heretofore rendered and performed for the benefit of the said Squire Davis by the negro woman slave of said Davis, Maria by name, about 38 years of age of a light mulatto color the said Squire the owner of said slave doth by this presents forever manumit emancipate and set free from the claims of which the said Davis and of all and every person claiming by through or under him the said negro woman slave Maria and her children: Jesse about 9 years old a bright mulatto boy, William about 7 years old a bright mulatto boy, Mary about 5 years old a bright mulatto girl, Adeline about 3 years old a bright mulatto girl. The munition acts herein before mentioned and that the said Maria by timely information given to her said owner Squire Davis 1836, while said Davis was overseer upon the plantation of one Louisa have her in said county and state did save the life of said Davis by then and there revealing to said Davis a conspiracy of the negro upon said plantation to take the life of said Davis and they the said negro had lately before taken that of their former overseer and that after said revelation the said negroes confessed said conspiracy against the life of said Davis— and that the said Maria hath for a long space of time been diligent about the business of said Davis and attention to said Davis during several long and severe spells of sickness and for diverse other meritorious acts done for the benefit of said Davis by the said Maria.
> Witness the hand and seal of the said Squire Davis the day and year first above written. Squire Davis
> Notarized State of Mississippi Jefferson County April 26, 1847, Clerk Gwinn M. Key
> Received for record in Floyd County, Indiana, January 19, 1858 by Samuel G. Harrison, Recorder[7]

In some cases a free African American owned titular slaves. That is, he or she purchased family members for the sole purpose of setting them free. This was true in the case of John Carter. Carter was a free "man of color" who resided in Louisville. On November 1, 1853, he purchased his wife, Betsy, along with their youngest child, Betty, from Robert Montgomery for the sum of $500. Over a period of time he purchased their other children as "it is the wish and desire of the said John Carter to release his said wife and four aforesaid children from all obligation or bonds of slavery … and to manumit and emancipate and set free …" his family.[8]

Often a white slave owner, who in some cases was the father, brought his slave-children to Floyd County with the sole intention of manumitting them. Following is the emancipation paper for Charles Henry Beckwith:

> Charles Henry Beckwith, Emancipation
>
> Know all men by these presents that I Quinos Beckwith of the County of Mississippi in the State of Missouri do of my own free will and accord hereby Emancipate and release from Slavery forever a certain Mulatto boy slave named Charles Henry Beckwith three years old on the 1st day of February, 1860. Said boy is of a very light colour in fact nearly white not having more than a sixth of negro blood. His eyes are at this time a light hazel colour but may change. He has a small mole on the inside of his right leg about half way between the knee and ankle. He has no other marks that are likely to last. The mother of the child is known by the name of Elizabeth Jackson and belongs to me.
>
> In testimony whereof I have hereto set my hand and seal this 15th day of August, 1860 at the City of New Albany in the State of Indiana where said boy now is. Quiros Beckwith, signed and sealed in presence of R. W. Rousseau and James G. Harrison, Notary.[9]

Many of those African Americans who applied for freedom papers in Floyd County for the first time or registered papers that had been granted them from another state had never been slaves. In many other societies over the centuries where slavery was condoned, the conquered became subjects of the conquerer and were taken away by him into slavery. Forced servitude in those situations was not necessarily based upon race. Slavery in America, however, was racist. The assumption was, therefore, that if one's skin was black, one was a slave. Given that assumption, it was of utmost importance for free people to carry proof of their freedom at all times. It is likely that some free people in Floyd County had no pressing need to carry proof of their freedom until the federal Fugitive Slave Act of 1850 and the state Exclusion Act of 1851 came into being. This may be why some of the freedom papers weren't recorded until the 1850s even though the person had been living in Floyd County for some time. H. G. Mosee and Peter Ross were examples of that. Or, these men may have lost their original papers or given them away to runaway slaves coming through Floyd County.

Many of the individuals who registered their freedom through the Floyd County court system were, in a sense, fugitives—fugitives who had come into Indiana, covered only by a thin veil of security. Their coming was built utterly on trust and courage — trust of the word of their former owner, trust that the white judge would not throw out their freedom papers from another state as being forged, trust in a free family member who promised to make payments on their purchase, trust that the word of their witness, sometimes a fellow African American, would be acceptable to the court, trust that the courts would look favorably on them. And there is absolutely no question that coming into the State of Indiana in such hard times took much courage. It took courage for European immigrants who crossed the ocean into the "new world," too. But for the most part, the European immigrant had a rather rosy and naive view of what he would find here. Blacks moving into "free" territory had few delusions of what they would encounter. But they came with the hope that relocation would give them and their offspring a better chance for freedom and autonomy.[10]

Appendix A: Transfers to Second Presbyterian Church, 1837–1852*

Name	Transferred From	Place	Date
James Brooks	1st Pres.	Cincinnati, OH	
John Loughmiller	Presbyterian	Shenandoah City, VA	
Mary Clipper	"	Bethlehem, IN	
William & Isabella James		Ripley, OH	
Martha Ainsworth	2nd Pres.	Cincinnati, OH	07/04/38
Mr. & Mrs. R.O. Snead	2nd Congrega.	Lowell, MA	03/18/38
Thomas & Eliz. Davis	3rd Pres.	Baltimore, MD	09/09/38
Wm. & Jane Anderson	Marine Church	Philadelphia, PA	09/09/38
Alice Morgan	2nd Church	New Jersey	09/09/38
James Brumler		Sth. Hanover, IN	10/28/38
Wm. M. Whistler	1st Pres.	Jeffersonville, IN	03/03/39
Wm. E. Stillwell	1st Pres.	Louisville, KY	03/03/39
John James & wife	Presbyterian	Cincinnati, OH	05/19/39
Mary Dubois	3rd Pres.	Pittsburgh, PA	05/19/39
D. W. Shyack		Pennsylvania	08/04/39
Catherine E. Bell	Congregational	Millford, NH	01/04/40
Sarah Connor	4th Pres.	Albany, NY	03/08/40
Wm. Morse & wife	Congregational	Marietta, OH	09/27/40
A.J. Lincoln		Vermont	01/03/41
Miss S. Seston	1st Pres.	Cincinnati, OH	04/18/41

New Albany Second Presbyterian Church Session Minutes, 1837–1852

Appendix A

Name	Transferred From	Place	Date
George Newes	3rd Pres.	Philadelphia, PA	06/27/41
George Philler		Greenville, PA	06/27/41
E. Brach	Pres. Church	Fayettville, NC	01/02/42
Elizabeth Walton	2nd Pres.	Louisville, KY	09/25/44
I.A. Jamisson		Mt. Sterling, IL	09/25/44
Benjamin Rankin	Pres. Church	Platt Co., MO	12/07/45
W. Burns	Asbury Meth.	Zanesville, OH	03/09/46
Lucy D. Bishop	2nd Pres.	Oxford, OH	08/29/47
R.O.C. Sneed	Constitutional Pres.	Evansville, IN	06/03/48
Emily Maria Brooks		Bloomfield, NJ	04/06/49
Joseph & Susanna Gale	Congregational	Pembroke, NH	11/26/49
Phoebe Cotlery	2nd Pres.	Delaware, OH	11/26/49
Abner B. Parmilee	Silver Creek Ch.	New Jersey	
Austin Gilbert	Congregational	Newbury, OH	09/06/50
Samuel King & wife	Presbyterian	Mt. Pleasant, OH	01/13/51
Catherine J. Atterbury	1st Pres.	Flint, MI	08/24/51
Dr. Joseph & Vi Graham	1st Pres.	Flint, MI	11/14/51
Curtis & Nancy Crane	Presbyterian	Mt. Pleasant, OH	03/29/52
Sarah Campbell	2nd Pres.	Oxford, OH	04/10/52
Martha Conner	1st Pres.	Erie, PA	12/20/52
John Dumont	Presbyterian	Mt. Pleasant, OH	12/20/52
Sarah Childs	1st Pres.	Carlisle, OH	12/31/52
Mary J. Nutting	United Pres. & Congregational Chs.	Melford, MI	12/31/52

Appendix B:
Sneed Anti-Slavery Memorial, 1840

Whereas the General Assembly did resolve most solemnly to refer the subject of slavery to the lower judicatories of the church, leaving it to them to take such order thereon as in their judgment will be most judicious and adapted to remove the evil,

Therefore, this Presbytery feels it incumbent upon them to make the following exposition of their views to the General Assembly, to the church and to the world.

I. We recognize the African race as a part of the human family, that God so loved as to give his Son to make atonement for their souls.

II. We consider ourselves bound by the great law of love to seek their best and highest good for time and eternity as truly as that of any other portion of the human family.

III. We consider the African slave trade as one of the most monstrous exhibitions of wickedness that the world has ever seen.

IV. We maintain the enslaving of the parents by violence and fraud an unutterable wickedness, [that] can never give any human being a right to enslave their posterity. As a consequence, whatever may have been the nature and propriety of ancient slavery, we can have no right to enslave the descendants of those Africans who were deprived by gross wickedness of the liberty which God gave them.

V. We therefore declare that we consider slavery as a hinous [sic] sin against God and our brother. Against God, as it is a violation of his law which requires us to love our brother as ourself, and to do to others, as we would that they should do to us. Against our brother, as it deprives him of the inalienable rights to life, liberty and the pursuit of happiness.

VI. We also consider slavery as a violation of the whole spirit of Christianity as it forces those for whom Christ died and Christians are bound to elevate, into a station of mental and moral debasement as it prevents them from acquiring the knowledge requisite to their reading the Word of God and places them in circumstances of strong temptation, so that the great mass of them sink down into the grossest wickedness, and as it subjects them to horrid cruelties and oppressions, which often come upon them at the caprice and rage of an irresponsible master.

VII. We consider the doctrine that the slave must be enlightened and prepared for liberty as a gross outrage upon common sense — as it is impossible to enlighten slaves — slaveholding law forbids it — and slaveholders are as much opposed to their instruction as their emancipation.

VIII. We consider the principle that the gospel will overturn slavery whilst the church tolerates it in her communion a delusion. Slavery so constantly lowers down the standard of piety and tempts both the master and the slave to such desperate wickedness that its direct tendency is to corrupt the gospel and banish it from a slaveholding community.

IX. We believe the result of the experiment in the West Indies proves that the only way to elevate the condition of the coloured race, is to emancipate them and give them mental and moral culture just as we do other heathen — and that they may be emancipated with perfect safety to the community in which they reside.

X. These being our views of American slavery, we hereby declare our solemn conviction that it is the duty of those who hold them in bondage, to give them their liberty if they would escape the displeasure of their great Savior.

XI. We solemnly declare our conviction that the church of Christ is in a high degree responsible for the continuance of slavery, and all its horrible enormities, by tolerating slaveholders in her communion by apologizing for it and by her efforts to hush to silence those whose consciences were tenderly opposed to it. She has averted the consciences of the slaveholders and upheld them in their evil cause.

XII. We would, therefore, exhort our beloved people, no longer by apologies for slavery or by a false testimony, on the subject to uphold the slaveholder in his wickedness, but on all proper occasions to testify against it as a violation of the gospel of Christ. We would enjoin our churches not to engage the services of ministers who hold slaves or who apologize for or justify it; and we would recommend to all our young men who are seeking the gospel ministry not to place themselves in any college or theological Seminary whose officers do not one and all in the most open and public manner testify against this sin without destroying their testimony by apologies.

XIII. We believe that our church has arrived at a crisis when her duty to God requires her to take strong ground against this sin. We deplore the fact that our

General Assembly did not testify against it and that some of our brethren still exert their influence to enduce us to be quiet on this subject.

Resolved, that this paper be laid before Synod with a request that they act upon it and further that it be published in the Cincinnati Observer, New York Observer and New York Evangelist.

Appendix C:
Floyd County African American Heads of Households, 1830

(Name, Male/Female, age range, number in household)

Baldwin, Gabriel, M, 55–100, 2.
Barrett, John M, 24–36, 3.
Brown, Westley, M, 36–55, 3.
Campbell, Elijah, M, 10–24, 3.
Campbell, John, M, 24–36, 6.
Carter, Washington, M, 24–36, 6. [George]
Cooke, Thomas, M, 36–55, 4.
Fendley, John, M, 24–36, 5.
Fendley, John, M, 36–55, 5.
Fendley, Maston, M, 24–36, 4.
Findley, Caesar, M, 55–100, 4.
Findley, Joseph, M, 24–36, 7.
Flood, Jesse, M, 24–36, 7.
Harris, Samuel, M, 24–36, 2.
Jackson, Edward, M, 55–100, 2.
Leach, Samuel, M, 24–36, 3.
Lewis, Wm., M, 36–55, 9.
Linney, John, M, 36–55, 3.
Martin, Patsy, F, 36–55, 3.
Martin, Samuel, M, 55–100, 4.
Medad, Anthony, M, 36–55, 8.
Might, Henry O., M, 10–24, 5.
Milton, Randall, M, 36–55, 8.
Mitchum, Jacob, (no age or sex shown), 2.
Mitchum, Arthur, M, 36–55, 4.
Mitchum, David, M, 24–36, 6.
Mitchum, Isom, M, 36–55, 11.
Mitchum, Nelson, M, 36–55, 9.
Mitchum, Nelson, M, 24–36, 6.
Mitchum, Pendleton, M, 24–36, 5.
Morrison, Wm., M, 36–55, 1.
Nickens, Lane, M, 10–24, 8.
Nickens, Moses, M, 24–36, 2.
Pettifoot, Right, M, 24–36, 2.
Potter, Barnaby, M, 36–55, 4.
Robertson, Isaac, M, 24–36, 5.
Ross, Peter, M, 55–100, 5.
Rouse, Thos., M, 24–36, 5.
Scott, Stephen, M, 55–100, 6.
Stewart, Henry, M, 24–36, 7.
Troublood, James, M, 36–55, 2.
Tyrell, Absolum, M, 55–100, 6.
Weaver, Wilson, M, 36–55, 9.
Woodward, Anthony, M, 24–36, 5.
Yoyster, Simon, M, 55–100, 1.

Appendix D: Floyd County African Americans in the Civil War

17th Reg. U.S. Colored Troops

Name

David F. Bush, 10th Battery, Private — died June 13, 1862
Daniel Oplinger, 11th Battery, Private — died July 10, 1864

Unassigned Colored Troops

Name	*Entered Service*
Colonel Brown	October 4, 1864
Henry Clay	October 5, 1864
John Cosbey	October 3, 1864

28th Reg. U.S. Colored Troops
(Three Year Service)

Name	*Mustered In*	*Out*
William Williams, Co. D, Musician	01/15/64	11/08/65
Doctor McClure, Private	01/15/64	killed at St. Petersburg, Virginia on 07/30/64
William McAtee	08/18/64	02/08/66
Oliver Prine	01/12/64	11/08/65
Joseph Williams, Co. A	01/15/64	died near Philadelphia on 08/27/64

Unassigned Recruits

Richard Graham	08/18/64
Jack Robertson	08/18/64
Alexander Samuels	10/12/64
William Wallace	08/31/64

8th Reg. Inf. U.S. Colored Troops

Name	Mustered In	Out
David Barrett	08/17/64	
John Foster	01/24/65	
John Jackson	10/14/64	
James E. Jinkes	01/17/65	
William Mars	01/24/65	
Isaac Myers	01/24/65	
George Smith	09/17/64	
James W. Thompson	12/28/64	
Jerry Williams	09/15/64	
Charles Evans	09/19/64	
Elijah Hart	10/01/64	
Enoch Machum (Enos Michum)	12/2/64	
James Stewart	11/13/65	

13th Reg. U.S. Colored Troops

George Christian	04/13/64	05/23/65
William Johnson	04/11/65	05/23/65

Unassigned Recruits

Jacob Dosier	10/26/64
John Turner	10/22/64

Appendix E: Freedom Papers, Bills of Sale, Deeds of Manumission

The following are listed in chronological order. For the sake of space, the papers have been summarized.

1847

Mary Buckner, Quintini Johnson and Rachel Johnson
Proof of Freedom Papers

B. F. Scribner and M. D. Tuly swore before Justice of the Peace Samuel G. Wilson that they had known Mary Buckner to be a resident of New Albany, Indiana, about two years. They testified that she and her daughters were reputed to be free "people of colour." Mary had arrived in the State of Indiana in 1843. Buckner was about fifty years old and her daughters by her first husband were Quintini, age seventeen, and Rachel, age fourteen. Buckner was described to be 5'½" tall and a very dark mulatto complexion with high cheek bones and heavy eyes.

The "Proof of Freedom" papers for Mary Buckner, Quintini and Rachel Johnson were signed and filed in Floyd County, Indiana, on September 11, 1847.[1]

Emanuel Moore (Carter)
Proof of Freedom Paper

The text of Emanuel Moore Carter's Proof of Freedom is found in the Epilogue.

1848

John Hagan
Proof of Freedom Paper

John Hagan came to Floyd County on or about April 29, 1844, and he remained there as a free man of color and citizen of the State of Indiana. Samuel Johnson was well acquainted with Hagan and testified on his behalf. Hagan was about fifty-one years old, "griff" or very dark mulatto complexion with a broad nose and thick lips. He had a large sunken scar on his forehead in the edge of his hair and a small one on the right cheek running from the outside corner of his right eye. He stood 5'7½" tall in his stockings and was rather stoutly built. On March 13, 1848, Samuel W. Owen, Recorder of Floyd County, gave him his "Proof of Freedom" that entitled him as a free person to be respected as such in person and property at all times and places in the due prosecution of his lawful concerns.[2]

Note: John Hagan was a farmer who purchased land in Franklin Township in the Oatman Plat and in New Albany Township in the Griffin Tract (West Union) in 1847 and 1848. The 1850 census shows that he was born in Alabama and that he had a property value of $1,000. His wife, Rachael, was born in Georgia. He had two children and, according to that census, there were four other African Americans living in his household who were probably working with him on the farm.

Rachel Sims
Manumission Papers

Rachel Sims' manumission papers originated in Weakley County, Tennessee, on June 8, 1847. The owner, James Sims, has died and had willed her freedom before his death. He had not left a written will, however, and therefore his heirs followed through with his spoken wishes and freed Rachel Sims. The manumission papers were signed by W. Wester, William Sims, B. B. Sims, John Sims, Wm. McCuian and Joseph David on June 8, 1847, and filed in Dresden, Tennessee, County of Weakley, August 2, 1848.[3]

Ann Mariah (Mary Ann) Clouster
Proof of Freedom Paper

On October 4, 1848, Jared C. Jocelyn notarized the signatures of William S. Culbertson and John S. Davis, who testified that they were well acquainted with Ann Mariah Clouster and knew her to be a free person of color and resident of the State of Indiana, who had come to Floyd County with her parents when she was a child. Clouster was described as being born in October of 1829, was of a dark mulatto complexion, 5'2¾" tall in her shoes and rather good looking. She had a scar on her left arm which was ¾" long and had lost one lower jaw tooth. She was married to Joseph Clouster. Samuel H. Owen, Floyd County Recorder, William S. Culbertson and John S. Davis declared Ann Mariah Clouster to be a free person of colour, a citizen of the State of Indiana and entitled to the "respect as such in person and property in the due prosecution of her lawful concerns at all times and places."[4]

Note: The 1860 census shows that Clouster remained in Floyd County and had a son, age thirteen, named Joseph Clouster, Jr.

1849

Peter Ross
Proof of Freedom Paper

Peter Ross was the son of Peter Ross, Sr., a farmer of Floyd County, with whom he had resided for nineteen years or since his birth on July 17, 1830. William C. Conner testified on behalf of Ross and said that he had known him for two years and knew him to be a free "person of color." Ross was 5'10" tall, dark brown or "griff" in complexion, rather stout, good teeth with the upper front teeth being apart from each other. He had rather "full eyes" and thick lips. The Proof of Freedom was signed and notarized by Jared Jocelyn, the Justice of the Peace in the year 1849. No further date was given.[5]

Note: The "Black Register" for Floyd County, Indiana, shows that Peter Ross, Jr., was born in Floyd County and registered at the age of twenty-three on August 20, 1853. He was described as being "black." Both of his little fingers were crooked. John Ross, his older brother, appeared with him as his witness and Peter gave his occupation as a "boatman," shown also by the 1850 census. The 1860 census showed that he was working as a steamboat fireman.

Other information about the Ross family includes the fact that on November 8, 1856, Peter Ross, Sr., signed his "Last Will and Testament" with an "X." His will was probated on April 10, 1858. It stated that he was a farmer and his heirs were: John, Peter, Jr., Thomas, Saul, Rome and Eli Ross. His heirs were to have the home place and seventy acres of land in Lafayette Township. Peter Ross, Sr., had inherited his land from Henry Ross.[6] Peter Ross, Sr., was born in North Carolina and all of his sons were born in Indiana.

Francis (Frank) Lewis
Deed of Manumission

Samuel Stubblefield, African American, purchased Frank Lewis in 1841 from Thomas Stute of Franklin County, Kentucky, for the purpose of setting him free. Frank was 5'5" tall with a scar on the left side of his chest. He was fifty-two years old in 1849, "speaks quick but stammers some," was healthy though lean. The "Deed of Manumission" was signed on March 12, 1849, with an "X" by Stubblefield and attested to by William B. Green and Henry Collins, City Judge of New Albany. The Deed was hand-delivered to Frank Lewis, setting him free.[7]

Andrew Pleasants
Proof of Freedom Paper

Andrew Pleasants was born free in Powhattan County, Virginia. He was registered in the Office of the Court of Hustings for the city of Richmond on March 11, 1839, and registered there again on September 30, 1846 (record no. 493). A true copy of the original "Proof of Freedom" was made at the Court of Hustings on May 29, 1849, by Charles Howard, Clerk, and witnessed by William Lambert, Mayor. The copy of the free papers for Andrew Pleasants was recorded in Floyd County on October 18, 1849, by Samuel H. Owen, Recorder.[8]

Note: The 1850 census for Floyd County, Indiana, shows that Pleasants was living in New Albany north of State Street with a wife, Ann, and three children named John H., Josiah and James. All of them were born in Virginia except James, who was born in Indiana. Pleasants' occupation was that of a boatman. He and his family were still in Floyd County at the time of the 1860 census, and Pleasants was still working as a boatman.

Sarah Sims
Proof of Freedom Paper

Sarah Sims applied to the Floyd County Court for her freedom papers on October 31, 1849. William Williams and Laben Williams, African Americans, testified as to her having been a resident of Floyd County since 1841. They had both known her for about sixteen years. Sarah was about eighteen years old in 1849, 5'4" tall, of a light mulatto complexion, broad, large white teeth in front, rather good looking and slender in build. William Williams and Laben Williams signed their names with an "X" and the "Proof of Freedom" was notarized by Samuel G. Wilson on October 31, 1849.[9]

Note: The Floyd County Census for 1850 shows that Sarah was born in Kentucky and that she was living with Thomas and Ann Sims.

Newell S. Mitchum
Proof of Freedom Paper

Newell S. Mitchum approached the Floyd County Court on November 23, 1849, along with witnesses John Bruner and William Speake, to receive his "Proof of Freedom" papers. Bruner and Speake testified that they had known Mitchum for five years and that he was a free man of color. Mitchum was twenty-one years old, 5'11½" tall with a rather slim build. He had a dark brown complexion with a flat nose and thick lips. His skin was badly pitted from smallpox. Newell Mitchum's "Proof of Freedom" was signed by John Bruner and William Speake and recorded in Floyd County on November 23, 1849.[10]

1850

Philip Sly
Proof of Freedom Paper

Philip Sly had been an indentured apprentice to Henry Bogert of Floyd County. After the time of his indenture had elapsed, he applied to the Floyd Circuit Court for proof of his freedom. He appeared with Henry Bogert, his testator, on January 31, 1850. Bogert swore that he was acquainted with Philip Sly, who was described as twenty-nine years old as of July 13, 1849. He was 5'2" tall in his boots, of a dark brown or "griff" complexion, broad shouldered, with a rather flat nose and thick lips. Sly had a scar from a cut on the outside of his left thumb. Sly received his "Proof of Freedom" papers on January 31, 1850. The document was signed by Stephen Beers, Justice of the Peace.[11]

Eliza Jane Morris and her son, New Year Branson Morris
Deed of Manumission

James H. Morris of the Parish of Carrol, State of Louisiana, "from motives of benevolence and humanity" manumitted and set free from slavery and the bonds of servitude Eliza Jane Morris, age thirty years and her son, New Year Branson Morris, age ten years. Eliza was described as being 5'2 or 3" tall, slender, with sharp features and a bright mulatto color. New Year was 4' tall, slender, very bright mulatto in color but with no other marks with which to identify him. James Morris set them both free on June 1, 1850, and registered the manumission papers in Floyd County, Indiana, where they were both residing at that time.[12]

Matilda O'Neil (O'Neal) and Walter B. O'Neil
Power of Attorney, Manumission Papers and Indentured Servant Record

A slave owner by the name of James M. Tucker from Franklin County, Mississippi, gave power to Thomas L. Head and Emeline M. Head of the Parish of Lafourch Interim, Louisiana, to act as his "Attorney in Fact" in regard to certain of his slaves, in this case — Matilda O'Neil and Walter B. O'Neil. On June 17, 1850, Tucker, "from motives of benevolence and humanity," manumitted and set free from slavery Matilda O'Neil and Walter B. O'Neil. Matilda turned thirteen years old on June 5, 1850. She was of a very light mulatto color and had blue eyes and dark brown hair that was slightly curled. One of her forefingers was disfigured from a cut. Walter was sixteen years old, of a very light mulatto complexion with blue eyes and sandy colored hair that curled slightly. The Manumission Papers and Power of Attorney were signed by James M. Tucker and notarized on June 17, 1850, in Franklin County, Mississippi.

On June 19, 1850, Thomas and Emeline Head appeared with Matilda O'Neil before Stephen Beers, the Justice of the Peace in Floyd County, Indiana, to file the Manumission Paper and place her as an indentured servant in the household of Presbyterian minister, Samuel K. Sneed. O'Neil was to work as an apprentice, to learn the "art and trade and mystery of housekeeping." She was to live in the Sneed household until June 5, 1855, her eighteenth birthday.

> During all which time the said apprentice shall and will faithfully serve her said Master, keep his secrets, obey all his lawful commands and shall do no damage to her said Master nor suffer any to be done by others if in her power to prevent it. She shall not absent herself from the services of her Master without his consent, but shall in all things behave herself as a good and faithful apprentice during the whole term aforesaid.

In turn Rev. Sneed agreed to teach and instruct O'Neil in the art of housekeeping, to read and write and use "arithmetic as far as the double rule of three," if O'Neil was capable. At the end of her term, Sneed was to provide O'Neil with two new suits of clothes and a new Bible. The Indenture record was signed on Wednesday, August 20, 1850, for

James M. Tucker by his Attorney-in-Fact and Samuel K. Sneed. Matilda O'Neil signed her name with an "X."[13]

1851

John Clien, Polly and her child Elizabeth, Jim, Sally, John, Eleanor and Ben
Proof of Freedom Papers

John Clien of Abbeville District, South Carolina, was granted his freedom papers through the act of a benefactor, Isaac Kennedy. Clien's wife, Elizabeth, a free woman, had died in 1843 or 1844 and had left behind her husband, John, and six children. Kennedy purchased Clien from the owner, John W. Ramsey, to prevent Clien from becoming separated from his children, who were freeborn by virtue of their mother's freedom. The names of Clien's children were: Polly (and her child, Elizabeth), Jim, Sally, John, Eleanor and Ben. Kennedy stipulated that Clien and his children should be allowed to pass through any state they wished in order to reach Indiana. He recommended the family as honest and industrious citizens.

The certificate was signed by the following citizens who vouched for the family by stating, "We the citizens of the state and district aforesaid do certify that we know John Clien and do recommend him as above." John Patterson, A. S. Graig, John Gray, Alex Stevenson, Andrew Nanly, J. H. Cobb, Will. I. Hammond, Henry F. Charles, John Charles, H. M. Stuckland, Samuel Jordan, F. Stedform, M.D., E. G. Kennedy, I. G. Kennedy, E. O. Reagran, John G. Dale and John M. Rining. The signatures were notarized in the Abbeville District of South Carolina on January 20, 1851.[14]

Franklin Locklayer
Proof of Freedom Paper

Franklin Locklayer, son of Thomas Locklayer, received his freedom papers from Limestone County, Alabama, and presented them for recording in Floyd County on March 14, 1851. John Hagan and Thomas Locklayer, both African American citizens of Floyd County, testified on his behalf. At the time of recording, Locklayer was nineteen years old, with his twentieth birthday to occur on July 15, 1851. He had a dark brown complexion and regular features, was well built and stood 5'5½" tall in his stockings. Locklayer had a raised scar across his breast 4" long and circular at the ends, being about half as wide in the middle as it was at the ends. Both of the testators, John Hagan and Thomas Locklayer, signed the document with an "X." Locklayer's "Proof of Freedom" was duly filed in Floyd County on March 14, 1851.[15]

Note: The 1850 Floyd County Census spells his name "Lockler" and shows that he was born in Tennessee.

Suckey Locklayer
Proof of Freedom Paper

Suckey Locklayer, wife of Thomas Locklayer, was once a slave belonging to James Sims of Limestone County, Alabama. Locklayer purchased her in 1827. However, the "Bill of

Sale," which had been lodged in the Limestone County, Alabama, courthouse, was mislaid or lost by the clerk. On April 6, 1844, the testators, Tandy R. Farrar, William Sims, David R. Scott and John Maples, appeared on behalf of Suckey and testified that they knew her when she was a slave belonging to James Sims. They were confident that Thomas Locklayer had been a free man of color for many years. They knew Suckey Locklayer to be a woman of good moral and honest character. Suckey's freedom papers were thereby procured in Limestone County, Alabama.

On March 14, 1851, Suckey Locklayer appeared before the Floyd County Recorder with her son, Franklin Locklayer, to record the certificate from Athens in Limestone County, Alabama, and receive her "Proof of Freedom." John Hagan, who had received his Freedom Papers three years earlier, appeared to testify for her. Suckey was described to be about fifty years old, she stood 5'2½" tall with a small dark scar on the back of the second finger of her left hand. She had two upper teeth broken, was stout with a dark brown complexion and "tolerably regular features."[16]

Note: According to the Floyd County "Black Register," Suckey was born in East Tennessee. The 1850 Floyd County Census gives her name as "Susan Lockler." In 1860 she was still living in Floyd County.

Thomas Locklayer
Proof of Freedom

Thomas Locklayer's freedom papers originated in Limestone County, Alabama. Isaac Hyde and John Maples testified that they were acquainted with Locklayer and that he was a man of color who had lived in Limestone County about twenty years. They claimed he had always "passed and been considered a free man." In 1827 Locklayer purchased his wife, Suckey, from James Sims. Suckey had never had any children previous to her purchase and all seven of their children had been born after the purchase. John Maples and Isaac Hyde signed the "Proof of Freedom" on April 6, 1844. On that same date Joshua P. Coman testified on behalf of Thomas, Suckey and their seven children, namely: Sarah Ann, Agny, Franklin, Amanda, May, James and Victoria.

On March 28, 1851, John Hagan, a neighboring farmer, appeared in the Floyd County Court on behalf of Thomas Locklayer. Locklayer was sixty-six years old, stood 5'2⅝" tall in his stockings, was rather stout with regular features and dark brown complexion. He had two front teeth broken off, one below and one above. His hair was short and his whiskers were turning white, but he had no other special marks.[17]

Note: The Floyd County "Black Register" showed that Thomas Locklayer was born in North Carolina. In the 1850 census his occupation was that of a farmer, but by the 1860 census he no longer appeared. Two of the children, Sarah Ann [Keniday] and Amanda, lived apart from the family and worked as laundresses.

William Henderson
Proof of Freedom Paper

William Henderson originally filed his Freedom Papers with the Floyd County Court on May 13, 1844. However, he must have lost, misplaced or given away his papers because after the passage of the Fugitive Slave Law and the state Exclusion Act of 1851, he appears again to receive his "Proof of Freedom." On March 22, 1851, William Ballard and Israel Frost, African American friends, swore that they were acquainted with William Henderson and that they had known him for fifteen years, since he was a child. He was twenty-one years old and stood 5'9–10" tall. He came to Floyd County from Lawrence County, Indiana, and they knew that he had a good moral character and was entitled to the protection of all good citizens. The 1844 document described Henderson as being 5'8¼" tall in his stockings with a scar over his right eye and a spot in the left eye. He was a rather stout person. Ballard and Frost signed their names with an "X." Isaac N. Akin of the Floyd Circuit Court notarized their signatures.[18]

Jesse Boyd and Children: Barbara Elizabeth, Martha Ann, John Amos Franklin and Farra Lawundia
Recommendation for Freedom Papers

Jesse Boyd, his wife, Sarah, and their four children intended to move to Indiana. Adam Wideman, the Magistrate of the District of Abbeville, State of South Carolina, recommended on February 1, 1851, "to all whom it may concern," that the bearers of the document, "Recommendation for Freedom," be allowed to pass over state lines into a nonslaveholding state. They "uniformly conducted themselves in a peaceable orderly industrious and civil manner and hold a high reputation in the Methodist Episcopal Church."

Jesse Boyd, age forty years, was the son of a free woman of color, Ann Boyd, who resided in Newberry District, South Carolina. Jesse's wife, Sarah, age thirty years, was also free born and the daughter of a free woman, Martha Sunard, who had resided in Newberry District for a long time. Because both Jesse and Sarah were born of parents who were free, they concluded their offspring were also free, namely: Barbara Elizabeth, age thirteen, Martha Ann, age ten, John Amos Franklin, age eight, and Farra Lawundia, age six. The couple were undoubtedly filing for their papers in order to protect themselves and their children from being separated and sold into slavery with the passage of the Fugitive Slave Law. The "Recommendation for Freedom" papers for Jesse Boyd and his children were filed in the Floyd County Recorder's Office on September 6, 1851.[19]

Sarah Ann Lucas
Proof of Freedom

Sarah Ann Lucas was nineteen years of age when she came before the Justice of the Peace, Jared C. Jocelyn, and the Floyd County Recorder, Samuel H. Owen, on October 8, 1851, to apply for her "Proof of Freedom" papers. (Sarah's birth date was August 20, 1851.) A. F. Israel and Benjamin Conner were New Albany citizens who testified on her behalf. They swore to having known Sarah for ten years and that "she had been generally reputed to be, and as they verily believe is a free person of colour and a citizen of the State of Indiana." Sarah was described as being of light mulatto complexion, 5'⅞" tall, rather stout, with two upper front teeth next to the eye teeth missing. Her "Proof of Freedom" was signed by Israel and Conner and notarized by Jocelyn on October 8, 1851.[20]

Note: Sarah's name appears in the Floyd County Negro Register in 1853.

Samuel Flinn, his wife, Louisa Flinn and Children.
Samuel's Children: James, George and Manda
Louisa's Children: Zion, Ellendar, Ann Louisa
Proof of Freedom Papers

The "Proof of Freedom" papers for the Flinn family originated in Abbeville District, South Carolina, and were signed and notarized by Matthew McDonald on February 10, 1851. The Testators were Bamone Barney, Isaac Kennedy, James H. Foster, Robert A. Crawford, F. W. M. Miller, John McKinerly, James Kepley and A. F. Conner. The witnesses testified that they were acquainted with Samuel and Louisa Flinn and knew them to be free born mulattoes. Samuel was born in Newberry District but had lived in Abbeville for thirty years. Flinn was able to do blacksmith work, shoe horses and was good at digging and walling wells. He was also good at plowing. Samuel and his wife were recommended as good and industrious people to the people of Indiana or to any other state through which they might sojourn. The "Freedom Papers" were filed in Floyd County by Samuel H. Owen and recorded on September 10, 1851.[21]

Isabella Glover and Children: Rebecca Glover, George Glover and John Glover
Proof of Freedom Papers

William Bradley, E. O. Beagin, George N. Pressley, M.D., Samuel Jordan and James H. Foster from the District of Abbeville in South Carolina all testified to the character and legal freedom of Isabella Glover. It was concluded, therefore, that by law her children were also free people. The Testators claimed Isabella was a member of good standing in the Methodist Episcopal Church and recommended her and her children "to the favorable notice and reception of strangers in either slave or nonslaveholding states where they may settle." The only description of the Glover family was to give their ages as of February 1, 1851. Isabella was fifty-five years old, Rebecca was twenty years, George was seventeen and John was eleven years old.

The "Proof of Freedom" was signed on February 1, 1851, in the District of Abbeville, South Carolina, by the five men named above and notarized by Matthew McDonald. The freedom papers were filed in the Floyd County Recorder's Office on September 10, 1851.[22]

Jemina (Mina) Stubblefield
Deed of Manumission

Jemina's owner, Seth Woodruff, purchased her from Jane Van DeGraff of Fayette County, Kentucky, on February 5, 1839, and brought her to New Albany. He decided twelve years later that in consideration of her faithful services and general good character and conduct, he would set her free from involuntary servitude. Jemina Stubblefield was married to Samuel Stubblefield, also of New Albany. She was described as a black woman, 5'4" tall with a running sore from a toothache on the left side of her face close to her nose. Her two fingers next to her little fingers on both hands were crippled from "rolling logs," and she was unable to straighten them. She appeared to be fifty but claimed to be forty-eight on August 1, 1850. Woodruff signed the Deed of Manumission setting Jemina free on April 11, 1850, delivered the deed to her on April 16, 1850. It was recorded in the Floyd County records on November 20, 1851.[23]

Note: The Floyd County Census of 1850 shows that Jemina, born in Kentucky, was a laundress. By 1860 she had acquired property valued at $300. Jemina was unable to read or write. Jemina's husband, Samuel, registered, according to law, with the authorities on August 4, 1853. At that time he was sixty-six years old. He was born in Virginia, had a scar on his left wrist and was described as being "black." The 1850 census shows he was a laborer with a real estate value of $300. His name was also found in the Floyd County recorder's office in probate records. He recorded his last will and testament on April 1, 1850. His will was probated on October 5, 1859, at the time of his death. His executor and only heir was his wife, Jemina. The will was witnessed by Henry Collins and Vinton S. Nunemaker.

Patrick Brown
Freedom Papers

The freedom papers for Patrick Brown originated with his owner, James Wright, on September 20, 1830, in Franklin County, Kentucky. A "Certificate of Freedom" was issued by Alexander H. Rennick, the Clerk of Franklin County, after Patrick's owner, James Wright, produced a "Deed of Manumission." Brown was between thirty-five and forty years old in 1830, of yellow complexion, 5'8" tall, with one of the upper four teeth missing and two others wide apart. The "Free Papers" for Patrick Brown were registered in Floyd County, Indiana, on December 11, 1851, by Samuel H. Owen, Recorder.[24]

1852

William Henry Washington Monroe
Proof of Freedom Paper

In approximately 1832, when William Henry Washington Monroe was a young boy, he moved to Grainger County, East Tennessee, with his mother, China Monroe. They were free people. In 1852 Monroe registered his freedom papers in Floyd County, Indiana, and it was recorded by Samuel H. Owen on March 17, 1852. David Jackson and Andrew Jackson McNally testified for him. Monroe was described as being twenty-three years old, 5'¾" tall in his stockings, rather stout built with features "tolerably regular," dark brown complexion with thick lips and two upper jaw teeth broken out with no other special marks. The Floyd County Recorder stated, "Being a free person of color, he is entitled to the protection of person and property in the due prosecution of his lawful concerns." The "Proof of Freedom" was signed on March 17, 1852, by David Jackson and Andrew Jackson McNally, in Floyd County, Indiana.[25]

Henderson Goen(s)
Evidence of Freedom Paper

Henderson Goen applied for and received his "Evidence of Freedom" papers on May 7, 1852. James A. Doll and John Knepfley swore that they had known him to be a resident of Floyd County for the past five years and a free "person of colour." Goen was twenty-one years old, having been born on June 19, 1830. He was 5'10¾" tall in his boots, of a light mulatto complexion with long hair "worn rather straight." He had a scar on the back of his left hand received from a cut with an axe, and a "scar on the little finger of his left hand through the nail from the end of his finger to nearly the second joint rendering the first joint stiff." The "Evidence of Freedom" was signed by Doll and Knepfley and notarized by Jared C. Jocelyn, Justice of the Peace, on May 7, 1852.[26]

Note: The Floyd County Census for 1850 shows that Goen was born in Indiana and was a boatman by occupation.

Hetty Whitten (formerly White)
Deed of Emancipation

Hetty Whitten's owner, John D. Conover, brought her to Floyd County with him from Mobile, Alabama. While in Floyd County, he had drawn up a "Deed of Emancipation" in 1850 but the Deed had apparently been lost or misplaced. Conover had another one drawn up "forever setting her [Whitten] free from all and every claim which I may have heretofore or may now to her services, to enjoy the same so freely and fully as if I had never had any interest in her said service." The Deed of Manumission was signed on June 1, 1852, by John D. Conover and notarized by William A. Scribner.[27]

Grantee: Melinda (or Malinda) Anderson
Grantor: Charles M. Thruston
Date recorded: September 1, 1852
Deed of Manumission

(Note: Because of its interesting detail and style, the following Deed is quoted in its entirety rather than summarized.)

I, Charles M. Thruston, from Louisville, Kentucky, make a solemn declaration that the servant girl named Malinda, the only daughter of a negro woman owned by me, was liberated by me when she was six or seven years old, and the deed of liberation and emancipation was delivered by me as my act and deed; but when my son in law, Lewis Rogers, was married to my daughter, Mary, Melinda went with Mary and I omitted to disclose the fact that she had been manumitted, the mother of Melinda having died about the time of Mary's marriage, I thought at some time when convenient, I would make Mary or the doctor a compensation equal to the value of Malinda so that she might be free in virtue of the (according to my) original intended purpose and promise as was in fact carried into execution by the deed of manumission aforesaid.

My motive for her emancipation was a sense of duty and feeling to one whom I stood and was much attached, and to save feelings that would be greatly tortures if I held Malinda in bondage. Having now paid or rather in "[?] a Rogen" and purchased her, so as to do justice to him as the husband of my daughter, I declare that said Melinda was when six or perhaps seven years old, absolutely and to all intents and purposes free and released from bondage in virtue of my deed of manumission and that the purpose of this paper is to declare the truth and to reassert her freedom in the most solemn manner, and that I claim no right or property in her, or her issue, and this Deed is to bear my testimony to that freedom, and to have a relation back to that freedom as given and granted more than two years ago. Knowing that the deed of manumission has been long lost, and not recorded, I with my own hand here thought proper to make this instrument for the purpose merely of protection to her, I reserved the right by the Deed of Manumission aforesaid to control her conduct and actions til she should be twenty-one years old which I now retain and desire only to hold her for her own permanent good until she arrives at the age which will be the 25th of December, 1854.

Description of Malinda: mullato, long hair, tall and well formed and the only child of Maria, long since dead. I purchased Maria of old Mr. Baryemon Stausbery, now dead.

Witness my hand and seal this June 23, 1851.

C. M. Thruston[28]

Sarah Craigg
Proof of Freedom Paper

Sarah Craigg had been an indentured servant to William Kirkwood, who had died. She, therefore, needed her "Proof of Freedom" because her indenture ended with Kirkwood's death. Somerville E. Leonard and R. R. Town attested to having known Craigg for five years and to the fact that she had been a resident of the State of Indiana during her indenture. Craigg was born on December 25, 1831, so at the time of application for her freedom papers she was twenty years old. She stood 5' tall, was rather stout and had a dark brown complexion. She had a scar on her forehead caused by falling into a cellar. Two other scars were found on her left arm, each 1" long, one caused by a burn and the other from a cut with glass. Craigg possessed a large mouth and irregular features. Sarah Craigg's "Proof of Freedom" was signed on October 15, 1852, by witnesses Somerville E. Leonard and R. R. Town and recorded in the New Albany records on that same day.[29]

Adelade Goram and children: Leonide Byrne, Cornelia Young, Tom Hamilton
Bill of Sale, Power of Attorney and Deed of Manumission

(Note: These manumission papers are interesting in that they involve a free "person of color" from New Orleans working through an attorney in Cincinnati in order to purchase a woman and her children for the purpose of setting them free.)

On June 14, 1851, for the sum of $5, H. R. W. Hill and Margaretta E. Hill, his wife, sold Adelade Goram and her three children, namely, Leonide Byrne, Cornelia Young and Tom Hamilton, to Violet Miller of New Orleans. The agreement of the sale was that the children were not to be emancipated until they reached the age at which the laws of Louisiana stated they could become free. The "Bill of Sale" was recorded in New Orleans on March 20, 1852. The witness to the signing of the document was C. J. Fone. The "Bill of Sale" included a "Power of Attorney" nominating John F. Wright of Cincinnati, Ohio, to emancipate Adelade Goram, age twenty-three and her child, Tom Hamilton, one year old. The "Power of Attorney" was signed by Violet Miller with an "X."

The emancipation papers described Gorman to be twenty-three years old and small in size. Her son, Thomas Hamilton, was eighteen months old and had a bright yellow complexion. The emancipation papers were signed by John F. Wright in Cincinnati, Ohio, on October 22, 1852. The Bill of Sale, Power of Attorney and both manumission papers were filed in the Floyd County, Indiana, recorder's office on October 30, 1852, by Samuel H. Owen.[30]

Octavious Young
Proof of Freedom Paper

Octavious Young was born a slave in Kentucky. He was purchased by Peyton A. Key and taken with his owner to Indiana. Young was an indented apprentice bound to Key until he turned twenty-one years of age, at which time he moved from Indiana back to Kentucky. He, however, continued to live with Key on the Ohio River and in Kentucky. Peyton A. Key and Somerville E. Leonard swore that they had known Young for twenty years and they both vouched for him being a free "person of color" and a citizen of Indiana. Young was described as being 5'6" tall, dark brown complexion, large mouth, bad teeth, a scar on his forehead, a scar across the big toe on his left foot that had been cut with an axe and another scar on the left ankle caused by "striking the right ankle against it." Octavious Young's "Proof of Freedom" papers were signed on November 1, 1852, by Peyton A. Key and Somerville E. Leonard and recorded as such.[31]

1854

Rebecca Bentley
Deed of Manumission

Rebecca Bentley's owner, Sarah A. Foy, of Port Gibson, Mississippi, set Bentley free on September 21, 1839. At the time, Rebecca was nine years old and the manumission took place in Cincinnati, Ohio. According to the record, Sarah A. Foy "forever relinquished all her rights, title and claim in and to Rebecca, her person, labour or services and of, in and to all and any estate or property which she may later obtain." The Deed of Manumission was witnessed by F. A. Waldo and notarized by Flamen Ball. It was received in New Albany, Floyd County, Indiana, May 2, 1854, and recorded by Samuel Owen.[32]

    Note: A few days later, on May 6, 1854, Rebecca registered with the Floyd County authorities.[33]

Morgan Black
Proof of Freedom Paper

Morgan Black's freedom papers originated in Augusta County, Virginia. They were signed in Staunton, Virginia, by the county clerk, Jefferson Kirney, and attested to by Justice of the Peace James A. Cockran. Black was described as being of dark complexion, 5'9" tall, twenty-one years of age and born free. A copy of his "Proof of Freedom" papers were filed and recorded in Floyd County, Indiana, on June 26, 1854, by Samuel H. Owen, Recorder of the Floyd County Court.[34]

Henry Lewis
Deed of Manumission

Harriet Warring had moved to Floyd County from New Orleans, Louisiana. She brought Henry Lewis with her, a slave whom she had purchased from George C. Taylor. Henry Lewis purchased his own freedom for the sum of $550. He was described as being a mulatto, forty years old and 5'7" tall.

Harriet Warring gave Lewis his freedom in the following words:

> I do hereby give, grant and release to the said Henry Lewis all my right title and claim and all the right title and claim of my heirs executors and administrators in and to the person labor and services of Henry Lewis and to any Estate or property which he may hereafter acquire or obtain.

The "Deed of Manumission" was signed by Harriet Warring on July 31, 1854, and notarized by Samuel H. Owen, Recorder of Floyd County, Indiana.[35]

Betsy Carter and Children: Sarah, Sally, Carey and Betsy
Bill of Sale and Deed of Emancipation

John Carter, a free man, purchased his wife and children from Robert Montgomery of Louisville, Kentucky, for a total of $1,700. The "Bills of Sale," which were signed on November 18, 1853, stipulated that Carter would make payments over a twelve-month period. The first "Bill of Sale" stipulated that Carter pay $500 for his wife, Betsy and the child, Betsy, age five years, by November 18, 1854. The second "Bill of Sale" stipulated the amount of $500 for Sarah, age fifteen years, be paid before January 1, 1855, $350 for Sally, age twelve years, due before January 1, 1856, and $350 for Carey, age eight years, payable before January 1, 1857. It was agreed that if John Carter were to die after he had fully paid off and discharged the first note, that his wife, Betsy and the child, Betsy, were to go free. Secondly, John was not to take possession of the three children until January 1, 1855. The "Bills of Sale" were both filed on June 12, 1856, in Louisville, Kentucky.

On that same day in June, Carter filed a "Deed of Emancipation." The deed states that he purchased his wife and youngest child from Robert Montgomery of Louisville, Kentucky, where they had been held as slaves, for the sum of $500, and that he had started the legal proceedings on November 1, 1853. On September 9, 1854, he purchased his remaining three children. It was Carter's wish, therefore, to

> release his wife and four aforesaid children from all obligation or bonds of slavery and to protect them against all claims that may hereafter be set up to property in them by his heirs or representatives, and now for ... natural love and affection, John Carter doth by these presents forever release from all bonds of slavery and manumit and emancipate and set free said Betsy Carter and her four children ... hereby for himself his heirs and representatives, relinquishing ... all claim which he may have acquired to his said wife and her children as slaves.[36]

John Carter signed the "Deed of Emancipation" on September 9, 1854, with an "X." John N. Tydings testified that he was acquainted with John Carter, knew him to be a free man, husband of Betsy Carter and father of the children.

1855

Ellen (no surname given)
Deed of Manumission

On October 9, 1855, "Ellen" purchased her freedom for the sum of $750 from Leander Merchant, George W. Boyd and William Denice of Mobile, Alabama. Ellen had moved from Mobile to New Albany, Indiana, where she must have earned the money to purchase her freedom. She was described as being twenty-one years old, 5'6" tall and of a brown complexion. "We do hereby give grant and release sell and convey unto the said female slave Ellen all our right title and claim to her person labor and services and to any property of whatsoever nature which she may hereafter acquire." The three owners worked through an attorney, George A. Chambers, in order to have the Deed of Manumission filed in the Floyd County recorder's office on October 9, 1855.[37]

Richard Buford
Deed of Manumission

The text of Richard Buford's Deed of Manumission can be found in the Epilogue.

1856

Elizabeth (no surname given)
Deed of Manumission

Douglas Campbell from Mobile, Alabama, hired Luke Wainwright as his attorney-in-fact to carry out his wishes regarding the emancipation of his slave, Elizabeth. Campbell's instructions were that his attorney was to take Elizabeth to Ohio or any other free state in the Union and there to emancipate her. Douglas Campbell signed the "Deed" on June 16, 1856, before Notary John Rolston in Mobile, Alabama (Deed Book vol. 4, p. 497).

Elizabeth was described in the Floyd County records as being twenty-three or twenty-four years old and of yellow complexion. The Deed of Manumission was received in Floyd County, Indiana, twelve days later — on June 28, 1856. It was notarized by Thomas M. Brown and recorded by James G. Harrison.[38]

Tina (no surname given)
Deed of Manumission

Tina, age twenty-five, had been owned by Mrs. M. W. Follin of Mobile County, Alabama, and at the time of Follin's death was sold to B. S. Skoats for $800 through the executor of the will, Gorham Davenport, on March 24, 1853. On September 26, 1855, Tina was sold to Willis L. Youman of Mobile for the sum of $800 for the purpose of setting her free. Manumission papers were carried out on July 30, 1856, "from motives of benevolence and diverse other considerations" made by the owner Willis L. Youman, who traveled with Tina to New Albany, Indiana, for the purpose of setting her free. The Deed of Manumission was signed by Willis L. Youman on July 30, 1856, and notarized by John H. Stotsenberg, a New Albany lawyer. They were verified by Salem P. Town.[39]

1857

William Lindsley, alias "Bill Slick"
Bill of Sale and Deed of Emancipation

William Lindsley, also known as "Bill Slick," was thirty-six years old at the time of his sale to Thomas A. Hasbrook and Thomas McQuinn. He was a dark mulatto color, 5'5–7" tall and possessing a rugged, stout body. He was sold by Hasbrook and McQuinn to Michael C. Kerr for the sum of $5 for the sole purpose of giving Lindsley his freedom by way of a "Deed of Manumission." However, Lindsley had to purchase his freedom for the sum of $350 payable to Samuel H. Owen, Floyd County Recorder, who in turn was to notify Kerr, who would pay the money over to Hasbrook and McQuinn.

Meanwhile, Kerr was instructed as follows: he was to "hire Lindsley out" or otherwise engage or dispose of him for Lindsley's own benefit, permitting him to work for his wages in order to raise the $350 for the purchase of his freedom. On the condition that Lindsley should neglect his duty, become idle or intemperate, he was to have a period of one year in which to raise and pay the $350. If he failed in this endeavor, Lindsley was to be reconveyed back to Hasbrook and McQuinn through Kerr. The "Bill of Sale" was signed by Hasbrook, McQuinn and Kerr on January 3, 1856.

On October 22, 1856, "negro Lindsley" paid to Samuel H. Owen the sum of $300 toward his freedom. On July 21, 1857, Lindsley paid the remaining $50 that was due on his "Deed of Emancipation." In accordance with the provisions of the "Bill of Sale," Kerr emancipated and set free William Lindsley, alias Bill Slick, "giving and granting him all the rights and privileges of a free 'man of color' and discharging him from all involuntary servitude." The "Deed of Emancipation" was signed by Michael C. Kerr, Samuel H. Owen and Thomas A. Hasbrook, notarized by Samuel Avery and recorded by James Harrison on July 21, 1857.[40]

Mary Ann Thompson
Freedom Paper

Mary Ann Thompson received her freedom papers in Floyd County, Indiana, on September 9, 1857, from Justice of the Peace Jared C. Jocelyn. Jocelyn claimed he had known Thompson for twenty years. During that time he knew her to be a free woman who had "conducted herself with propriety." Thompson was almost twenty-six years old, 4½ to 5' tall and had a scar on the right side of her face below the right eye. In addition, her right arm was stiff. Thompson's "Freedom Papers" were signed by Jared C. Jocelyn and notarized by James Harrison on September 9, 1857.[41]

1858

Maria Davis and Children: Jesse, William, Mary and Adeline
Deed of Manumission

The text of the Deed of Manumission for Maria and her children is found in the Epilogue.

Note: The 1860 Census for Floyd County shows that Maria was single, age fifty-one and a laborer. She had real estate valued at $1,000 and personal property with a value of $2,000. Her children, William, age twenty years, and Jesse, age twenty-two years, were farm hands. All four of her children had personal property valued at $1,000 each.

Nelson Fisher
Freedom Paper

The emancipation of Nelson Fisher originated in New Orleans, Louisiana, with his owner, Atticus Slaughter, who sent him to the State of Ohio for the purpose of setting him free. Honorable Judge John Burgoyne of the Hamilton County, Ohio, Probate Court manumitted Nelson Fisher on April 24, 1857. A certified copy of the "Free Papers of Nelson Fisher" was received of record on June 2, 1858, in Floyd County, Indiana, and duly recorded.[42]

Note: John Burgoyne, Judge of the Probate Court of Hamilton County, Ohio, was a staunch abolitionist who was known for working in favor of the slave. According to Levi Coffin in his *Reminiscenses,* Burgoyne had many slaves come through his probate court who were brought to Cincinnati by their white fathers in order to emancipate them.[43] Coffin was often called upon to help relocate them. The Floyd County Census for 1860 shows Fisher to be thirty-five years old and a steward on the riverboats. His name also appears in the Floyd County Black Register along with those of his children, Margaret, William and May.

Samuel Casey
Deed of Manumission

Samuel Casey, a sixty-three year old "slave for life," had to pay $200 to procure his freedom. He paid said sum to his owner, John Crabb, on June 19, 1858, who in turn declared him "a free man from this time hence forth and forever from all claims for services." The "Deed of Manumission" was signed on June 19, 1858, notarized by Salem P. Town and recorded on July 6, 1858 by James G. Harrison.[44]

Elsie Willett
Deed of Manumission

Samuel K. Snead [Sneed], born in Jefferson County, Kentucky, and a citizen of New Albany from 1832 to 1853, purchased Elsie Willett in 1832 and took her to New Albany. Sneed "retained her in his family" until July 4, 1839, when Willett turned eighteen. With

Sneed's knowledge and consent at that time Willett became a free woman. In the "Deed of Manumission" Sneed confirmed that Willett was taken by him to Indiana with full knowledge of the laws of the state on the subject of slavery. He intended that she should become free.

Willett's physical description on December 16, 1858, was of a thirty-seven year old "negro" woman with a large robust frame, light brown or copper complexion and about 5'5–6" tall. With the "Deed of Manumission" filed on December 16, 1858, Sneed gave and conveyed to Elsie Willett all his right, title and interest in her as a slave for life. At the time of recording of the deed, Willett was living in Louisville, Kentucky. The "Deed of Manumission" was witnessed by J. W. Reineking and Edward W. Hurlbut, both members of the Presbyterian church in New Albany. It was notarized by James G. Harrison and recorded on December 16, 1858.[45]

1859

William Fenwick
Bill of Sale and Deed of Manumission

This "Deed of Manumission" included a "Bill of Sale" wherein R. J. Ormsby sold William Fenwick to his wife, Ellen Fenwick, a free woman, for the sum of $800 cash on August 25, 1859. On August 27, 1859, Ellen set William free by "Deed of Manumission." The "Bill of Sale" and "Deed of Manumission" were recorded in Floyd County by James G. Harrison.[46]

1860

Emily Gatewood and Judy Price
Deeds of Manumission and Proof of Freedom Papers

The Last Will and Testament of Elizabeth J. Field recorded in Jefferson County, Kentucky, directed that her executor should emancipate and set free "her negro woman, Emily Gatewood," and "her negro woman, Judy Price." William R. Vance, the Executor of the Estate of Elizabeth J. Field, therefore emancipated and set free Emily Gatewood and Judy Price on June 1, 1860. Gatewood was a "negro" woman with dark complexion, 5'1" tall and about thirty-eight years old. Judy Price was of dark complexion, 5'4" tall and about thirty-four years old. The "Deed of Manumission" and the "Proof of Freedom" were recorded in Floyd County by James G. Harrison on the same day, June 1, 1860.[47]

Charles Henry Beckwith
Freedom Paper

The text of Charles Henry Beckwith's Freedom Paper is found in the Epilogue.

1861

Indiana (no surname given)
Power of Attorney and Deed of Manumission

A "Power of Attorney" originated in Bolivar County, Mississippi, on behalf of the owner of a slave named only "Indiana." John P. Hughes appointed Henry McDongal of New Albany, Indiana, to take charge of and conduct Indiana to New Albany. Indiana was a bright mulatto girl, age twenty-three. She had been held in slavery by Hughes, and he desired to give her freedom. However, the laws of Mississippi prohibited emancipation of slaves by a deed or a will. He, therefore, hired McDongal to conduct Indiana to New Albany in safety and to be her agent as long as she chose to remain in New Albany. The "Power of Attorney" gave McDongal the authority to proceed with establishing Indiana's freedom through the courts in the State of Indiana or any other state in which she chose to travel with the consent of McDongal. The "Power of Attorney" was signed January 12, 1860, by John P. Hughes.

A "Deed of Manumission" was granted to "Indiana, a slave girl" on February 5, 1861, by John P. Hughes from motives of benevolence and humanity. On that day Hughes set her free forever from the bonds of servitude. R. M. Weir and J. S. Richey witnessed the Deed and it was signed by Henry McDongal on behalf of John P. Hughes.[48]

1862

William H. Johnson
Proof of Freedom Paper

William H. Johnson, age thirty, made application for his proof of freedom papers on July 24, 1862, with Daniel White of New Albany testifying on his behalf. White testified that he had known Johnson for ten years and knew him to be a free man of color, of good honest and industrious character, deserving of the patronage and protection due all good citizens. Johnson's "Proof of Freedom" was signed by Daniel White before Josiah Gwin, Floyd County Recorder.[49]

Harry G. Mosee
Proof of Freedom Paper

Harry G. Mosee, age thirty, came before the Clerk, Salem P. Town, on August 8, 1862, to apply for a certificate of freedom. John S. Richey certified that he had known H. G. Mosee for ten years and knew him to be of good character and deserving of the protection of all good citizens. "Proof of Freedom" papers were granted H. G. Mosee on August 8, 1862.[50]

Note: The 1860 census shows that Mosee was born in Kentucky and that he was thirty-seven years old. His occupation as a porter most likely required him to carry his freedom papers on his person. Bill Mosee, age thirty and born in Tennessee, lived with him.

1864

Mary Harris and child Florence Harris
Deed of Manumission

William H. Gaslin of Louisville, Kentucky, manumitted and set free from the bonds of servitude Mary Harris, age twenty years, and her one-year-old daughter, Florence. Gaslin signed the manumission paper on July 22, 1864, in the presence of George V. Hawk and Justice of the Peace Jared Jocelyn, who also served as notary. Josiah Gwin recorded the papers on July 26, 1864 in Floyd County, Indiana.[51]

William Morris
Emancipation Papers

The text of William Morris' Emancipation Paper is found in the Epilogue.

Notes

Chapter 1

1. New Albany was formally established in 1813. Floyd County was formed on January 2, 1819, having been carved out of Harrison County to the west and Clark County to the north and east.

2. Howard H. Peckham, *Indiana: A Bicentennial History* (N.Y.: W.W. Norton & Co., Inc., 1978), p. 38. See also the *New Albany Daily Ledger,* "Slavery in the North," December 3, 1855, p. 2, c. 2, quoting the *American Almanac.*

3. Earl Saulman, "A History of The Blacks in Harrison County," unpublished, Harrison County Sheriff's Tax Book, p. 2. The John Oatman Plat is located in Franklin Township, Floyd County, but was originally a part of Harrison County. Saulman has independently compiled a voluminous history of African Americans in Harrison County primarily by studying court records. His "History" can be found in the Harrison County Library, Corydon, Indiana.

4. *New Albany Daily Ledger,* December 27, 1860, p. 3. c. l.

5. Probate Records, Floyd County, Indiana, 1819–1837, Will Book "A," Last Will and Testament of George Wheeler, p. 89.

6. Probate Records, Floyd County, Indiana, Will Book "B," Last Will and Testament of Mary Rice, Signed August 6, 1836, probated November 14, 1836, p. 236.

7. *Ibid.*, Last Will and Testament of Ann Kirkwood, Signed November 1, 1859, probated December 24, 1859, p. 138–139.

8. *New Albany Daily Ledger*, January 18, 1861, p. 3, c. 2.

9. Floyd County Court Records, Recorder's Office, Deed Book "E," p. 583.

10. Miscellaneous Court Records, Floyd County, Indiana, Indenture Record Book "A," p. 5. The 1850 census shows Barbara Ann Neil living with Thomas and Ann Sims and records her birthplace as "Kentucky." All subsequent indenture records are found in Indenture Record Book "A," pp. 11, 12, 16, 20, 30–31, 33, 34 and 151, respectively.

11. Henrietta Buckmaster, *Let My People Go* (Columbia, South Carolina: University of South Carolina, 1992), p. 35. The Mason-Dixon line was the boundary line as surveyed by Charles Mason and Jeremiah Dixon between Pennsylvania and Maryland. Before the Civil War and the end of slavery, it became a popular way to refer to the line of demarcation between slave and free states. Runaways not only headed north but many slaves who lived near the great westward migration routes also latched on to wagon trains that passed through. One Lexington, Kentucky, paper expressed dismay that besides running north, runaways were heading for California. *Lexington Express*, May 27, 1852, reprinted in *Frederick Douglass' Paper*, August 13, 1852, p. 2, c. 3.

12. Besides escape, African Americans also resisted enslavement in many other ways. As Harrison puts it, slaves resisted by purchasing their freedom, by doing as little as possible, feigning illness or injury, deliberately inflicting injury on themselves and sometimes going so far as committing suicide, fighting back, rising up against owners in organized attacks and destroying property. Lowell H. Harrison, *The Anti-Slavery Movement in Kentucky* (The Kentucky Bicentennial Bookshelf, 1978), p. 80.

13. A historical marker has also been placed at the Garrison slave pen site.

14. *New Albany Daily Ledger,* March 16, 1862, p. 2, c. 1; March 16, 1863, p. 2, c. 1. As late as March 1863 two or three "negroes" were kidnapped in New Albany, taken to Kentucky and sold into slavery.

15. *Kentucky's Black Heritage* (Frankfort, Ky.: Kentucky Commission on Human Rights, 1971), n.p.

16. George H. Yater, *200 Years at the Falls of the Ohio* (Louisville, Ky.: Heritage Corporation of Louisville and Jefferson County, 1979), p. 81.

17. Allan M. Trout, "The Civil War in Kentucky, 1861–1865; Louisville: A Foot in Each Camp," *Courier Journal Magazine* (Louisville, Ky: *Courier Journal*, November 20, 1960), n.p.

18. Yater, p. 42. See also *Louisville Daily Courier*, July 14, 1855, p. 4, c. 3 and p.1, c. 2. "The time of the Circuit Court was occupied in the trial of Latapie, on the charge of attempting to abduct slaves." Also, "Trials in Criminal Court: Harboring Slaves, *Commonwealth vs. Stephen Latapie*; also, *Commonwealth vs. William Jetter.* (Pen Bogert, Reference Specialist, The Filson Club Historical Society, Louisville, Ky.)

19. Helen T. Catterall, *Judicial Cases concerning American Slavery and the Negro*, I (Washington: Carnegie Inst., 1926–29), pp. 365–68.

20. *New Albany Daily Ledger,* January 18, 1861, p. 3. c. 2. "The Free Negro Law of Kentucky."

21. William Hosea lived in New Albany at 350 Market Street and on the northeast side of 8th Street above Sycamore at various times. *New Albany City Directory and Business Mirror for 1856–57* (New Albany: A. C. Grooms & W. T. Smith, 1856). *New Albany City Directory, City Guide & Business Mirror for 1860* (New Albany: E. Coy & Co., 1860).

22. *Louisville Daily Courier*, January 8, 1857, p. 2, c. 3.; *New Albany Daily Ledger*, January 8, 1857, p. 3, c.1.

23. John Brown Diary, 1821–1822, The Filson Club Historical Society, Louisville, Kentucky, March 4, 1822, p. 37, unpublished. *Cf.* also *Louisville Public Advertiser*, January 9, 1833, which refers to objections raised by Louisville to Jeffersonville and New Albany harboring slaves. Reference found in Richard C. Wade, *Slavery in the Cities* (N.Y.: Oxford Univ. Press, 1964), p. 220. Additionally, it was reported in the *Louisville Courier* that Mr. Slocum, the New Albany marshal, was accused of "running off" slaves in Kentucky, although the *New Albany Tribune* denied it. *Cf. New Albany Tribune,* September 13, 1853, p. 3, c. 1.

24. "Two young Men of New Albany Arrested on Suspicion of Running Off Slaves," *New Albany Daily Ledger*, August 14, 1860, p. 3, c.1.

25. Although Wilbur H. Siebert published his research on the Underground Railroad in 1898, he and his students continued to interview people well into the twentieth century. The remainder of his research is stored in the archives of the Ohio Historical Library in Columbus, Ohio.

26. B. F. Scribner, *How Soldiers Were Made* (New Albany, Indiana, 1887), p. 12.

27. Charles Henry Ambler, *A History of Transportation in the Ohio Valley* (Glendale, Calif.: The Arthur H. Clark Co., 1932), pp. 246–248. Until the Union Army blocked the railroad route from Louisville to Nashville, this railroad route to the South replaced the river route as the primary means of shipping supplies.

28. James Smith to Sam Smith, May 16, 1861. Isaac P. Smith Letters and Papers. The letters and papers of Isaac P. Smith and his family have been preserved and are in the possession of a descendant, Timothy Kate Sorrow. Many of the letters were written during the Civil

War period. The collection also contains many sermons, political speeches and documents of that period.

29. *Ibid.*

30. Miscellaneous Court Records, Floyd County, Indiana, May 12, 1864, Indenture Record Book, p.121.

31. George Winston Smith, "Fugitive Slave Laws," *Collier's Encyclopedia*, 10 (The Crowell-Collier Pub. Co., 1965 ed.), p. 449. "Some Southern papers claim that under the Fugitive Slave law 'aiding and abetting the escape' means writing, speaking and publishing against slavery as it induces the escape of slaves and is therefore a penal offense." *Frederick Douglass' Paper,* August 25, 1851, p. 3, c. 1.

32. *New Albany Daily Ledger*, November 12, 1850.

33. *Ibid.,* November 15, 1850.

34. "The Last of the Fugitive Slave Case," *Ibid.,* November 30, 1850, p. 2, c.1.

35. *Ibid.,* November 27, 1850, p. 2, c.1. This fugitive slave case aroused much feeling and excitement in New Albany. Merchants even referred to the case in their advertisements claiming, "The slavery question being settled, it is deemed necessary that the people should turn their attention to matters of a more personal nature. Therefore, all you that want New Goods at very low prices call at "Julius Dufour's." *Ibid.,* September 28, 1850, p. 2, c. 5–6.

36. Charles Money, "The Fugitive Slave Law in Indiana," *Indiana Magazine of History*, XVII (September, 1921), 270–281. Also, Wilbur H. Siebert collection, Special Report No. 3, 1889–90, to Prof. Albert Bushnell Hart at Harvard, from J. F. Hutchinson.

37. *New Albany Daily Ledger,* September 25, 1854, p. 3, c. 1. Editors of the *Ledger* claimed the *Tribune* editors supported the abolitionist movement and showed this by wanting to reopen the Fugitive Slave Law issue. The *Tribune* also reported that Rev. Whitten of Indianapolis expressed his abolitionist sentiments at the Methodist Conference by saying that "every man who supported the Fugitive Slave Law, from Franklin Pierce down to the lowest black-hearted rascal, ought to be hung."

38. *Ibid.,* December 12, 18, 19, 1862 and February 3, 1863.

39. Letter written April 23, 1861, by James Smith, New Albany, to his brother Sam Smith living in New Jersey. Isaac P. Smith Letters and Papers.

40. *New Albany Daily Ledger*, April 16, 1861, p. 3, c. 2.

41. "Runaway Slaves," *Ibid.,* March 5, 1863, p. 2, c. 2.

42. *Ibid.,* August 28, 1855, p. 2, c. 2; also, *Louisville Daily Courier,* "Runaway Arrested," September 13, 1855, p. 4, c. 4.

43. *New Albany Daily Ledger,* August 28, 1855, p. 2, c. 2.

44. Letter from John Bishop to the Secretary of the American Home Missionary Society, May 1, 1852, American Home Missionary Society Papers, Amistad Research Center, Tulane University. Bishop worked as a missionary for the Society after leaving New Albany. The American Home Missionary Society, located in New York, was formed out of a spirit of the evangelical Christians to purge the "wild west" of its wrongs and to give it some moral shape. It was an ecumenical effort primarily made up of Congregationalists and New School Presbyterians. Rudolph states that most of the men who served the Society as missionaries were New England men who disliked slavery. L. C. Rudolph, *Hoosier Zion* (New Haven: Yale University Press, 1963), p. 49.

45. John Howard, "Memoirs of John Howard," unpublished, 1903–04. The original copy of the "Memoirs" is held at the Howard Steamboat Museum, 1101 East Market Street, Jeffersonville, Indiana.

46. Vida Newson, "Phases of Southeastern Indiana History," *Indiana Magazine of History,* XX (March, 1924), 55–56; and William M. Cockrum, *Pioneer History of Indiana* (Oakland City, Indiana: Oakland City Press, 1907), pp. 605–606.

Chapter 2

1. *Louisville Daily Courier,* June 30, 1855, p. 4, c. 4.
2. *New Albany Daily Ledger*, March 11, 1857, p. 2, c. 2. This article, originally published in the *Jeffersonville Republican*, shows that an abolitionist group existed in nearby Jeffersonville, Clark County.
3. *New Albany Daily Ledger*, February 3, 1863, p. 2, c. 1.
4. *Ibid.,* November 14, 1862, p. 2, c.1.
5. *Ibid.*, January 26, 1861, p. 3, c. 1.
6. *Ibid.*, February 2, 1861, p. 3, c. 1.
7. *Louisville Public Advertiser,* July 9, 1841. Pen Bogert, Reference Specialist, The Filson Club Historical Society, Louisville, Kentucky.
8. *New Albany Daily Ledger,* October 29, 1862, p. 2, c. 2; April 8, 1862, p. 2, c. 3, tells of a black church in nearby Jeffersonville that was burned.
9. *Ibid.*, August 7, 1865, p. 2, c. 1.
10. Henry Ellis Cheaney, "Attitudes of the Indiana Pulpit and Press Toward the Negro: 1860–1880," Ph.D. Dissertation, University of Chicago, June, 1961, p. 445.
11. *New Albany Tribune,* undated article, p. 8. Copy found in Vertical file "Newspapers, *New Albany Ledger,*" Stuart B. Wrege Indiana History Room, New Albany–Floyd County Public Library.
12. *New Albany Daily Ledger*, October 30, 1862, p. 2, c. 1. The man was sentenced to the county jail for sixty days.
13. It is believed that "Little Jimmie" Trueblood and his wife, who were Quakers and lived four miles Northeast of Salem, used their home to hide fugitives. Another Underground Railroad operator, Thomas H. Trueblood, lived West of Salem. It is not known what their relationship to the editor was. See Herman Rave, "Hectic Days When the 'Underground Railroad' Flourished in Southern Indiana," County Jottings, *Louisville Daily Courier,* May 29, 1927. See also Harvey Morris, *The Underground Railroad, History of Washington County* (Salem, Ind.: Washington County Historical Society, 1993).
14. The term "Black Republican" was used abusively by the Democrats who accused the Republicans of trying to bring total equality to the races.
15. *New Albany Tribune,* December 6, 1852, p. 2, c. 1.
16. *Ibid.*, August 30, 1852, p. 3, c. 2. The *White River Standard* took J. B. Norman to task in a letter to the *Tribune*. Norman had complained that the *Standard* was slandering him. The *Standard* retorted, "It is possible that J. B. Norman has conceived the idea that he has a respectable standing in society. Monstrous!!"
17. While New Albany resident and African American George Washington Carter was digging for gold in California, his sons ran the family barber shop on lower Main Street, and the *Tribune* editor chided Norman that:
Wash Carter's boys charge no more for shaving the face of a mean man than of a decent one. It must therefore be quite clear that the editor of the *Ledger* can get cleaned upon as reasonable terms as a respectable gentleman like ourself. Our neighbor need have no fears that he will be turned out — they are used to the smell of brimstone down there. [*New Albany Tribune*, August 14, 1852, p. 2. c. 2.]
18. *Ibid.*, December 8, 1856, p. 2, c. 1; *New Albany Tribune*, Dec. 8, 1856, p. 3, c.1.
19. *Ibid.*
20. Generally, the Republican party became the party of the reformist type — the anti-slavery protestant.
21. Field McChesney, "The *Ledger* Is Monument to Early Editor," *New Albany Tribune*, date unknown. Vertical file "Newspapers, *New Albany Ledger,*" Stuart B. Wrege Indiana History Room, New Albany–Floyd County Library.

22. *Ibid.*

23. Victor M. Bogle, "A View of New Albany Society at Mid-Nineteenth Century," *Indiana Magazine of History*, LIII (June, 1957), n. 119, p. 118.

24. *New Albany Daily Ledger,* May 4, 1865, p. 2, c. 1.

25. *Ibid.*

26. *Ibid.*

27. "Upper" and "Lower" are terms used in New Albany to describe "East" and "West" in street designations and are terms used interchangeably in this book.

28. James Smith, New Albany, to Sam Smith in New Jersey, April 23, 1861. Isaac P. Smith Letters and Papers. "A New Albany citizen, J. P. Gillespie, had to flee Louisiana to avoid being lynched as an abolitionist." *Cincinnati Daily Gazette*, January 6, 1860. Gillespie, Captain of a group of border guards, had been in the rescue party involving David and Charles Bell of Harrison County, Indiana, who were arrested and jailed for helping a slave escape. Gillespie's guards were re-activated in Floyd County at the outbreak of the Civil War.

29. *Ibid.*

30. *New Albany Daily Ledger,* August 1, 1851, p. 1, c. 5.

31. Cheaney, p. 94. See also *New Albany Tribune*, June 20, 1853 p. 2, c. 3 and June 27, 1853, p. 2, c. 2.

32. Cliffton J. Phillips, *Indiana in Transition* (Indianapolis: Indiana Historical Bureau, 1968), p. 18.

33. *New Albany Daily Ledger,* May 12, 1853, p. 3, c. 2.; May 17, 1853, p. 2, c. 1; June 20, 1853, p. 2, c. 3; June 27, 1853, p. 2, c. 2.

34. *Ibid.*

35. *Ibid.*

36. Floyd County Marriage Record Index, 1819–1837, February 30, 1841. Jack Gaston to Polly Smith. "Finney" was the witness. "Jack being colored and Polly being white this license was returned by the justice as null and void." No signature was made by the justice.

37. *New Albany Daily Ledger,* August 9, 1860, p. 3, c. 1.

38. *Ibid.*, August 13, 1860, p. 3, c. 1.

39. Emma Lou Thornbrough, *The Negro in Indiana Before 1900* (Bloomington, Indiana: IU Press, 1993), p. 187. See also *New Albany Daily Ledger,* October 31, 1862, p. 2, c. 1, which recounts how an Indiana regiment stationed below New Albany refused a number of runaways entry onto the Indiana shore, saying "that their object in going to war was not to make Indiana an asylum for negroes."

40. *New Albany Daily Ledger*, October 20, and November 21, 1862.

41. *Ibid.*, November 10, 1862, p. 2, c. 1.

42. *Ibid.*

43. The *New Albany Tribune* gives its reaction to the Exclusion Act of 1851 in several articles. See May 12, 1853, p. 3, c. 2 and May 17, 1853, p. 2, c. 1, for examples.

44. *New Albany Daily Ledger,* August 7, 1860.

45. *Ibid.*, July 22, 1862, p. 1, c. 3.

46. *Ibid.*, July 23, 1862, p. 2, c. 1.

47. *Ibid.*

48. *Ibid.*

49. *Ibid.*, August 4, 1862, p. 2, c. 2.

50. *Ibid.*, August 1, 1862, p. 2, c. 2.

51. Alexander Martin, unpublished diary written during the Civil War, October 6, 1861–April 5, 1865, partial copy stored in the Stuart B. Wrege Indiana History Room, New Albany–Floyd County Public Library. The original diary is in the private collection of Grace McKee. Martin's house at 920 East Oak Street is still standing today.

52. *New Albany Daily Ledger,* December 26, 1865, p. 2, c. 1; May 7, 1868, p. 2, c. 3.

Chapter 3

1. Stephen A. Douglas was the leader of the Democratic Party for many years. He was the candidate of the Northern branch of the split Democratic Party in the 1860 presidential election when Lincoln was elected.
2. James Smith to Sam Smith, October 3, 1860. Isaac P. Smith Letters and Papers.
3. The Missouri Compromise of 1820 permitted Missouri to enter the Union as a slave state and also forbade slavery in the Louisiana Purchase. The Compromise remained in effect until 1854 when Douglas had the restriction against slavery in the new territories removed through the Kansas-Nebraska Act. He received a lot of criticism for his support of this Act.
4. James Smith to Sam Smith, October 3, 1860, Isaac P. Smith Letters and Papers. The presidential race of 1860 shows the following Floyd County, Indiana, vote: Douglas, 1,888; Lincoln, 1,151. The presidential race of 1864 shows the following vote in Floyd County: McClellan, 2,055; Lincoln, 1,457. Betty Lou Amster, *New Albany on the Ohio, Historical Review, 1813–1963* (The New Albany Sesquicentennial, Inc., 1963), Appendix C, p. 145.
5. James M. McPherson, *Ordeal by Fire* (N.Y.: A. Knopf, 1982), p. 96 and 123. John Charles Fremont was the first Presidential candidate of the new Republican party in 1856. During the Civil War he was commander of the Western Department of the Union forces. He became a hero in the eyes of abolitionists when, on August 30, 1861, he declared that all slaves belonging to citizens involved in the rebellion were freed.
6. James Smith to Sam Smith, September 21, 1860. Isaac P. Smith Letters and Papers.
7. Wesley G. Scott, "The Scott Family: A Pioneer Family of Kentucky and Indiana," Scottsville, Indiana. Unpublished, bound in the Stuart B. Wrege Indiana History Room, New Albany–Floyd County, Indiana.
8. Mary S. Davis Collins, "New Albany, with a Short Sketch of the Scribner Family," *Indiana Magazine of History*, XVII (September, 1921), p. 222. See also L. A. Williams, *History of the Ohio Falls Cities and Their Counties,* II (Cleveland: L. A. Williams & Co., 1882), p. 87.
9. Carlyle R. Buley, *The Old Northwest* (Bloomington: IU Press, 1950), n. 397, p. 620, quoting the *New Albany Chronicle* as found printed in the *Cincinnati Gazette,* March 10, 1821.
10. L. A. Williams, II, p. 213.
11. Miscellaneous Court Records of Floyd County, Indiana, Indenture Record Book "A," p. 46. *Cf.* Appendix E for the manumission record of Jemina Stubblefield.
12. W. Sherman Savage, *Controversy Over the Distribution of Abolition Literature 1830–1860* (Jefferson City, Missouri: The Assoc. for the Study of Negro Life and History, Inc., 1938), p. 121. Quoting the *Globe,* 36th Congress, 1st Session, Vol. 29, I, 16.
13. Hugh C. Bailey, *Hinton Rowan Helper: Abolitionist-Racist* (Montgomery, Ala.: Univ. Of Alabama Press, 1965), p. 55.
14. Hinton Rowan Helper, *The Impending Crisis in the South* (Miami, Fla.: Mnemosyne Pub. Co., Inc., rep. 1969), pp. 155–156.
15. Marion Clinton Miller, "The Anti-Slavery Movement in Indiana," Ph.D. Dissertation, University of Michigan, 1938, p. 235. See also Hugh Talmage Lefler, *Southern Sketches* (Charlottesville, Virginia: The Historical Pub. Co., Inc., 1935), p. 5.
16. Bailey, p. 20, making reference to C. Eaton, *Freedom of Thought in the Old South* (Durham, 1940), pp. 47, 186.
17. Savage, p. 123, quoting from *State vs. Daniel Worth* in Jones report (N.C.) VII, 488. See also Lewis Tappan, *The Evangelical War Against Slavery* (Cleveland: Case Western Reserve, 1969), pp. 334–355.
18. *New Albany Daily Ledger,* August 3, 1860, p. 2, c. 1.
19. *Ibid.,* March 19, 1860, p. 3, c. 2 and March 21, 1860, p. 2, c. 1. The *Ledger* made an error, using the word "Helferite" rather than "Helperite." However, some of Helper's ancestors spelled their name "Helfer" and "Hefler." See Lefler, *Southern Sketches,* n. 100.

20. Bailey, p. 41. Helper cultivated friendships with leaders in the Republican Party, including Horace Greeley, editor of the *New York Daily* and *Weekly Tribune*. As a result, Greeley was convinced of the potential political influence of *The Impending Crisis* and gave his endorsement.

21. William H. Seward was an anti-slavery Whig/Republican and at one time governor of New York and later Secretary of State under President Lincoln. He gave Helper's writings support although it is believed Seward never read *The Impending Crisis*. (See Lefler, p. 23.)

22. *New Albany Daily Ledger,* March 21, 1860, p. 2, c. 1. The 1850 Floyd County census lists a farmer, Morgan Saunders, with a $700 property value, who was born in Indiana but whose wife and children were born in Kentucky. He had a mulatto girl, Sarah Justice, living with his family; Sarah Justice was attending school. The 1860 census shows that Morgan still lived in Floyd County. It also shows Henry Sanders, a German immigrant, living in the sixth ward, and two John Sanders, one born in Kentucky and the other an immigrant from Scotland.

23. Lefler, p. 13, quoting Helper, *Impending Crisis*, n.p.

24. Bailey, p. 52, quoting Lewis Tappan to Helper, September 8, 1859, as found in William Henry Anthon, "Book of Letters Relative to the Publication of *The Impending Crisis*," New York Public Library.

25. Thornbrough, *The Negro in Indiana Before 1900*, p. 58.

26. Miller, p. 49, quoting *The African Repository,* VIII, 31.

27. Joe William Trotter, Jr., *River Jordan* (Lexington, Ky.: The University Press of Kentucky, 1998), p. 34.

28. Samuel Conn, *Centennial Sermon: A Historical Sketch of the First Presbyterian Church in New Albany, Indiana* (New Albany, Ind.: Grant, Faires & Rodgers Printers, 1876), p. 17.

29. *New Albany Gazette,* July 5, 1833, as reprinted in the *African Repository IX*, p. 186. (Miller dissertation, pp. 48–49.)

30. *New Albany Daily Ledger,* January 20, 1851, p. 2, c. l.

31. *Ibid.*, July 5, p. 2, c. 3.

32. *Ibid.*, August 9, 1851, p. 2, c. 3, "The Colored Convention." See also, *Ibid.*, September 9, 1851, p. 2. c. 2. Reporting on the same meeting, the article states that the "colored freemen meeting" was held in Pendleton, Madison County, Indiana, and was attended by about sixty people from different parts of the state. They met in the Pendleton Methodist church to discuss colonization due to the Exclusion Act that had just been passed. The majority wanted to remain in their native land. See also *Frederick Douglass' Paper*, July 24, 1851, p. 2, c. 4.

33. William W. Findley and his family emigrated to Caldwell, Liberia, from Covington, Indiana, on May 15, 1851. A letter from William W. Findley to Rev. J. Mitchell, May 12, 1852, was reprinted in the *New Albany Daily Ledger,* August 6, 1852, p. 2, c. 4. Covington is on the Indiana border near Danville, Illinois.

34. *Ibid.*, pp. 55–91.

35. *Ibid.*, May 11, 1863, p. 2, c. 2; "Rev. W. W. Hibben of Madison, Indiana, is now operating as an agent of the American Colonization Society for Indiana." Also, *Ibid.*, May 14, 1863, refers to the colonization effort being good for the white citizens of Indiana. See additionally March 14, 1864, p. 2, c. 1 and March 24, 1864, p. 2, c. 1.

36. *New Albany Daily Ledger*, October 24, 1855, p. 2, c. 2 and 3.

37. *Frederick Douglass' Newspaper*, "Letter to Frederick Douglass from Byrd Parker," February 17, 1854, p. 3, c. 2–3.

38. Louis Filler, "Anti-Slavery Movements in the United States," *Colliers Encyclopedia*, II (Crowell-Collier Pub. Co., 1965), p. 330.

39. Rundlette Kensell Palmer, "A History of Alna Maine," p. 583; Nell Walker, "A Brief History of Old Alna," December, 1970, unpublished; Records compiled by the DAR and presented to the Maine Historical Society by Maine Chapter of the DAR, which include Alna village cemetery records; U. S. Census records for Alna, Lincoln County, Maine, 1840 and 1850.

40. John L. Myers, "The Antislavery Agency System in Maine, 1836–1838," *Maine Historical Society Quarterly,* Vol. 23, No. 2 (Orono, Maine: U. Maine Orono, Fall, 1983), pp. 58–59.

41. Myers, p. 71.

42. *Russell's Commercial Gazette,* Boston, April 1, 1843. Paul, a fugitive slave, was given money by a group of abolitionists in Bath, Maine, for his stage fare for about 100 miles. "Paul is the second fugitive slave that has passed on this route to New Brunswick this winter. He charged us not to publish him till he got to Canada." The article is signed by Pelig Wadsworth. *Cf.* Elizabeth Freeman Reed, "Newspaper Notes on the Growth of the Anti-Slavery Movement in Maine, 1944." The Center for Maine History, Portland.

43. The 1840 and 1850 Maine Census records show several generations of "John Doles" in Alna, Lincoln County, Maine. Austin Willey, in *The History of the Anti-Slavery Cause in State and Nation*, claims that one Eben Dole, an evangelical from Maine, gave half of the sum needed for the release of William Lloyd Garrison in 1830 when he was arrested and put on trial for libel in Baltimore. Garrison had published a statement accusing a shipmaster of Newburyport, Massachusetts, of domestic piracy, that is, transporting slaves from the North to the Deep South. John Dole could also have been a part of the Eben Dole family. If so, he may have been recruited by the Tappan brothers or Theodore D. Weld. *Cf.* Bertram Wyatt-Brown, *Lewis Tappan and the Evangelical War Against Slavery* (Cleveland: Case Western Reserve, 1969), Ch. 5, n. 3, p. 94.

44. Myers, pp. 74–77.

45. J. M. Guthrie, "Sesquicentennial Scrapbook: The U.G. Railroad," *Jeffersonville Evening News* (Jeffersonville, Indiana, February 28, 1967), n.p.

46. Miller, p. 66.

47. *Ibid.*, p. 66.

48. With the exception of Cass County, which is in north central Indiana, all of the named counties are in the eastern part of Indiana, with Jay, Wayne, Franklin, Dearborn and Union bordering the State of Ohio.

49. Miller, p. 7.

50. *Ibid.*, p. 66, quoting Prof. D. L. Dumond, *Birney Letters.*

51. William H. Cockrum, *Pioneer History of Indiana*, pp. 601–602.

52. *Ibid.*, pp. 602–603.

53. *Ibid.*, p. 603.

54. William M. Cockrum, *History of the Underground Railroad* (Oakland City, Ind.: J. W. Cockrum Printing Co., Heritage Books, 1915), p. 195. Also found in Jacob Piatt Dunn, *Indiana and Indianans* (Chicago and N.Y.: American Historical Society, 1918), and in Miller's dissertation, where he makes reference to John Dole sprinkling capsicum on the trail of a fugitive to thwart the use of dogs (Quoting Cockrum, p. 199).

55. *Ibid.*, pp. 194–217.

56. *Ibid.*, p. 217.

57. Cockrum, *Pioneer History of Indiana*, pp. 606–608.

58. *New Albany Daily Ledger,* May 15, 1855, p. 2, c. 2; see also "A Bold Attempt Though Unsuccessfully Made by Five Slaves to Runaway," *Louisville Daily Courier,* May 15, 1855, p. 4, c. 2, for more details of the story.

59. Cockrum, *Pioneer History of Indiana,* pp. 600–601.

60. *Ibid.*, pp. 605–606.

Chapter 4

1. Levi Coffin, *Reminiscences of Levi Coffin* (N.Y.: Arno Press, 1968 rep.), pp. 644–645.
2. Floyd County Deed Book W, May 14, 1849, pp. 594–595.

3. Floyd County Deed Book 36, December 10, 1889, pp. 545–546.

4. Session records were kept by the individual congregations. Each congregation in turn belonged to a presbytery that met regularly twice a year or as needed. The original united Presbytery of Salem, (the first presbytery to function in Indiana), included the following missionary stations: New Albany, Bethlehem, Pisgah (at New Washington), New Lexington, Blue River, Charlestown, Bethany, Hopewell, Washington, Salem, New Providence (now Borden), Columbus, Sand Creek and Nazareth. Even though the Old and New schools split in 1837, they both continued using the name "Presbytery of Salem" until April 8, 1847, when the Old School changed its name to "Presbytery of New Albany." Locally, on October 10, 1867, the Salem Presbytery (N.S.) drew up their part of the agreement to reunite with the New Albany Presbytery (O.S.). *Salem Presbytery Minutes* (N.S.), April 4, 1861–April 9, 1870, III, p. 194. It wasn't until a New Albany Presbytery (O.S.) meeting at Seymour in 1868 that a bond of union took place on the local level between these Old and New school churches. Until the reunification, they each had their separate newspapers. The Old School published in *Presbyterian of the West,* and the New School in *Christian Herald.*

5. Victor B. Howard, "Sectionalism, Slavery and Education — New Albany vs. Danville, Kentucky," *The Register of the Kentucky Historical Society*, v. 68, #4, October, 1970, p. 294. *Cf.* also F. E. Mayer, *The Religious Bodies of America* (St. Louis, Missouri: Concordia Publishing House, 1961), p. 244. Howard and Mayer agree that the New School represented the northern view on slavery. *Cf.* also Buley, *The Old Northwest*, I, p. 440. Buley stated that the "New School men flirted with abolitionism." He also claimed that in the Old Northwest the Old School/New School division over slavery was not such a major factor as in some other parts of the country, and Indiana members were practically unanimous in their opposition to it. See L. C. Rudolph, *Hoosier Zion* (Bloomington: IU Press, 1995), p. 120. The *Ledger,* trying always to paint all anti-slavery people as abolitionists, criticized John McMillan Stevenson, pastor of First Presbyterian (O.S.), 1849–1857, for expressing his strong anti-slavery views from the pulpit. *New Albany Daily Ledger,* December 11 1856, p. 2, c. 1, and *New Albany Tribune,* December 15, 1856, p. 2, c. 2.

6. *New Albany Second Presbyterian Church Minutes of Session, 1837–1865,* Vol. I, June, 1838. Rev. Lyman Beecher was a guest preacher at Mt. Tabor campground. Lyman was not only the father of Harriet Beecher Stowe, author of *Uncle Tom's Cabin,* which in 1852 set the world on fire with its spirit of abolitionism, but he was also president of Lane Seminary, Cincinnati, Ohio, during a time of great upheaval and rebellion in the student body over the issue of slavery. Harriet Beecher married Calvin Stowe, a professor at Lane. *Uncle Tom's Cabin* was dramatized in August, 1852, but not put on stage at the Music Hall in New Albany until March 14, 1865, and in November 1867. *New Albany Daily Ledger,* March 14, 1865, p. 2, c. 3; November 6, 1867, p. 2. c. 1, and advertisement same page.

7. Samuel K. Sneed to American Home Missionary Society, September 1 (?), 1855. Vertical File, "Presbyterian Church," Stuart B. Wrege Indiana History Room, New Albany–Floyd County Public Library.

8. *Cf.* Victor B. Howard, *Conscience and Slavery* (Kent, Ohio: Kent State University Press, 1990), for more detail regarding the "Old School — New School" differences.

9. Frederick Irving Kuhns, "The AHMS in Relation to the Anti-Slavery Controversy in the Old Northwest, 1826–1861," Ph.D. Thesis, Billings, Montana, 1959, pp. 13–38.

10. Minutes of Second Presbyterian Church Sessions, 1837–March 1865, Vol. 1, p. 31.

11. The anti-slavery memorial was accepted by the following vote: "Yea's": Rev. Samuel K. Sneed, Rev. William C. Rankin, Rev. S. Kittridge, Rev. C. R. Fisk, A. Huston, A. McKinney, John Loughmiller, D. Brown, A. Weiss. There was one "Nay," that of E. L. Dunbar. *Presbytery of Salem Records* Vol. I, October 1, 1840. This Memorial was adopted at Indianapolis, October 9, 1840, by the Indiana Synod, *Records of the Synod of Indiana* I, pp. 489, 492–496. Generally, the American Home Missionary Society missionaries were the ones who framed and worded the anti-slavery resolutions within the presbyteries.

12. Salem Presbytery (N.S.) included churches in New Albany, Evansville to the west, Bedford to the north, and Madison to the east. Even though they discussed slavery and its consequences at nearly every meeting during the antebellum era, their Presbytery minutes, as printed in the *Ledger,* never mentioned these discussions or the anti-slavery overtures made to the General Assembly. No doubt the Presbytery chose to eliminate these references for their own protection; they did not have a friend in the editor of the *Ledger,* J. B. Norman. See *New Albany Daily Ledger,* October 8, 1857, p. 3, c. 2, for an example of Presbytery Minutes recorded in the local newspaper.

13. George R. Wilson, *Early Indiana Trails and Surveys,* Indiana Historical Society Publications, VI, No. 3 (Indianapolis: C. E. Pauley & Co., 1919), p. 355. Although Springville no longer exists, it was the headquarters for those opposed to slavery in Indiana as early as 1807. Many of the area settlers came to the Indiana Territory "to get free from a government which does tolerate slavery." (Annals of Congress, 10 Cong., 1 Sess., I, 27.) One of the trails leading into Springville from the west came within nine miles of New Albany and actually crossed into Floyd County at its northeastern corner. Springville was very close to what we today know as Charlestown, Indiana.

14. L. A. Williams, II, p. 144.

15. Rudolph, *Hoosier Zion,* p. 49.

16. Ashbel S. Wells to Absalom Peters, American Home Missionary Society, 1830. American Home Missionary Society Papers, Amistad Research Center, Tulane University. Wells remained in the New Albany area for four years.

17. Miscellaneous Court Records of Floyd County, Indiana, Indenture Record Book A, pp. 93–94. For fifty years the Methodist preacher Peter Cartwright was the presiding elder in the Kentuckiana region. He testified in his autobiography that in Kentucky, the rules about traveling preachers and slavery were enforced. Whenever a traveling preacher became the owner of a slave, he was required to record a "bill of emancipation" or a pledge that he would free the slave; otherwise he had to forfeit his ministerial office. Peter Cartwright, *Autobiography of Peter Cartwright, the Backwoods Preacher* (New York: W. P. Strickland, Inc., 1857).

18. M. C. Miller, p. 32, quoting *Doctrine and Discipline of the United Brethren in Christ,* p. 81. A record of the purchase of the slaves Betsey and Letina is found in Harrison County, Indiana, Deed Book A, February 16, 1811, p. 29, research of Earl Saulman, "A History of the Blacks in Harrison County," p. 2. It is unknown at this time whether or not Pfrimmer's purchase of slaves was for the sole purpose of granting them freedom.

19. Rev. Black returned to Pittsburgh where he became pastor of the Reformed Presbyterian church and was involved in the colonization effort before his death. Rev. Sneed remained in the Salem Presbytery working for the American Home Missionary Society until 1853 when he received a call to preach at Walnut Street Presbyterian Church in Evansville, Indiana, also in the employ of the Society.

20. John Bishop, Bedford, Indiana, to the American Home Missionary Society, May 1, 1852. American Home Missionary Society Papers, Amistad Research Center, Tulane University.

21. *Ibid.,* August 2, 1852.

22. The Atterbury family lived at 504 East Main and later on the north side of upper Main between Ninth and Tenth streets. A *New Albany Daily Ledger* article of August 7, 1860, mentions the fact that at a time when Rev. Atterbury and his family were out of town, a neighbor spied a man inside Rev. Atterbury's house. Supposing he was a thief, the neighbor called upon the police to investigate. Even though the house had been watched and surrounded, and the police then searched inside, the man was never found and the newspaper suggested that "he must have hidden himself very well."

23. *New Albany Tribune,* January 22, 1853, p. 2, c. 1.

24. Henry Little to American Home Missionary Society, August 21, 1847, American Home Missionary Society Papers, Amistad Research Center, Tulane University.

25. *New Albany Daily Ledger,* July 28, 1857, p. 3, c. 1. The *Ledger* called John G. Fee a "violent abolitionist." Fee was often mobbed and abused by Kentuckians when he was preaching. *Cf.* also *Ibid.*, March 2, 1858, p. 3, c. 1, which speaks of Fee being dragged from the pulpit and abused while at the same time a colporteur named Jones, who was with him, was stripped and whipped. In 1851 Fee appealed to the charity of northern abolitionists for funds to erect a "free" church in Bracken County, Kentucky (one that does not tolerate slavery and admits whites to the membership), and that money should be sent to the American Home Missionary Society for this cause. *Frederick Douglass' Paper,* November 27, 1851, p. 1, c. 6. *New Albany Daily Ledger,* April 29, 1852, p. 2. c. 1. In the spring of 1852 Fee was chairman of an anti-slavery convention held in Cincinnati. Vice-chairmen were George W. Julian, Stephen C. Stevens, both of Indiana — and Frederick Douglass.

26. Rudolph, *Indiana Letters: Abstracts,* August 21, 1847, pp. 337–338 and 446.

27. L. A. Williams, II, p. 200. *Cf.* also "A Brief History of the Primary Class of the First Presbyterian Sunday School," pamphlet. It has been thought that a Sunday school in West Union was established by Rev. Robert L. Baeck in April, 1865, when in fact, according to Second Presbyterian session records, it had its beginning as a mission earlier than that. Rev. Thomas Spencer was appointed missionary of the church in this endeavor in 1862. In 1870, "An urgent appeal came from the colored people of West Union to come out there and help them form a Sunday School...." Possibly it was revived at that time. First and Second Presbyterian churches united in this effort.

28. Rev. Horace C. Hovey, *Church History of the New Albany Presbytery*, pamphlet. Vertical file, "Presbyterian Church," Stuart B. Wrege Indiana History Room, New Albany–Floyd County Public Library. The mission was still functioning in 1873 when records show $125 was contributed for the support of the State Street Mission. The building is still shown on the Sanborn Insurance Map of 1891. Also, in 1870, African Americans in Jeffersonville requested the Presbyterians in New Albany to help them organize a church. The latter promptly named a committee to investigate and make recommendations. (Minutes, 1870, Presbytery of New Albany, pp. 16–17 and 70–71.)

29. William H. Gibson, Sr., *History of the United Brothers of Friendship, Pt. II* (Louisville, Ky.: Bradley & Gilbert Co., 1897), p. 23. This may explain why it was possible for Second Presbyterian church to function as a refuge for blacks in a town that was so anti-black biased.

30. One Presbyterian pastor who got into trouble for his anti-slavery work was T. B. McCormick from Mechanicsville, Indiana, in the vicinity of Evansville. McCormick, a Cumberland Presbyterian Minister, boasted openly about his involvement with the Underground Railroad. Governor Powell of Kentucky requisitioned Governor Wright of Indiana to deliver up McCormick; McCormick had to flee the state.

31. Rev. John G. Atterbury, *God in Civil Government,* A discourse preached in the First Presbyterian Church, New Albany, November 27, 1862 (New Albany, Ind.: George E. Beach, Printer, 1862.)

32. Coffin, pp. 644–645.

33. Cheaney, p. 348, quoting the "Minutes, Presbytery of New Albany," 1872, p. 159.

34. *Ibid.*

35. Third Presbyterian Church, formed from Second Presbyterian when it became too large, carried an anti-slavery personality with it. They had a guest preacher, the Rev. Bevin, on Sunday, October 27, 1861. The *Ledger* accused Bevin of being an abolitionist and claimed he was more suited to the "precincts of Oberlin than New Albany." Bevin apparently attempted to convey the idea that the Civil War was being carried on by God for the benefit of blacks. "Such sermons may suit some locations, but are out of place here," claimed the *Ledger*.

36. *Presbyterian Reunion: A Memorial Volume, 1837–1871,* (N.Y.: Dewit C. Lent & Co., 1870), pp. 442–43.

37. *New Albany Daily Ledger,* May 22, 1858, p. 3, c. 1.

38. Hannah Johnson, born in 1785 in Maryland, was married to Richard Johnson, a laborer, also born in Maryland. The 1850 census shows they owned their own home.

39. Levi Welch was a woodcutter and lived north of the city at the edge of West Union. Mortimer Welch, born in South Carolina, in 1820 lived with them and worked on the river. The Welch family was related to the Findley family through marriage. Eli Welch, a son of Levi, married Mary J. Findley, the daughter of Josiah and Mary Findley. Mary J. Welch was buried in the Findley family graveyard in Franklin Township. The grave stone is still legible and records Mary's birth as December 5, 1839, and her death as March 27, 1861.

40. William Finney was named by Jacob Cummings, a runaway slave, as one of the African American men who helped him in his flight through Floyd County and may have been related to Amanda Finney (*Cf.* Chapter 5). Dr. Clapp was born October 5, 1792, in Hubbardstown, Massachusetts. He brought Amanda Finney to New Albany with him. Clapp died in New Albany December 17, 1862. At one time Oliver Wendell Holmes visited him in New Albany and spoke at the Lyceum. Holmes was well known for being an abolitionist.

41. Born in Ohio, Harriett Hill Carter knew George and Ann and probably traveled with them from Scioto County, Ohio, to New Albany. She and Edward Carter, her husband, lived with George and Ann for a time before moving to their own home. Edward, a barber, was born in Virginia. George and Ann named a daughter and a son after Edward and Harriett. *Cf.* Chapter 8 for more information about the Carter family.

42. *The Messenger,* New Albany, Indiana, July, 1904, 5th year, No. 8, upon the death of Abby H. Smith. Isaac P. Smith Letters and Papers.

43. *New Albany Daily Ledger,* March 4, 1858, p. 2, c. 1.

44. The Lincoln Campaign Club began in earnest in 1860. The membership consisted primarily of Presbyterians and Methodists, the officers being: F. D. Danneker, secretary, James Kelso, Assistant Secretary, J. J Brown, treasurer and A. M. Hancock, corresponding secretary. Other members of the club included: Benjamin Lockwood, John D. Rogers, Dr. G. L. Gibbs, James C. Davis, Dr. Muer, John Renshaw, Brad Scribner, John S. McDonald, John Griggs, James M. Day, Isaac Davis, Hezekiah Beeker, George Townsend, John Armstrong, W. F. Schoen, Captain J. P. Frank and David Gerlitz. First Ward Whig members included William M. Wier, J. C. Jocelyn, William A. Scribner, Sam Dorsey, Elijah Sabin, F. A. Hutcherson, Jeremiah Warner, Peleg Fiske, J. B. Wilson, James Pearce, William S. Hillver, William C. Conner and William A. Clapp. At least half of that list had membership in one of the Presbyterian churches.

45. The railroad's use as a means of escape for the enslaved fugitive will be discussed in Chapter 6.

46. Edwin McMasters Stanton (1814–1869), was a Democrat and a strong Unionist. He was Attorney General of the United States under President James Buchanan and in 1861 became legal advisor to President Lincoln's Secretary of War, Simon Cameron. On January 20, 1862, Stanton became Secretary of War.

47. Brooks Genealogy Book, p. 66. Hargrave Archives, D. C. #537, Folder 1, DePauw University Archives and Special Collections.

48. *New Albany Daily Commercial,* December 17, 1867. Reprint of a memorial sermon given by the Rev. R. C. Hovey at the time of the death of James Brooks.

49. Frank F. Hargrave, *A Pioneer Railroad of Indiana* (Lafayette, Indiana: Wm. B. Binford Printing Co., 1932), p. 152.

50. Southern Indiana Genealogical Society, Vol. VIII, No. 3.

51. *New Albany Daily Ledger,* November 16, 1857.

52. At one of Lyman Beecher's camp meetings, 200 people came forward. One of Lyman's sons, Henry Ward Beecher, was a Presbyterian pastor in Lawrenceburg and Indianapolis who had attended Amherst and Lane Seminary. A dramatic speaker, he preached in New Albany at John Street Methodist Church, and the newspaper poked fun at his "theatrical performance." *Frederick Douglass' Paper* told of an incident in which H. W. Beecher was presented with a new carriage by members of his congregation after the passage of the Fugitive Slave

Law. When Beecher acknowledged the gift he said, "And now that you have been kind enough to give me a carriage I'll tell you what I intend to do with it. The very first slave that is making his escape from slavery and asks me to help him on shall have a seat in that carriage, and if there is no one else to drive him into Canada, I will get on the box and take the reins myself." Among the contributors were some whose views were opposed to Beecher's. *Frederick Douglass' Paper,* August 5, 1852, p. 2, c. 3, quoting from the *Commonwealth.*

53. Buckmaster, p. 92.

54. There were many links between New Albany Presbyterianism and Lane Seminary, all of which show that many Presbyterians there had an anti-slavery mind-set. Professor Diarca Howe Allen was asked to preach the dedicatory sermon at Second Presbyterian in New Albany in 1850. He was a professor of Sacred Rhetoric and Systematic Theology at Lane Seminary from 1840 to 1867. Allen was unable to fulfill the obligation, and Rev. D. W. Fisher, a New School preacher from Cincinnati, preached the dedication sermon in Allen's stead. Allen was born in Lebanon, New Hampshire, on July 8, 1808. He was educated at Dartmouth and Andover Seminary and later wrote a biography of Lyman Beecher. It has already been mentioned that John Bishop and his father, Robert H. Bishop, had a connection with Lane Seminary. (Lowell H. Harrison, pp. 68–69.) The abolitionist, John G. Fee, had been a Lane classmate of John Bishop's (1842–1845). Born in Bracken County, Kentucky, Fee was well known for his Underground Railroad activity. The Salem Presbytery (N.S.) appointed a delegate to attend the annual examination of students at Lane (Salem Presbytery Minutes, Vol. II, p. 305), and supported them financially. Lane Seminary sent students to assist the Salem Presbytery (N.S.) at Mitchell and Lawrenceport and possibly other mission stations in the Presbytery. *Ibid.*, p. 379.) Thomas E. Thomas, professor at the New Albany Theological Seminary, taught at Lane after the Civil War from 1871 to 1875.

55. The school was also known as Ayres University or Indiana Theological Seminary.

56. Meeting at New Albany on November 7, 1843, Salem Presbytery Records, June 30, 1843–November, 1846, pp. 60–61.

57. Howard, "Sectionalism, Slavery & Education," p. 293.

58. Erasmus Darwin MacMaster, "Speech in the General Assembly of the Presbyterian church," May 30, 1859, (Cincinnati, 1859), p. 6.

59. *Ibid.*, pp. 20–21.

60. In 1845 the Old School Presbyterian Assembly compromised on the slavery issue by ruling that slavery was not sinful in every case, but denounced, instead, the evils often attached to slavery. By condemning abolitionism as tending to perpetuate evils, the Assembly preserved a balance that satisfied almost all parties (General Assembly *Minutes*, Old School, 1845, p. 17). See Howard, "Sectionalism, Slavery & Education," p. 292.

61. The 1856–57 New Albany City Directory lists Professor Thomas as living on the north side of Oak Street between East Ninth and Tenth street.

62. Howard, "Sectionalism, Slavery and Education," p. 308.

63. *Ibid.*

64. John Finley Crowe was the founder of Hanover College in 1827 and although it remained Old School, he fit the mold of a New School man on the slavery issue. He, along with other Old School men, looked upon slavery as a sin against God that must be purged from church and country to avert condemnation. While living in Shelbyville, Kentucky, he was the editor of an anti-slavery newspaper sponsored by the Kentucky Abolitionist Society, *Abolition Intelligencer and Missionary Magazine. Cf.* Lowell H. Harrison, *The Anti-Slavery Movement in Kentucky.* When things got too hot for him in Kentucky, he moved across the river into Jefferson County, Indiana. The American Home Missionary Society supported him in his missionary endeavors there. In 1827 he was part of the Salem Presbytery committee, which adopted a memorial to the General Assembly requesting they take a stronger stand on the Slavery Resolution of 1818. (Records of the Synod of Indiana I, pp. 31–51)

65. LeRoy J. Halsey, *McCormick Seminary, 1812–1896* (Chicago, Ill.: McCormick Seminary

Press, 1893), p. 57. A full list of students who graduated from New Albany Theological Seminary can be found in *McCormick Theological Seminary of the Presbyterian Church; General Catalogue, 1830–1912* (Chicago: McCormick Theological Seminary, 1912), pp. 3–20.

66. James G. K. McClure, *1848–1932, The Story of the Life and Work of the Presbyterian Theological Seminary, Chicago* (Chicago: Lakeside Press, R. R. Donnelly & Sons, 1929), p. 24.

67. He also organized another Methodist church, built of logs, in Greenville Township known as Shrader's Chapel. Shrader came to Floyd County in 1828 with his four brothers; the brothers lived outside New Albany on Paoli Pike.

68. A history of Centenary Methodist Church written in 1875, called "The Centenary Advocate," said that the old and quaint Wesley Chapel building was [still] being occupied in 1875 by Dr. Aug. Knaefel [Knoefel] as a warehouse for drugs." (L. A. Williams, II, p. 188.) See Chapter 7 for more information about August Knoefel.

69. Donald Mathews, *Slavery and Methodism, a Chapter in American Morality, 1780–1845* (Princeton, N.J.: Princeton University Press, 1965), pp. 168–169. On January 5, 1839, an antislavery society was formed at Neil's Creek in Jefferson County, Indiana, led by an abolitionist, Rev. Lewis Hicklin, of the Methodist Church. There were eighty-two charter members, thirty-two of which were women. Forty meetings were held before the group disbanded in 1845. (Miller dissertation, p. 69. *Cf.* also "Anti-Slavery History of Jefferson County, [Indiana]" Historic Eleutherian College, Inc., rep., 1997.) The Neil's Creek group may have been the closest organized anti-slavery group to Floyd County, unless one existed in Clark County led by Dr. Nathaniel Field.

70. In 1853, Centenary Methodist invited two ministers of the Society of Friends from Upper Canada, Nicholas Brown and his wife Margaret, to speak at a meeting. The Quakers were, of course, the primary organizers of aid to fugitive slaves as they reached Canada. This undoubtedly was the topic of the program and part of a circuit of lectures asking for monetary assistance to meet the growing need in Canada. *New Albany Tribune*, January 1, 1853, p. 3.

71. *Ibid.*, December 3, 1852, p. 3, c. 1, and December 7, 1852, p. 3, c. 1. Centenary gained sixty new members through the December 7 revival.

72. F. C. Holliday, pastor, Wesley Chapel, *The History of Annexation*, unpublished, Vertical File "Methodist Church," Stuart B. Wrege Indiana History Room, New Albany–Floyd County Public Library.

73. In a speech by Senator A. A. Hammond before the Indiana Senate, he argued vehemently against the clergy. He said, " [The abolitionists'] efforts would have been powerless but for the aid they have received from a much more powerful as well as dangerous class. I refer to that class of political teachers who belong to the ministry, and who claim to speak by authority." *Brevier Legislative Reports* by Ariel and W. H. Drapier, IV, No. 2 (Indianapolis, January 16, 1861), p. 21.

74. *June 20, 1817 — The Beginnings of Methodism and a History of Wesley Chapel*, unpublished booklet (New Albany, Indiana, 1908).

75. *New Albany Tribune*, November 12 and 13, 1856. In 1857 he was elected President of Hamline College, St. Paul, Minnesota. In 1861 he became State Superintendent of Public Instruction of Minnesota. In 1862 he enlisted in the Minnesota Third Regiment and was commissioned chaplain. In 1864 he became editor of the *Central Christian Advocate*. *Cf.* also David W. Johnson, *Hamline University, A History* (St. Paul: North Central Pub. Co., 1980), pp. 45–47.

76. Miller, p. 225, quoting Matlack, *The Antislavery Struggle and Triumph in the Methodist Episcopal Church*, pp. 277–279.

77. *New Albany Daily Ledger*, November 17, 1856, p. 2, c. 1.

78. *Ibid.*, November 13, 1856, p. 2, c. 2.

79. *Ibid.*, November 18, 1856, p. 2, c. 1–2.

80. *Ibid.*, July 30, 1857, p. 2, c. 1. Cheever felt so strongly about the evils of slavery that he suggested slaveholders themselves be done away with rather than that slavery be allowed to continue.

81. *Ibid.*, November 18, 1856, p. 2, c. 1.
82. *New Albany Tribune*, November 20, 1856, p. 2, c. 2 and 3.
83. *Ibid.*, December 11, 1856, p. 3, c. 2; December 15, 1856, p. 2, c. 2.
84. *New Albany Daily Ledger*, October 5, 1857, p. 3, c. 3.
85. *Ibid.*
86. *Ibid.*, quoting the *New Albany Tribune*, October 6, 1857.
87. Freeman Dailey Bovard, "Benjamin Franklin Crary, D.D.," *Methodist Review*, XII (March, 1896), Fifth Series, pp. 176–190.
88. *Ibid.*, pp. 184–188.
89. *New Albany Daily Ledger*, August 26, 1857, p. 3, c. 1.
90. *Ibid.*, January 27, 1858, p. 3, c. 1, and January 29, 1858, p. 3, c. 1.
91. *Ibid.*, March 26, 1858, p. 3, c. 1, and April 28, 1858, p. 3, c. 1.
92. A letter from the Freedmen's Aid Society was preserved and placed in the Wesley Chapel archives at DePauw University. During November 1866, the letter had been distributed to various leaders in the New Albany Methodist church to be acted upon.
93. Lawrence Mark Lipin, "Producers, Proletarians and Politicians: Opposition and Accommodation in the Small Industrializing City, 1850–1887," Ph.D. Dissertation, University of California, Los Angeles, Univ. Microfilms, 1989, p. 108. The names of Methodist members are handwritten into the record books of Wesley Chapel, which are stored at the Roy O. West Library, DePauw University.
94. Dummer Hooper was born on November 2, 1803, in Durham, Maine, and married Annabella Brown. He established a shipyard in New Albany in 1837 that closed in 1850. He was a city councilman and represented the 4th Ward in 1840–1841 and the 5th Ward from 1857 to 1859. He was the New Albany street commissioner in 1855 to 1856, a member of Wesley Chapel M. E. Church and a Mason. He lived at 316 Lower Fourth Street, across from the Reising Brewery.
95. "Journal of William S. Hooper," written from 1858 to 1868. Entry of October 11, 186_ (year unknown), pp. 171–172. A brother, S. K. Hooper, was a member of the 23rd Regiment of New Albany volunteers. Stuart B. Wrege Indiana History Room, New Albany–Floyd County Public Library.

Chapter 5

1. Alan L. Bates, et al., "Falls Cities Ferries: A Note," *Indiana Magazine of History*, XCV (September, 1999), 255–283.
2. Unpublished WPA Report, "Floyd County Court Records," p. 4. Stuart B. Wrege Indiana History Room, New Albany–Floyd County Public Library. "Morrison" may have been the William Morrison listed in the 1830 Floyd County census who lived by himself and was in age group 36–55 years.
3. Patrick Shields' name appears in the Harrison County Tax Book of 1811 since Floyd County had not yet been formed out of Harrison County. *New Albany Tribune*, "Early City History," December 24, 1934, p. 2; L. A. Williams, II, p. 266; Saulman, "A History of the Blacks in Harrison County."
4. The 1850 census shows that Jeremiah Clark was mulatto and born in Virginia. His wife, Amy, was white and born in Kentucky. He was a farmer with a property value of $1,000.
5. L. A. Williams, II, p.260.
6. *New Albany Daily Ledger,* January 3, 1867, p. 2, c. 3, "The Early History of Floyd County," quoting from the first records of Floyd County court proceedings, May 10, 1819. The court was held in the home of Seth Woodruff.
7. L. A. Williams, II, p. 245.

8. *Corydon Democrat,* April 12, 1905, p. 1, c. 1.

9. Samuel Cummings, *The Western Pilot, Containing Charts of the Ohio River and of the Mississippi* (Cincinnati: George Conclin, 1847), p. 52.

10. L. A. Williams, II, p. 219.

11. Floyd County Miscellaneous Index Grantor Book 1: February 17, 1820.

12. The spellings "Findley" and "Finley" are used interchangeably throughout early records to denote the same people. Two variations are even to be found in a single early document to denote the same person.

13. Frederick P. Griffin, *History of Corydon & Harrison County Indiana, A Scrapbook of Newspaper Clippings,* Vol. 1 (Jasper, Ind.: Printing Services, Inc., 1991), *Corydon Democrat,* January 31, 1918, p. 128.

14. Floyd County Recorder's Office, Deed Book D, p. 545.

15. Joseph's heirs were: Patsy Findley, her husband Fleming Mitchim, and a child, Hannah Mitchim; Paul Findley, his wife Polly, and a child, Peter Findley; Jinsez Findley and her husband, Henry Freeman; Isaac Findley, his wife, Suzannah Findley and Nancy Findley. *Ibid.,* Deed Book T, pp. 453–454.

16. *Ibid.,* Deed Book 13, p. 149.

17. The Findley Cemetery is on private property, which is now managed by Lee Hubert. The land surrounding the cemetery has been in the Hubert family for more than 100 years.

18. The 1850 census shows that Josiah Findley's family included his wife Malinda, his mother, Hannah, born in Virginia, and the following children: James S., Mary Jane, John W., Amanda C., Sarah E. and Nancy Ann. By 1860 the family had added five more children: Philip, Secretia, William, Emeline and Josiah. Finley's mother, Hannah, had died. Also, James S. had married, moved next door and listed "cooper" as his occupation. Findley children buried with their mother are: John W.: b. 10-20-1841, d. 7-4-1861; Nancy A.: b. 4-3-1850, d. 7-9-1861; Philip, b. 10-10-1858, d. 7-16-61; Sarah E.: b. 8-24-1846, d. 8-16-1863; Mary J.: b. 12-5-1839, d. 5-27-1861; William E.: b. 11-1-1834. d. 12-12-1861; Martha, d. 2-18-1860. One grandchild is buried with the family: Mary E., daughter of Eli and Mary J. Welch: b. 2-3-1860; d. 8-22-1861. The tombstones use the spelling "Finley." However, deed records use the spelling "Findley."

In 1870 Josiah, even though he had sold the original home place, still lived in Franklin Township on a farm. His nineteen-year-old son, Josiah, had married and was farming with him. Josiah, Sr.'s real estate was valued at $5,000.

19. Some early Stinson family members are buried in this plot but their names were not registered with the county coroner. Those whose names were registered are: Florence Stinson, D.O.D. August 28, 1887, Cora Stinson, D.O.D. July 18, 1900, and Eva Stinson, D.O.D. May 10, 1901.

20. Floyd County Deed Record Index Grantee Book I; Deed Book B, p. 409, July 16, 1824.

21. See Appendix E for Frank Lewis' Deed of Manumission.

22. *New Albany Daily Ledger,* August 24, 1860, p. 3, c. 1.

23. *Ibid.,* November 21, 1862, p. 2, c. 2.

24. *New Albany Evening Tribune,* June 26, 1905, p. 4, c. 2.

25. *New Albany Daily Ledger,* January 3, 1867, p. 2, c. 3. Article titled "The Early History of Floyd County," quoting the first records of Floyd County court proceedings of May 10, 1819. The court was held in the home of Seth Woodruff.

26. L. C. Rudolph, *Hoosier Faiths, A History of Indiana Churches and Religious Groups* (Indianapolis, Ind.: Indiana University Press, 1994), p. 563. Quoting Minutes of the Indiana Conference of the AME Church (Bloomington, Ind.: Indiana African American Historical and Genealogical Society, 1990.)

27. *Cf.* the Epilogue and Appendix E for examples of free people purchasing freedom for others.

28. Alexander Martin, Captain of the 38th Indiana Volunteers. Unpublished diary written during the Civil War between June 30, 1863 and April 5, 1865. The original diary remains in the private collection of Grace McKee. A copy is found in the Stuart B. Wrege Indiana History Room, New Albany–Floyd County Public Library.

29. Mrs. M. Arthur Payne, "Sketches of New Albany, Indiana and Vicinity," State Librarian, Piankeshaw Chapter DAR, January, 1959, pp. 198–201.

30. Hargrave, *A Pioneer Railroad of Indiana*, p. 15, quoting *New Albany Tribune* editor Milton Gregg, July 7, 1854.

31. "Butchertown" was a community within the boundaries of West Union; it contained tanneries, a glue factory and tallow works, two breweries, stockyards, many slaughterhouses and several brickyards. The "Apple Tree Garden" was a German Beer Garden where the Germans held picnics, parties and songfests. Names associated with the slaughterhouses were: Faugerousee and Sloemers, who ran the stockyards, Schuler, Frank Manus, Benjamin Mertz, HB & Brothers Graybrook, John Everbach, Charles Umbreit, Wolfe, John Enslinger, Philip Schartz, Bill Endres, Knight, Laib, Erdman and Louis Hartman. More information about Hartman follows; he is named in black oral history as one who helped fugitives.

32. Floyd County Recorder's Office, Bk. 10, p. 376, February 6, 1864; Bk. 18, p. 55, January 30, 1871; Bk. 28, p. 275, June 9, 1883.

33. The John E. Bezy family has an oral history which states that Mary Walker and/or her children were sewn up in feather ticks in order to cross the Ohio River in a wagon on the ferry. If this is so, they would have come to Floyd County before the end of the Civil War. Willis was born in Virginia, as were his parents. Mary was born in Kentucky, but her mother was born in Virginia.

34. Floyd County Deed Book 20, p. 164, Book 21, p. 42 and Book 30, p. 464. The land was located as follows: 1873 WD, $350, 17 acres of SE ¼ of NW ¼ of Sec. 32 Twn. 2 Range 5. Later they purchased a roadway for $15.

35. Floyd County Death Records, Book H-8, p. 33.

36. Caleb C. Dayton built a tavern on Old Vincennes Road called the "Rising Sun Tavern." It was built of logs and was a stagecoach stop between New Albany and Vincennes.

37. Information on Ellis and Mary Walker came from census and courthouse records and also from Frank Didelot, John Bezy and Joanne LaFollette Hale, all of whom had ancestors who were early pioneers in Floyd County; those three knew of the Walkers and their burial site through family oral history. The burial ground is on property now owned by Joanne LaFollette Hale.

38. *Historic Indiana, Indiana Properties Listed in the National Register of Historic Places, 1999–2000*, (Indianapolis: State of Indiana Division of Historic Preservation and Archaeology, 1999), p. 50. A picture of Quinn's house in Wayne County is shown with the caption, "Quinn organized the Bethel AME Church in Richmond and played a significant role in the Underground Railroad efforts."

39. *Louisville Public Advertiser*, July 9, 1841. "We learn from the *New Albany Gazette* that the African Church in that city was destroyed by fire on Tuesday night — supposed to have been the work of an incendiary."

40. Coy D. Robbins, *Reclaiming African Heritage at Salem, Indiana* (Bowie, Maryland: Heritage Books, Inc., 1995), pp. 74–75.

41. Rudolph, *Hoosier Faiths*, p. 563.

42. Along with the greater influx of blacks into Floyd County after the Civil War, other black churches began springing up such as Jones' Chapel (now Jones Memorial AME Zion), which organized in 1868. Father R. R. Briddle, an elderly black preacher from Louisville, helped with the organizational meetings that were held in London Hall at the corner of Lower Fourth and Main streets. The first church was built at Lafayette and Spring streets. In 1867 a group of members from the black Baptist church broke away and formed Second Baptist Church.

43. William Dove had already been working in Indiana in the mid–1850s. He reported to William P. Quinn in 1856 regarding educational statistics within the Indiana Conference of the AME Church. Lori B. Jacobi, "More Than a Church: The Educational Role of the African Methodist Episcopal Church in Indiana, 1844–1861," Wilma L. Gibbs, ed., *Indiana's African American Heritage,* p. 8.

44. *New Albany School Fund Record,* I, August 11, 1831, p. 107. See Carl Arthur Zimmerman, "A History of the School, City of New Albany, Indiana," M.A. Dissertation, Indiana University, 1932, p. 42.

45. Though the AME church was active in educating African American children in Floyd County beginning in the mid–1840s, both the 1850 and the 1860 census show that roughly twenty-five percent of the black population, age twenty years and above, was illiterate.

46. "Hannibal's Retreat," *The Appeal, A National Afro-American Newspaper* (St. Paul, Minnesota, July 25, 1891.)

47. *Ibid.,* III, July 9, 1869, p. 74.

48. *Ibid.,* III, September 19, 1870, p. 120. See Zimmerman, p. 153. This Olden Street School was destroyed in the cyclone of March, 1917.

49. *Ibid.,* p. 157.

50. *Ibid.,* pp. 155–156.

51. The Division Street School, located at the corner of Division and Green streets in New Albany, is owned by the New Albany–Floyd County Consolidated School Corporation. The building has been set aside for restoration as a museum and learning laboratory to preserve and honor the legacy of the African American public school experience in Indiana.

52. C. Peter Ripley, ed. "Blacks and Politics," *Black Abolitionist Papers,* III (Chapel Hill: University of North Carolina Press, 1985–93), p. 43.

53. Robbins, p. 105.

54. Just prior to the arrest of Calvin Fairbank for helping the Louisville slave, Tamar, to escape, Fairbank had been seen at the "Centre Street church for colored persons ... where Bird [Byrd] Parker preaches, shaking hands with Wash Spradley." Randolph Paul Runyon, *Delia Webster and the Underground Railroad* (Lexington: The University Press of Kentucky, 1996), p. 151.

55. *Frederick Douglass' Paper,* July 15, 1853, p. 2, c. 7–8 and p. 3, c. 2. See also November 18, 1853, p. 3, c. 6.

56. *Frederick Douglass' Paper,* July 22, 1853.

57. *Ibid.,* December 16, 1853, p. 3, c. 4.

58. *Ibid.,* December 30, 1853, p. 3, c. 2; May 12, 1854, p. 4, c. 2, 3 and 6. Jones and Bonner used William P. Quinn as a reference in their advertisements. They openly acknowledged the fact that Jones' house was used as a "station" for slaves on their way to Canada.

59. Gibson, p. 42. *Cf.* also Ripley, *Black Abolitionist Papers,* I, Speech by J. W. C. Pennington. Pennington wrote that black leaders who lived north of the Ohio River began establishing organizations early in the nineteenth century.

60. The Carters have a strong history of involvement with membership in lodges over the years as is evidenced by the lodge-affiliated symbols carved on their tombstones in West Haven Cemetery, New Albany.

61. *New Albany Daily Ledger,* June 9, 1884, p. 4, c. 2. Henry Clay died on June 5, 1884, at age seventy-eight of pneumonia. He is buried in West Haven Cemetery. His tombstone together with a large, obelisk family monument depicts the symbol of the Masonic Lodge. Floyd County Coroner Record #419.

62. *Ibid.,* December 29, 1865, p. 2, c. 2. The black Free Masons gave a well-attended festival at one of the churches in West Union. John Sanders was listed as one of the leaders.

63. Iris. L. Cook, WPA interview, "More about the Underground Railroad in Southern Indiana," May 1936, Observation of Margaret Webb's Father, pp. 2–3. In the midst of the depression of the 1930s, the Federal Writers' Project, created under the Works Progress Admin-

istration (WPA), provided work for jobless writers and researchers. This agency urged former slaves to speak up and to tell what they remembered of life under slavery. Field workers interviewed former slaves wherever they might be found. More than 2,000 former slaves participated in this program. Belinda Hurmence (ed.), *My Folks Don't Want Me to Talk About Slavery* (Winston-Salem, N. C.: John F. Blair, 1984), p. xi.

64. *New Albany Daily Ledger*, December 16, 1861, p. 2, c. 1; and *Ibid.*, July 11, 1865, p. 1, c. 4, "The Negro and the War."

65. *Ibid.*, July 8, 1863, p. 1. c. 3.

66. *Ibid.*, December 21, 1863, p. 2, c. 1.

67. See Appendix D for a roster of enlisted men from Floyd County. W. H. H. Terrell, Adjutant General Indiana, *Roster of Enlisted Men, 1861–1865*, Vols. 7 & 8 (Indianapolis: M. Douglass, 1867).

68. *New Albany Daily Ledger*, September 28, 1864.

69. William Frank Dawson's Civil War records remain with his granddaughter, Mary Garvin, who lives in New Albany.

70. Amster, p. 51.

71. George and Nancy Stinson are buried in the New Albany National Cemetery in Sec. C, Grave 3088. George died on March 12, 1913, and Nancy died on June 18, 1923.

72. *New Albany Daily Ledger,* December 12, 1862, p. 2, c. 1.

73. *Ibid.*, July 22, 1862, p. 1, c. 5; December, 12, 1862, p. 2, c. 1 regarding contrabands being forced to perform menial jobs; and *Ibid.*, April 5, 1864, p. 2, c. 2, about contrabands in Indianapolis regiments deserting and leaving for Canada.

74. The *Reveille*, April 14, 1864. This newspaper was published particularly for the injured and sick soldiers. *Cf.* also *New Albany Daily Ledger*, February 11, 1865, p. 2, c. 2 and May 13, 1865, p. 2, c. 1.

75. *New Albany Daily Ledger*, January 26, 1899, p. 4 for mention of Nichols' pension; death notices found in *The Louisville Herald*, January 30, 1915, p. 10, c. 4; *New Albany Daily Ledger,* January 29, 1915; *New Albany Daily Tribune*, February 5, 1915, p. 8, c. 2.

76. Mary Bayer Stauble, "Lucy Nichols," *Southern Indiana Genealogical Society* (newsletter), Vol. XXI Nr. 1, January 2000, pp. 39–43, XXI Nr. 2, April 2000, pp. 85–88.

77. *New Albany Daily Ledger*, 1908. "Aunt Polly Campbell ending days in Poorhouse." Vertical file "Blacks," Stuart B. Wrege Indiana History Room, New Albany–Floyd County Public Library. Matilda Gresham, *The Life of Walter Gresham*, I and II (Chicago: Rand McNally, 1919). Gresham does not mention Polly and her services, although the *Ledger* article at the time of Polly's death says General W. Q. Gresham was nursed by Polly in New Albany when he convalesced after his injuries suffered at the Battle of Peach Tree Creek.

78. Floyd County Coroner's Record, 1881, p. 2, line 8. Patsy Lindsey was born in Virginia. Isaac P. Smith Letters and Papers; *Louisville Courier Journal,* January 27, 1999, Metro Section, regarding Timothy Kate Sorrow, who is the author of a drama about Patsy Lindsey titled "The Patsy Lindsey Story."

79. *New Albany Daily Ledger*, January 19, 1863, p. 2, c. 1.

80. "Hannibal's Retreat," *The Appeal*, Minneapolis, St. Paul, Minn., July 25, 1891.

81. It is no longer known for sure why the New Albany men were in New Orleans at this crucial time in history, but there is one good possibility. Steamboats from New Orleans regularly plied the Ohio River and brought Southern newspapers to New Albany. In 1861 the Confederate authorities published recruitment notices and sponsored mass meetings in New Orleans to promote the enlistment of free blacks into a separate regiment to assist in protecting New Orleans. *True Delta*, April 23, 1861, a New Orleans newspaper, advertised meetings of free blacks to discuss the possibility of participating in the Confederate war effort. On April 26, 1861, Jordan Noble put an ad in the same paper advertising for Home Guards. *Cf.* Mary F. Berry, "Negro Troops in Blue and Gray: The Louisiana Native Guards, 1861–1863," in Donald G. Nieman, ed., *The Day of the Jubilee: The Civil War Experience of Black South-*

erners (New York: Garland Pub., Inc., 1994), p. 23. The Carter brothers, both barbers who had been educated, must have read the newspaper and heard in their busy shop along New Albany's Main Street about the formation of black troops in New Orleans. Additionally, they fully believed that they would not be recruited for military service in Indiana. They may have had relatives or friends living in New Orleans—slaves or free people. If so, these New Albany men could have traveled down the Mississippi to join the Guard as a show of support. Unless they had a friendly contact in New Orleans who paved the way for them, the relationship of the Carter brothers to the Confederate leaders, both white and black, must have been complicated. Free blacks who had come from north of the Ohio River would have been suspected of being spies. Whatever the reason, these New Albany men became a part of the Native Guard that was formed initially to protect New Orleans. Randall M. Miller and John David Smith, ed., *Dictionary of Afro-American Slavery* (N.Y.: Greenwood, Press, 1988), p. 136. *Cf.* also Joseph Thomas Wilson, *The Black Phalanx, A History of the Negro Soldiers of the United States in the Wars of 1775–1812 and 1861–1865* (Hartford, Conn.: American Publishing Company, 1890), p. 176; Robert Ewell Greene, *Black Defenders of America, 1775–1973* (Chicago: Johnson Publishing Co., 1974), pp. 355–356.

    82. Manoj K. Joshi and Joseph P. Reidy, "To Come Forward and Aid in Putting Down This Unholy Rebellion: The Officers of Louisiana's Free Black Native Guard During the Civil War Era," Donald G. Nieman, ed., *The Day of Jubilee* (N.Y.: Garland Pub. Co., 1994), p. 178.

    83. Mary F. Berry, "Negro Troops in Blue and Gray," in Nieman, *The Day of* Jubilee, p. 30. *Cf.* Also Noah Andre Trudeau, *Like Men of War: Black Troops in the Civil War, 1862–1865* (Boston: Little, Brown & Co., 1998), p. 24. Though fear of reprisal may have induced them, historically the men of the home guard were loyal first and foremost to the city of New Orleans.

    84. Greene, p. 356. Joshi and Reidy, p. 179. A recruiting agent, G. S. Denison, observed in a letter to Secretary Salmon P. Chase that Butler was recruiting three classes of free men: "Those who have received freedom from their owners, those who are made free by the present military courts, and all who come in from the enemy's lines." (Trudeau, p. 27, quoting from Marshall, ed., *Private and Official Correspondence*, 2:328.) The men from New Albany do not fit in any of those categories and present a strange puzzle indeed. The fact that these Northern black men put on the uniform of a Southern group of soldiers comes as a surprise but clearly points out the complications involved in a civil war.

    85. Berry, p. 32. Trudeau, p. 46.

    86. Joseph Thomas Wilson, p. 212. The Confederates coveted this strategic area.

    87. Capt. Hannibal Carter to Col. N. W. Daniels, February 8, 1863, filed with J. A. Pickens to Major General Banks, January 5, 1863. Letters Received, 6th USCI, Regimental Books & Papers USCT, Record Group 94, National Archives, Washington D. C. (Found in Joshi, pp. 188–189.) See also Ira Berlin, et al., *Free at Last* (N.Y.: The New Press, 1992), pp. 255–257, 437–438.

    88. Berry, pp. 39–40. It was believed that General Banks, who was assigned to the area following Butler, was strongly influenced by Southern plantation owners. See Dudley Taylor Cornish, *The Sable Arm* (N.Y.: W. W. Norton & Co., Inc., 1966), p. 127.

    89. Hannibal C. Carter, "Declaration for Original Invalid Pension," October 28, 1887, Cook County, Illinois.

    90. *New Albany Daily Ledger,* June 13, 1863, p. 2, c. 1.

    91. Hannibal's regiment had to deal with extreme prejudice that involved Major General Nathaniel P. Banks who worked toward a goal of removing the black officers and replacing them with white men. Rather than be dismissed by Banks' Order No. 126, Hannibal resigned. James G. Hollandsworth, Jr., *The Louisiana Native Guards* (Baton Rouge: Louisiana State University Press, 1995), pp. 70–75.

    92. Eric Foner, *Reconstruction: America's Unfinished Revolution, 1863–1877* (N.Y.: Harper and Row, 1989), p. 353.

    93. William C. Harris, *The Day of the Carpetbagger* (Baton Rouge, Louisiana: Louisiana State University Press, 1979), pp. 441–451.

94. *George Donnell v. State of Mississippi*, 48 Miss. 661-82 (1873).
95. Harris, pp. 448–449.
96. *The Appeal*, July 25, 1891.
97. Hannibal C. Carter is buried in Sec. 38, Lot 12, grave #2 at Mt. Olivet Cemetery in Chicago, Illinois. There is no gravestone or civil war veteran's marker at the site. His daughter, Claudia C. Carter, paid for the gravesite.
98. Mss. 116, The Wilbur H. Siebert Collection, Interview with the Reverend Jacob Cummings, September, 1894: Ohio Historical Society.
99. *New Albany Daily Ledger*, August 23, 1866, p. 2, c. 1.
100. In 1833 Henry Clay, a well-known black citizen, was allowed to take a white man, Benjamin Conner, to court on a charge of "trespassing, assault and battery." Conner had accused Clay of making noises and disturbing the Methodists during their worship. In order to stop the disturbance, Conner assaulted the plaintiff. Clay, with the help of Attorney Dewey Elderkin, was able to win his suit against Conner but was awarded only $1 instead of the $500 he asked for.
101. L. A. Williams, II p. 556. In May of 1858, a fire destroyed the railroad machine shop. Henry Clay contributed $40 to help rebuild it. *New Albany Daily Ledger*, May 21, 1858, p. 3, c. 1.
102. John Hill later moved to Indianapolis with Willie, one of George Washington Carter's sons, and set up business in a barber shop with them at the Bates Hotel at 14 N. Illinois Street.
103. 1860 U. S. Census for Floyd County, Indiana. Other African Americans living near the New Albany–Salem Railroad station in the Upper First, Second and Third Wards not mentioned above were Frank Carpenter, Suckey (Suzie) Locklayer, Alex Pell, John W. Edmonds, both boatmen, and Bill and Harry Mosee.
104. See Chapter 8 for more information about George Washington Carter. The *Frederick Douglass' Paper* reports on various incidents of runaway slaves traveling by way of "over the ground rails" to reach freedom in the north. See, for example, *Frederick Douglass' Paper*, October 20, 1854, p. 1, c. 2.
105. *New Albany Daily Ledger*, January 12, 1856, p. 3, c. 1.
106. *Ibid.*, July 25, 1862, and July 29, 1862.
107. *Ibid.*, May 31, 1862, and June 6, 1862.
108. *Ibid.*, December 9, 1856, p. 3, c. 1.
109. Iris L. Cook, unpublished WPA report, May 19, 1936, pp. 1–2, Vertical file, "Indiana: Underground Railroad," Stuart B. Wrege Indiana History Room, New Albany–Floyd County Public Library.
110. *Ibid.*

Chapter 6

1. *New Albany Daily Ledger*, April 24, 1862, p. 2. c. l.
2. James Smith to Sam Smith, cited earlier. Isaac P. Smith Letters and Papers.
3. *New Albany Daily Ledger*, December 18, 1862, p. 1, c. 1.
4. Cockrum, *History of the Underground Railroad*, pp. 610 & 614.
5. There are many accounts recorded in the newspaper of runaway slaves crossing over into southwestern Indiana. Some examples are: *New Albany Daily Ledger*, February 12, 1857, "An alleged fugitive slave has been arrested in Bloomington. He is thought to have come from Gibson County [Indiana]. He has been taken to Louisville, Kentucky." See also, *Ibid.*, April 5, 1864, p. 2, c. 2: "Twelve negro slaves ran away from Henderson, Kentucky, last week. Scarcely a day passes that some of the slaves in that vicinity do not skedaddle." See also, *Ibid.*,

April 7, 1864, p. 2, c. 3: "American citizens of African descent nightly skedaddle across the river into Indiana from Daviess County, Kentucky. Many of them from the U. S. Army."

6. Buckmaster, pp. 77–79.

7. Morris, *The Underground Railroad, History of Washington County*, p. 54.

Thomas H. Trueblood's home on Cox Ferry Road, four miles west of Salem, and on "The Reid Line," was one of the first major "safe houses" to which the runaways using the central route were brought after crossing the Ohio River. Reid was the son of a Reformed Presbyterian minister. See also Arville L. Funk, "The Hoosier Scrapbook," *The Louisville Times*, October 4, 1976, n.p.; Mona Robinson, *Who's Your Hoosier Ancestor?* (Bloomington: IU Press, 1992), p. 59.

8. Henry Lester Smith, "The Underground Railroad in Monroe County," *Indiana Magazine of History*, XIII (September, 1917), p. 294.

9. *Cf. New Albany Daily Ledger*, April 27 1858, p. 3, c. 1; May 6, 1858, p. 3, c. 1; August 2, 1858, p. 2, c. 1; August 14, 1858, p. 2, c. 2; October 25–30, 1858; November 3, 1858, p. 3, c. 2.; September 4, 1860, p. 3, c. 1.

10. Wilma Gibbs (ed.), *Indiana's African American Heritage*, Xenia E. Cord, "Black Rural Settlements in Indiana Before 1860" (Indianapolis, Indiana: Indiana Historical Society, 1993), p. 101.

11. Regarding the Underground Railroad and Madison, Indiana, there are many stories. For example, in 1973 improvements were being made on Indiana Highway No. 7 near Madison. Work was delayed due to the discovery of a tunnel that originated in a stone house located on a farm six miles north of Madison in Lancaster Township. *Indianapolis Star*, 1973, n.p.

12. *Frederick Douglass' Paper*, August 27, 1852, p. 1, c. 2, quoting the *Louisville Democrat*, August 10, 1852.

13. *New Albany Daily Ledger*, October 12, 1857, p. 3, c. 1.

14. *Ibid.*, April 20, 1864, p. 2. c. 2.

15. Miller, p. 36.

16. *New Albany Daily Ledger*, September 30, 1856, p. 3, c. 1.

17. Lewis C. Baird, *History of Clark County, Indiana* (Indianapolis, Ind.: B. F. Bowen & Company, Pub., 1909), p. 386.

18. Rudolph, *Hoosier Faiths*, pp. 77–78.

19. *Ibid.*, pp. 65–66.

20. Miller quoting *The Indiana True Democrat*, November 4, 1852. See also Baird's *History of Clark County, Indiana* for Dr. D. L. Fields' information on his father. The son denied that his father ever played a role in the Underground Railroad and claimed he remained neutral on the issue of slavery and freedom. "He [Dr. Nathaniel Field] determined to abide by the law, creating and maintaining the institution, until abrogated by the moral sense of the masters themselves. He opposed slavery on moral and religious grounds, and appealed to the reason and conscience of the slaveholder and the slave." p. 413.

21. Coffin, p. 644.

22. By the 1840s, Cassius M. Clay was well-known for being an opponent of slavery. He was primarily influenced by the abolitionist William Lloyd Garrison and published an anti-slavery newspaper, the *True American*, in Lexington, Kentucky, among other anti-slavery activities. He wrote his memoirs, *The Life of Cassius Marcellus Clay*, in 1886.

23. Randolph Paul Runyon, *Delia Webster and the Underground Railroad* (Lexington, Ky.: The University Press of Kentucky, 1996), pp. 152–53. Thomas B. Sinex of New Albany reported in the *New Albany Daily Ledger* on November 19, 1851, that Fairbank and Tamar took passage on the New Albany and Salem Railroad and got out at Salem, where Fairbank paid their fare. This is contrary to testimony taken from the Louisville police court on Monday, November 17, 1851, which stated that Joseph Gibson saw the accused in a buggy with a negro woman go by his house at New Providence, Indiana (present-day Borden). Fairbank wrote a letter to Frederick Douglass giving his own view of what happened. *Frederick Douglass' Paper*, Novem-

ber 21, 1851. January 1, 1852, February 26, 1852, and March 11, 1852, papers include letters from him asking for financial help in getting him out of prison.

24. H. A. Edson, "An Indiana Pioneer," *The Princeton Review* (Princeton: J. M. Sherwood, 1877), VI, 86–87.

25. *Ibid.*

26. L. A. Williams, II, p. 519.

27. Wilbur H. Siebert, *The Underground Railroad, From Slavery to Freedom* (New York: The MacMillan Company, 1898), p. 134.

28. *New Albany Daily Ledger*, February 3, 1863, p. 2, c. 1. Fifteen "Negroes" who had been given their freedom papers by a Michigan regiment near Lexington, Kentucky .... crossed the river from Louisville to take the Underground Railroad north through Indiana. Six of them were arrested at Silver Creek.

29. Mss. 116, The Wilbur H. Siebert Collection, Letter from John Thomas, 5 April, 1896: Ohio Historical Society. See also Luke W. Thomas, "The Thomas Family," *Indiana Magazine of History*, XXIII (December, 1923), pp. 350–355.

30. Mss. 116, The Wilbur H. Siebert Collection, Letter from D. J. Leeper, 13 December, 1895: Ohio Historical Society.

31. Amster, p. 13.

32. For more detail about the ferry system between Louisville and Southern Indiana, see Bates, pp. 255–283.

33. Catterall, I, p. 347, *Waltham v. Oldham*, October 1839. The owner of the ferry that ran between Louisville and Jeffersonville was sued for damages when he allowed a slave to use his ferry to reach the Indiana shore, from which he continued his flight to Canada.

34. *New Albany Daily Ledger*, February 2, 1857, p. 2, c. 1.

35. *New Albany Daily Ledger*, June 11, 1857, p. 2, c. 2.

36. Certificate provided by Miss Nettie Irwin, 42 East Fifth Street, New Albany, Indiana, and included in Tyler Veasey, "Ind. Underground Railroad," WPA Report, unpublished. See Vertical file "Indiana; Underground Railroad," Stuart B. Wrege Indiana History Room, New Albany–Floyd County Public Library.

37. *New Albany Tribune*, May 28, 1853, p. 3, c. 1 and p. 4, c. 1.

38. Tyler Veasey, "Ind. Underground Railroad," WPA report, unpublished, p. 6. Vertical file, "Indiana: Underground Railroad," Stuart B. Wrege Indiana History Room, New Albany–Floyd County Public Library.

39. Harold Sabin, "Underground Railroad Had Many Routes and Stations in Indiana," *Indianapolis Star* (Indianapolis, Indiana, April 6, 1996), n.p.

40. Pen Bogert, Reference Specialist, The Filson Club Historical Society, Louisville, Kentucky.

41. Logan Esarey, *A History of Indiana from Its Exploration to 1850* (Indianapolis: Hoosier Heritage Press, 1970), p. 627.

42. George P. Rawick, *The American Slave: A Composite Autobiography*, VI (Westport, Connecticut: Greenwood Pub. Co., 1972), pp. 145–146A. See also WPA Interview of George Morrison by Iris Cook at his home, 25 East 5th St., New Albany, Indiana.

43. Blassingame, John W., ed. *Slave Testimony: Two Centuries of Letters, Speeches, Interviews and Autobiographies* (Baton Rouge: Louisiana State University Press, 1977), pp. 432–436. Isaac Throgmorton was interviewed in Canada in 1863 at age fifty-four.

44. *New Albany Daily Ledger*, April 30, 1860, p. 3, c. 1.

45. *Ibid.*, February 20, 1856, p. 2, c. 2.

46. *Ibid.*, December 12, 1862, p. 2, c. 1.

47. *Ibid.*, December 18, 1862, p. 1, c. 1.

48. *Ibid.*, August 10, 1859, p. 2, c. 1.

49. Catterall, I, p. 358, *Gordon v. Longest*, January, 1842; I, p. 315, *Edwards v. Vail*, April 1830; I, pp. 425–426, *McClain v. Esham*, June 1856. In June of 1860, a runaway slave was caught

in the hold of a steamboat docked at Paducah, Kentucky. *New Albany Daily Ledger,* June 29, 1860.

50. Buckmaster, p. 198.

51. Esarey, p. 726.

52. Hargrave, pp. 152–153.

53. *Louisville Daily Courier,* September 7, 1855, p. 4, c. 3; September 8, 1855, n.p., n.c.; September 10, 1855, p. 1, c. 1. Also, *New Albany Daily Ledger,* September 11, 1855, p. 2, c. 1. In 1847 the Board of Directors of the New Albany–Salem Railroad was made up of the following men: William Lindley from Washington County, Stephen Hale, E. Newland, John Gordon, James Brooks, R. Crawford, John Brown, Peter Tellon, James Montgomery, H. B. Shields, S. E. Leonard, Thomas Conner, James Collins, Jr., and R. H. Campbell, all from New Albany, *The New Albany Democrat,* July 8, 1847, p. 1, c. 1. In 1857 R. H. Campbell, John T. Creed and James M. Haines were assistants in management to James Brooks, *New Albany Daily Ledger,* March 5, 1857, p. 3, c. 1.

54. According to William W. Garrott, who began working for the railroad at age thirteen, the first trains were especially slow-moving. As a train boy, he would leave the front end when it reached an orchard near Orleans, fill his pockets with apples, and swing aboard the rear coach as it came by. From an interview with Mr. Wm. W. Garrott, born August 28, 1843, Frankfort, Indiana. Folder 6, Frank Flavious Hargrave Archives on James Brooks, DePauw University Archives and Special Collections.

55. Esarey, p. 626.

56. W. W. Borden, *Personal Reminiscences of Mr. W. W. Borden* (New Albany, Indiana: The Tribune Company, 1901), n.p. The Borden family came from Rhode Island and established an inn which also served as a stagecoach stop. The New Albany–Salem Railroad tracks ran next to the Borden Inn in Borden, Indiana.

57. *New Albany Daily Ledger,* December 3, 1856, p. 2, c. 2.

58. *Ibid.,* January 23, 1861, p. 3, c. 1.

59. *Ibid.,* August 31, 1861, p. 2, c. 2. "Four fugitive slaves passed through here on their way to Tennessee yesterday. They were captured north of here."

60. *Ibid.,* July 29, 1862, p. 2, c. 2.

61. *Ibid.,* April 18, 1860, p. 3, c. 1.

62. Stuart Seely Sprague, "Slavery's Death Knell: Mourners and Revelers," *The Filson Club History Quarterly,* 65 (October, 1991), p. 450.

63. Thomas Carter Perring, "The New Albany–Salem Railroad — Incidents of Road and Men," *Indiana Magazine of History,* XV (December, 1919), p. 346. This article does not claim that she was a runaway slave. The incident is mentioned only because it shows that it was possible for a person to be shipped out of the New Albany depot in a crate.

64. James Smith to Sam Smith, October 3, 1860. Isaac P. Smith Letters and Papers.

Chapter 7

1. Margaret Webb spoke to this issue in a presentation to the Southern Indiana Genealogical Society in July, 1987. Her presentation is recorded in Floyd County Genealogical Society Minutes, Vol. VIII, NR 3.

2. Rawick, vol. 6, pp. 214–217. Mr. Woodson was living at 905 [?] 4th Street in New Albany at the time of the interview.

3. *New Albany Tribune,* August 21, 1947. The Second Baptist Church Underground Railroad oral history information was primarily gathered from the vertical files in the Stuart B. Wrege Indiana History Room, from the *New Albany Daily Ledger,* from the *New Albany Tribune,* from Ruth Bledsoe, whose father, Rev. H. A. King, was the pastor there from 1937

Notes—Chapter 7

to 1963 and from Kathleen Wilkerson, whose family has held lifelong membership in Second Baptist Church, gives tours of the church, and has kept the oral history intact.

4. The 1850 census lists 208 blacks in Jeffersonville Township, 130 in the town of Jeffersonville itself and 24 in Utica Township.

5. Watson was established in 1872, but undoubtedly African Americans were already living in that rural area before then.

6. "First Presbyterian Church History," Charlestown, Indiana, pamphlet.

7. "The Underground Railroad and Church History," unpublished pamphlet, 1995, Second Baptist Church, 300 East Main Street, New Albany, Indiana. The pamphlet is published for use at New Albany's annual Harvest Homecoming celebration.

8. *Ibid*. See also Tyler Veasey, "Clock in Steeple High Above Main Street Faithful After 99 Years," *New Albany Tribune*, 1949.

9. *New Albany Tribune,* July 30, 1852, p. 3, c. 1 & 2.

10. *Ibid*.

11. *New Albany Daily Ledger*, May 24, 1851, p. 2, c. 1. It was announced that Second Presbyterian was almost completed. An iron fence, a bell and the clock were yet to be added. Finally, in March 1856, the "Big Ben of New Albany" with four faces was installed by Mr. Penfeld. It could be seen over one-half mile away. The original bell had two clappers, one manipulated by the clock's mechanism to strike the hours and another manually operated to summon church worshippers. Oral tradition suggests the bell, when manually operated, was used to signal those waiting to cross from the other side of the river. "The Rev. H. A. King believes that the bells' peals might have been used as signals during the Civil War 'slave freeing business' that existed in and around New Albany." Tyler Veasey, "Clock in Steeple High Above Main Street Faithful After 99 Years," *New Albany Tribune*, March 1949. The hand-manipulated bells were also used to announce the death of President Abraham Lincoln.

12. *New Albany Daily Ledger*, July 31, 1865, p. 2, c. 1. See also *Ibid.*, January 23, 1863, p. 3, c. 1, regarding free "negroes" flocking to New Albany.

13. "The Underground Railroad and Church History."

14. Elizabeth Nunemacher, "Nursing During Civil War," Vertical file "Civil War," undated editorial, Stuart B. Wrege Indiana History Room, New Albany–Floyd County Library. John R. Nunemacher, president of the school trustees in 1862, leased the school administration building for use as the headquarters for the military hospitals during the Civil War. See *New Albany Tribune*, October 7, 1948.

15. Both the *Tribune* office and the DePauw House were damaged by fire September 21, 1860. This fire put the voice of the Republican Party out of business for a time. No *Tribune* newspapers are available in the local library for further research of the fire. The *New Albany Daily Ledger* did not speculate as to how the fire started.

16. There are several reasons why the building may not be on the list of hospitals: It may have been due to its small size or possibly it was used as a hospital on a temporary basis and only late in the war. Injured and sick African American soldiers were kept isolated from the white soldiers in the hospitals. Either they were in separate wards or were placed in their own building. African American soldiers could have also been treated in the DePauw Hotel/hospital with this information not having been made public. As it was, there was a good deal of controversy in New Albany about the sick and injured black soldiers and where they were to be treated. Some of those addresses of hospitals used exclusively for black soldiers were Hospital No. 5 (Anderson College), on Main between Lower Third and Fourth streets and on a boat docked at the wharf which was deemed "unseaworthy." The DePauw Hotel was converted to a hospital in 1886, from the DePauw Trust Fund, and called the United Charities Hospital. (*Cf. New Albany Daily Ledger,* November 10, 1862, p. 2, c. 1.)

17. Vertical file "Wars. Civil War, I and II," Stuart B. Wrege Indiana History Room, New Albany–Floyd County Public Library.

18. Testimony of Lloyd Fischer given to the author in 1998. Mr. Fischer drew a rendering of the tunnel as he remembered it. The drawing is now in the possession of the author.

19. *New Albany Ledger Standard*, March 14, 1877, p. 4, c. 2. The stable was given the name "Sweet Gum Stable" by a wagoner who saw the huge number of steamboat loads of Harrison County sweet gum used to build it.

20. "The Underground Railroad and Church History," p. 5.

21. Floyd County Deed Book F, p. 702; Deed Book H, p. 274.

22. Floyd County Deed Book 12, p. 252.

23. Indiana Department of Natural Resources, National Register of Historic Places, "Sweet Gum Stable," prepared by Camilla R. Dieber, Program Assistant, July 7, 1995, p. 6.

24. *New Albany Ledger Standard*, April 24, 1877.

25. *New Albany Daily Ledger*, June 6, 1865, p. 2, c. 2; June 7, 1865, p. 2, c. 2; June 8, 1865, p. 2, c. 1; June 26, 1865, p. 2, c. 2.

26. *Ibid.*, August 24, 1865, p. 2, c. 2.

27. *New Albany Ledger Standard*, March 14, 1877, p. 4, c. 2.

28. Buckmaster, pp. 370–373.

29. *Ibid*.

30. Dieber, Indiana Department of Natural Resources, p. 5.

31. Chapter 8 will include information about a German immigrant, Louis Hartman, who lived at the corner of State and Cherry streets and who is linked to the Underground Railroad in oral tradition.

32. WPA Report, May 19, 1936, unpublished. Iris L. Cook interview of Sarah Merrill at 1710 Monon Avenue, New Albany, Indiana.

33. Morris, p. 58.

34. Lon McCoy, "Road to Freedom," *Homespun Magazine*, I, No. 5 (April 1949), p. 3. See also *New Albany Daily Ledger*, July 12, 1855, p. 2, c. 1: Two runaway slaves, the property of Messrs. Mayes, of Taylor County, Kentucky, were captured a few days since about twenty-five miles back of Jeffersonville.

35. *New Albany Daily Ledger*, February 27, 1851, p. 2. c. 1.

36. Esarey, p. 627.

37. *Cf.* the map of Floyd County on p. 60.

38. McCoy, p. 3.

39. Burrell Grundy had several brothers. One eventually settled in Corydon and another in the black settlement near Chambersburg, south of Paoli, Indiana.

40. Over the years many other names have been used for State Street and its extension — Paoli Pike — such as: The Plank Road, New Albany and Vincennes Turnpike, Pool's Pike (J. S. Pool & Co. Marble Works was located at 118 State Street) and later, Route 150. The black cemetery on Paoli Pike never had an official name and was referred to in the original deed as "The Colored Peoples' Grave Yard." However, through the efforts of teachers and students at S. Ellen Jones Elementary School in New Albany, the cemetery is being cleaned and restored and has been given a new name, "Freedomland." It contains more than three hundred graves.

41. The New Albany City Directory of 1872–73 describes Louis Hartman's dwelling as being on the west side of State Street between Cherry and Ealy in West Union.

42. *Cf.* the document on p. 110, which details the oral tradition of the Underground Railroad passed down in the Grundy family.

43. Pearl also told a story about a "still" being hidden in the "third basement" of 1401 State Street during prohibition. Officials from Indianapolis would travel to New Albany because they knew a flow of alcohol was coming from there. Someone in New Albany city government would warn people "the Feds" were on their way and the word would be passed. These officials were "up against a wall" and could not locate the still(s). Someone asked them if they had tried looking in any of the "third basement" houses. They found one at 1401 State Street. New Albany police raided the house on more than one occasion during prohibition.

44. Floyd County Deed Records: Bk. 37, p. 48, Dec. 1, 1928; Bk. 30, p. 544, July 11, 1885; Bk. 20, p. 203, Nov. 20, 1873; Bk. 11, pp. 10–11, May 9, 1864; Bk. 5, p. 814, October 10, 1857, Bk. 1, p. 101, Feb. 3, 1853.

45. *New Albany Tribune,* October 13, 1949. *Cf.* also Vertical file "Buildings No. 1," Stuart B. Wrege Indiana History Room, New Albany–Floyd County Public Library.

46. *New Albany Tribune,* October 13, 1949. When I-64 was built, it cut through the Old Vincennes Road that now circles around and under I-64 before it joins with the old section again. Before that, however, the Old Vincennes Road led straight toward August Knoefel's summer hotel.

47. *Cf.* The document of the Grundy oral history on p. 110.

48. L. A. Williams, II, pp. 290–291.

49. *New Albany Daily Ledger,* July 15, 1863, p. 2, c. 2.

50. *New Albany Daily Ledger,* July 10, 13 and 15, 1863. The *Daily Louisville Democrat,* July 11, 1863, p. 2, c. 2, omits any mention of Glenn's son and claims Rev. Glenn fired on the Rebels from his yard. His wife dragged him into the house at which point the Rebels burst open the door, wounded him in both thighs and set the house on fire. His wife and other ladies in the house dragged him out to an orchard and thus saved him from being roasted alive, claimed the Louisville paper.

51. Tyler Veasey, "Reminiscence of Morgan's Raid in Harrison County," District #5, Harrison County, unpublished WPA report, quoting County Atlas "History of Harrison County" (Corydon, Ind.: F. A. Bulleit, 1906), p. 50.

52. *The Charter and Ordinances, of the City of New Albany, Indiana* (New Albany, Ind.: M. Gregg & Sons, City Printers, 1855), p. 34.

53. Smith was also responsible for designing First Presbyterian Church on Bank Street, the Collins house, the John Conner home, which is today the Masonic Lodge, and the Montgomery house at Sixth and Main streets.

Chapter 8

1. Pen Bogert, Reference Specialist, The Filson Club Historical Society, Louisville, Kentucky.

2. U. S. Census Records, Floyd County, Indiana, 1830; Floyd County Recorder, Grantee/Grantor Books I, 1826–1835. The bulk of Burford's land was in Section 30, Range 5, Township 2. He lived in Mercer County, Kentucky, before moving to Harrison County, Indiana, where he married Isabet Shields.

3. *New Albany Daily Ledger,* February 5, 1857, p. 3, c. 2.

4. Miscellaneous Court Records, Floyd County, Ind. Indenture Record Book A, pp. 30–31.

5. The original *Register of Negroes and Mulattoes in Floyd County* remains in New Albany with the Carnegie Center for Art and History.

6. *City Guide and Business Mirror* (New Albany: E. Coy & Co.), 1859, p. 82.

7. Lipin, pp. 45–46.

8. *New Albany Daily Ledger,* July 6, 1859, p. 2, c. 1; *Louisville Daily Democrat,* July 6, 1859, p. 2, c. 1; *Louisville Daily Courier,* July 6, 1859. Louisville newspaper research courtesy of Pen Bogert, Reference Specialist, The Filson Club Historical Society, Louisville, Kentucky.

9. *Ibid.* Once runaway slaves were able to reach Cincinnati, they could get help from the free black community, Quakers and other abolitionists and eventually reach Canada.

10. *Louisville Daily Journal,* February 13, 1861. Pen Bogert, Reference Specialist, The Filson Club Historical Society, Louisville, Kentucky.

11. *Ibid.*

12. Louisville City Court record #33, p. 197, February 12, 1861. The case was brought to trial on May 11, 1861, Order Book of Jefferson County Circuit Court, Book #9, p. 82. McIntosh was tried and found guilty on a felony charge of aiding slaves to escape and was sentenced to five years in the Kentucky penitentiary at hard labor. On May 14, 1861, with the help of an attorney, he filed a "Motion to Set Aside." This Motion was continued to May 17, 1861, when it was overruled, and McIntosh was taken to the prison in Frankfort, where he started serving his sentence in June 1861. Pen Bogert, Reference Specialist, The Filson Club Historical Society, Louisville, Kentucky.

13. Register of Prisoners, Kentucky State Penitentiary, 1861–1866. Microfilm #7009891, KDLA. *Commonwealth vs. H. McIntosh*, Franklin Circuit Court, June 1862, Case file #981. Grand Jury indictment for felony. Offense was "feloniously escaping from commitment in the Kentucky Penitentiary." Pen Bogert, Reference Specialist, The Filson Club Historical Society, Louisville, Kentucky.

14. *New Albany Commercial*, June 28, 1868, titled, "A colored Enoch Arden case."

15. United States Census Records, Floyd County, First Ward, 1860.

16. Lipin, pp. 45–46. Close to thirty percent of the total number of servants in New Albany, many of whom were African American, lived on the northern edge of the business district in this general area, which was near the railroad station.

17. Pen Bogert, "Making Their Way to Freedom," Filson Club Lecture delivered September 23, 1999, Louisville, Kentucky.

18. The announcement of this convention appeared in all the local newspapers including those in New Albany. *New Albany Tribune*, June 26, 1852, p. 3, c. 1.

19. Savage, p. 124. The conflict over the distribution of abolitionist literature through the mail continued as the Civil War progressed. The conflict between the North and the South boiled down to freedom of speech on the one hand, and the protection of property guaranteed by the Constitution of the United States on the other hand.

20. Gibson, pp. 32–34.

21. A quotation from a letter written by Barbara Clayton Clark, a Carter descendant, on May 30, 1982, to "Significa," *Parade Magazine*, 750 Third Avenue, New York, New York 10017, regarding a brief biography she was writing of Hannibal C. Carter. A copy of this letter and biography are found in Vertical File, "Black History," the Stuart B. Wrege Indiana History Room, New Albany–Floyd County Public Library.

22. U.S. Bureau of the Census, Floyd County, Indiana, 1860.

23. Carter Woodson, *A Century of Negro Migration* (N.Y.: Russell & Russell, 1969), p. 57, quoting Evans, *A History of Scioto County, Ohio*, p. 643. A Peter Carter purchased land as early as 1806 in Ross County, Ohio, just north of Scioto County where Chillicothe is located. It is not known whether Peter was related to George Washington Carter.

24. Carter descendant Barbara Clayton Clark reported that the Carters were people with a lot of presence and savvy. It has also been suggested that through African American newspapers, information and "signals" regarding the Underground Railroad were passed on by members of the Carter family.

25. *New Albany Tribune*, May 6, 1878.

26. Miscellaneous Index to Grantor and Grantee Records, Books 1 & 2, Floyd County, Indiana, Recorder's Office.

27. *New Albany Daily Ledger*, August 2, 1860, p. 2, c. 3.

28. *Louisville Courier*, January 21, 1861.

29. *New Albany Daily Ledger*, May 6, 1878. The article goes on to say that George Washington Carter found prejudice against blacks to be more pronounced in Canada than in the United States and he gave this as a reason for returning to New Albany. However, others might not have agreed with this assessment. Jehu Jones, a black Lutheran clergyman who moved to Toronto in 1839, was "struck by the apparent lack of prejudice and the abundant opportunities that he found in Canada, and he marveled that information about life there was not more

wide-spread among northern blacks." Ripley, p. 76. At an anti-slavery meeting in Toronto, Canada, it was established that 30,000 blacks resided in Canada. A resolution was passed inviting fugitive slaves to come to Canada (*New Albany Tribune,* April 3, 1852, p. 3, c. 1.)

30. *New Albany Daily Ledgers*: September 20, 1955, p. 2, c. 2; December 17, 1955, p. 3, c. 1; June 4, 1958, p. 3, c. 1; July 17, 1958, p. 3, c. 1; August 2, 1958, p. 3, c. 1; September 23, 1961, p. 2, c. 2; September 27, 1961, p. 2, c. 3.

31. *Ibid.,* May 6, 1878.

32. *New Albany Tribune,* May 4, 1878.

33. George Washington Carter is buried in Fairview Cemetery, Plat 2, Range 7, Lot 15, Cemetery Record #7146.

34. *New Albany Daily Ledger*, July 23, 1917, p. 1, c. 7, "New Albany Sustains Loss of Benefactor"; July 26, 1917, p. 1, c. 3, "Citizens Pay Last Tribute to Louis Hartman."

Chapter 9

1. Some recent writers have even called the Underground Railroad an absolute myth. See Mark C. Carnes, et al., *Mapping America's Past* (N.Y.: Henry Holt, 1996), pp. 106–7.

2. James Hoffmeier, *Israel in Egypt*, as quoted by David Van Biema, "In Search of Moses," *Time*, December 14, 1998, p. 82.

Epilogue

1. The Exclusion Act of 1851 is explained in Chapter 2.

2. *New Albany Daily Ledger*, August 25, 1857, p. 3, c. 1. Another case involving the same issue occurred in Floyd County, The State of Indiana vs. Elizabeth Washington. Washington was charged with breaking the law by "coming into the State." The District Prosecutor, Alexander Dowling, tried the case in the Floyd County Common Pleas Court. Attorneys Otto and Davis represented Washington. The next day this case was dismissed. *Ibid.*, October 5 and 6, 1859, p. 3, c. 1.

3. Miscellaneous Court Records of Floyd County, Indiana, Book of Indentures, p. 70.

4. *New Albany Tribune*, June 20, 1853, p. 2, c. 3. Several days later the *Cincinnati Commercial* noted that a forced migration out of the State of Indiana was evident from the many "negro" families at the docks with all of their worldly possessions. *New Albany Tribune* quoting the *Cincinnati Commercial*, June 27, 1853, p. 2, c. 2.

5. Miscellaneous Court Records of Floyd County, Indiana, Book of Indentures, p. 4. The 1850 census for Floyd County shows that Carter was born in Virginia. His wife, Melinda, and three children, Preston, Martha and Eliza, were born in Indiana. The two oldest children were attending school. The witnesses for Emanuel Carter, Messrs. Clapp, Key, Brook and Day were all Presbyterians. He, therefore, may have had a connection to one of the Presbyterian Churches in New Albany.

6. *Ibid.*, p. 24. No date of entry into the Floyd County records is given.

7. *Ibid.*, p. 89.

8. A summary of the John Carter Deed of Emancipation and two Bills of Sale can be found in Appendix E.

9. *Ibid.*, p. 103.

10. A summary of the Floyd County Freedom and Manumission Papers is found in Appendix E. Carolyn Eve, the Floyd County Recorder, has microfilmed the entire "Book of Indentures." The freedom papers, as well as indenture records, can be viewed in the Stuart B. Wrege Indiana History Room at the New Albany–Floyd County Public Library.

Appendix E

1. Miscellaneous Court Records of Floyd County, Indiana, Book of Indentures, p. 2.
2. *Ibid.*, p. 5.
3. *Ibid.*, p. 21.
4. *Ibid.*, p. 49.
5. *Ibid.*, p. 14.
6. Probate Records, Floyd County, Indiana, Book "B," p. 9.
7. Miscellaneous Court Records of Floyd County, Indiana, Book of Indentures, p. 14. The 1850 census shows that Lewis was living with Stubblefields. He was a "laborer," born in Virginia and unable to read or write. The Stubblefields lived in the same neighborhood as the George Washington Carter family. The 1860 census shows that Lewis moved out of the Stubblefield home after Samuel died. Lewis was a wood sawyer with a real estate value of $200.00. Precilla, ninety-five years old, lived with him. She was born in Virginia and both Frank and Precilla were listed as "paupers."
8. *Ibid.*, p. 23.
9. *Ibid.*, p. 23.
10. *Ibid.*, p. 23.
11. *Ibid.*, p. 24.
12. *Ibid.*, p. 27.
13. *Ibid.*, pp. 31–32.
14. *Ibid.*, p. 42.
15. *Ibid.*, p. 38.
16. *Ibid.*, p. 35.
17. *Ibid.*, p. 36.
18. *Ibid.*, p. 38.
19. *Ibid.*, p. 43.
20. *Ibid.*, pp. 45–46.
21. *Ibid.*, p. 44.
22. *Ibid.*, p. 44.
23. *Ibid.*, p. 46.
24. Miscellaneous Court Records for Floyd County, Indiana, Book of Indentures, p. 47.
25. *Ibid.*, p. 48.
26. *Ibid.*, p. 50.
27. *Ibid.*, p. 50.
28. *Ibid.*, p. 52.
29. *Ibid.*, p. 59.
30. *Ibid.*, p. 55–57.
31. *Ibid.*, p. 58.
32. *Ibid.*, p. 61.
33. *Register of Negroes and Mulattoes in Floyd County*. Carnegie Center for Art and History.
34. Miscellaneous Court Records of Floyd County, Indiana, Book of Indentures, p. 64.
35. *Ibid.*, pp. 77–78.
36. *Ibid.*, pp. 72–74.
37. *Ibid.*, p. 68.
38. *Ibid.*, p. 75.
39. *Ibid.*, p. 77.
40. *Ibid.*, p. 83.
41. *Ibid.*, p. 87.
42. *Ibid.*, p. 95.
43. Coffin, p. 377.

44. Miscellaneous Court Records of Floyd County, Indiana, Book of Indentures, p. 91.
45. Miscellaneous Court Records of Floyd County, Indiana, Book of Indentures, pp. 93–94. Samuel K. Sneed was pastor of First Presbyterian Church and then Second Presbyterian Church in New Albany when it formed in 1837. He also worked for the American Home Missionary Society as an itinerant missionary.
46. *Ibid.*, p. 96.
47. *Ibid.*, p. 101.
48. *Ibid.*, p. 104.
49. *Ibid.*, p. 108.
50. *Ibid.*, p. 108.
51. *Ibid.*, p. 123.

Bibliography

I. Books

Abajian, James De T., ed. *Blacks in Selected Newspapers, Censuses and Other Sources: An Index to Names and Subjects.* Boston: G. K. Hall, 1977.
Ambler, Charles Henry. *A History of Transportation in the Ohio Valley.* Glendale, California: Arthur H. Clark, 1932.
Amster, Betty Lou. *New Albany on the Ohio, Historical Review, 1813–1963.* The New Albany Sesquicentennial, 1963.
Bailey, Hugh C. *Hinton Rowan Helper: Abolitionist-Racist.* Montgomery: University of Alabama Press, 1965.
Baird, Lewis C. *History of Clark County, Indiana.* Indianapolis: B. F. Bowen, 1909.
Barnes, Gilbert Hobbs. *The Antislavery Impulse 1830–1844.* New York: Harcourt, Brace & World, 1964.
Berlin, Ira, et al. *Free at Last: A Documentary History of Slavery, Freedom and the Civil War.* New York: The New Press, 1992.
Bigham, Darrel E. *Towns and Cities of the Lower Ohio.* Lexington: University of Kentucky Press, 1998.
_____. *We Ask Only a Fair Trial: A History of the Black Community at Evansville, Indiana.* Bloomington: Indiana University Press, 1987.
Biographical and Historical Memoirs of Mississippi, v. I. Chicago: Goodspeed, 1891.
Blassingame, John W., ed. *Slave Testimony: Two Centuries of Letters, Speeches, Interviews and Autobiographies.* Baton Rouge: Louisiana State University Press, 1977.
Boles, John B. *Black Southerners, 1619–1869.* Lexington: University Press of Kentucky, 1984.
Borden. W. W. *Personal Reminiscences of Mr. W. W. Borden.* New Albany, Indiana: The Tribune Company, 1901.
Breen, T. H. and Stephen Innes. *Myne Owne Ground.* New York: Oxford University Press, 1980.
Broadwater, Robert. *Desperate Deliverance.* Altoona, Pennsylvania: Daisy, 1998.
Buckmaster, Henrietta. *Let My People Go.* Columbia: University of South Carolina Press, 1992.
Buley, Carlyle R. *The Old Northwest.* vs. I & II. Bloomington: Indiana University Press, 1950.
Carnes, Mark C., John A. Garraty, et al. *Mapping America's Past.* New York: Henry Holt, 1996.
Cartmell, T. K. *Shenandoah Valley Pioneers and Their Descendants.* Berryville, Virginia: Chesapeake, 1963.
Cartwright, Peter. *Autobiography of Peter Cartwright, the Backwoods Preacher.* New York: W. P. Strickland, 1857.

Catterall, Helen T. *Judicial Cases Concerning American Slavery and the Negro*. Washington: Carnegie Institution, 1926–29.
Charter and Ordinances of the City of New Albany. New Albany, Indiana: M. Gregg & Sons, 1855.
Cockrum, William M. *History of the Underground Railroad*. Oakland City, Indiana: J. W. Cockrum, Heritage Books, 1915.
_____. *Pioneer History of Indiana*. Oakland City, Indiana: Oakland City Press, 1907.
Coffin, Levi. *Reminiscences of Levi Coffin*. New York: Arno Press, 1968.
Coleman, J. Winston, Jr. *Slavery Times in Kentucky*. Chapel Hill: The University of North Carolina Press, 1940.
Conn, Samuel. *Centennial Sermon: A Historical Sketch of the First Presbyterian Church, New Albany, Indiana, Given in the Church*. New Albany, Indiana: Grant, Fares & Rodgers, 1876.
Cornish, Dudley Taylor. *The Sable Arm*. New York: W. W. Norton, 1966.
Cox, LaWanda. *Lincoln and Black Freedom, A Study in Presidential Leadership*. Columbia: University of South Carolina Press, 1981.
Crenshaw, Gwendolyn J. *"Bury Me in a Free Land": The Abolitionist Movement in Indiana, 1816–1865*. Indianapolis: Indiana Historical Bureau, Third Printing, 1993.
Cummings, Samuel. *The Western Pilot*. Cincinnati: George Conclin, 1847.
Curtis, Anna L. *Stories of the Underground Railroad*. New York: The Island Workshop Press, 1941.
Dickey, J. M. *A Brief History of the Presbyterian Church in the State of Indiana*. Madison, Indiana: Arion, 1828.
Drimmer, Melvin, ed. *Black History, A Reappraisal*. Garden City, New York: Doubleday, 1968.
Dunn, Jacob Piatt. *Indiana and Indianans*. Chicago & New York: American Historical Society, 1918.
Edson, Hanford A. *Contributions to the Early History of the Presbyterian Church in Indiana*. Cincinnati: Winona, 1898.
Esarey, Logan. *A History of Indiana, from Its Exploration to 1850*. Indianapolis: Hoosier Heritage Press, 1970.
Foner, Eric. *Free Soil, Free Labor, Free Men*. Oxford: Oxford University Press, 1970.
_____. *Reconstruction: America's Unfinished Revolution, 1863–1877*. New York: Harper & Row, 1989.
Gara, Larry. *The Liberty Line*. Lexington: University of Kentucky Press, 1961.
Gibbs, Wilma, ed. *Indiana's African American Heritage*. Indianapolis: Indiana Historical Society, 1993.
Gibson, William H. *History of the United Brothers of Friendship, Part II*. Louisville: Bradley & Gilbert, 1897.
Greene, Robert Ewell. *Black Defenders of America, 1775–1973*. Chicago: Johnson, 1974.
Gresham, Matilda. *The Life of Walter Gresham, 1832–1895*. Chicago: Rand McNally, 1919.
Griffin, Frederick P. *History of Corydon and Harrison County, Indiana: A Scrapbook of Newspaper Clippings*. Jasper, Indiana: Printing Services, 1991.
Haffner, Gerald O. *Everyday Life in Indiana's Old Capitol, 1813–1825*. New Albany: Indiana University Southeast, 1976.
Halsey, LeRoy J. *A History of The McCormick Theological Seminary of the Presbyterian Church*. Chicago: McCormick Seminary Press, 1893.
Hargrave, Frank F. *A Pioneer Railroad of Indiana*. Lafayette, Indiana: Wm. B. Binford, 1932.
Harris, William C. *The Day of the Carpetbagger*. Baton Rouge: Louisiana State University Press, 1979.
Harrison, Lowell H. *The Anti-Slavery Movement in Kentucky*. The Kentucky Bicentennial Bookshelf, 1978.

Helper, Hinton Rowan. *The Impending Crisis in the South*. Miami: Mnemosyne, rep. 1969.
Herron, Shawn M. "Portland." *A Place in Time: The Story of Louisville's Neighborhoods*. Louisville: *Courier-Journal*, 1989.
Hollandsworth, James G., Jr. *The Louisiana Native Guards*. Baton Rouge, Louisiana, 1995.
Holliday, Rev. F. C. *Indiana Methodism*. Cincinnati: Hitchcock & Walden, 1873.
Howard, Victor B. *Black Liberation in Kentucky, Emancipation and Freedom, 1862–1884*. Lexington: The University Press of Kentucky, 1983.
_____. *Conscience and Slavery*. Kent, Ohio: Kent State University Press, 1990.
Hurmence, Belinda, ed. *My Folks Don't Want Me to Talk About Slavery*. Winston-Salem, North Carolina: John F. Blair, 1984.
Indiana Historic Sites and Structures Inventory: City of New Albany Interim Report. New Albany: City of New Albany, Indiana, September, 1994.
Indiana Historic Sites and Structures Inventory: Floyd County Interim Report. Carol Tobe, pre., Indianapolis: March 1978.
Johnson, David W. *Hamline University, a History*. St. Paul: North Central, 1980.
Katz, William Loren. *The Black West*. New York: Simon & Schuster, 1996.
Kentucky's Black Heritage. Frankfort: Kentucky Commission on Human Rights, Galen Martin, exec. dir., 1971.
Lefler, Hugh Talmage. *Southern Sketches*. No. 1. Charlotteville, Virginia: The Historical Publishing Co., 1935.
Lesick, Lawrence Thomas. *The Lane Rebels: Evangelicalism and Antislavery to Antebellum America*. Metuchen, New York: Scarecrow, 1980.
Lucas, Marion B. *A History of Blacks in Kentucky, from Slavery to Segregation, 1760–1891*. vol. 1. Lexington: The Kentucky Historical Society, 1992.
McClure, James G. K. *1848–1932, The Story of the Life and Work of the Presbyterian Theological Seminary, Chicago*. Chicago: Lakeside Press, R. R. Donnelly & Sons, 1929.
McCormick Theological Seminary of the Presbyterian Church; General Catalogue, 1830–1912. Chicago: McCormick Theological Seminary, 1912.
McPherson, James M. *Ordeal by Fire*. New York: A. Knopf, 1982.
Martin, Asa Earl. *The Anti-Slavery Movement in Kentucky Prior to 1850*. Louisville: The Standard Printing Company of Louisville, 1918.
Mathews, Donald G. *Slavery and Methodism, A Chapter in American Morality, 1780–1845*. Princeton, New Jersey: Princeton University Press, 1965.
Mayer, F. E. *The Religious Bodies of America*. St. Louis: Concordia Publishing House, 1961.
Miles, Frank. *There's No Presbyterian Church on Presbyterian Avenue*, 1986. Madison, Indiana: The 175th Anniversary History Committee, 1990.
Miller, John W. *Indiana Newspaper Bibliography*. Indianapolis: Indiana Historical Society, 1982.
Miller, Randall M., and John David Smith, ed. *Dictionary of Afro-American Slavery*. New York: Greenwood, 1988.
Miller, William Lee. *Arguing About Slavery*. New York: Knopf, 1996.
Moebs, Thomas Truxtum. *Black Soldiers — Black Sailors — Black Ink: Research Guide on African-Americans in the United States Military History, 1526–1900*. Chesapeake Bay, [Virginia]: Moebs, 1994.
Morris, Harvey. *The Underground Railroad, History of Washington County*. Salem, Indiana: Washington County Historical Society, 1993.
Murray, Andrew E. *Presbyterians and the Negro: A History*. Philadelphia: Presbyterian Historical Society, 1966.
Nevin, Alfred, ed. *Encyclopedia of the Presbyterian Church in the United States of America*. Philadelphia: Presbyterian Encyclopedia Co., 1884.

New Albany City Directory and Business Mirror for 1856–57. New Albany, Indiana: A. C. Grooms & W. T. Smith, 1856.
New Albany City Directory, City Guide & Business Mirror for 1860. New Albany, Indiana: E. Coy & Co., 1860.
New Albany Directory, City Guide & Business Mirror, 1863–64. New Albany, Indiana: Williams & Co., 1863.
New Albany Directory for 1871–72. New Albany, Indiana: John R. Nunemacher, 1871.
Nichols, Charles H. *Many Thousands Gone.* Bloomington: Indiana University Press, 1969.
Nieman, Donald G. *The Day of the Jubilee: The Civil War Experience of Black Southerners.* New York: Garland, 1994.
Palmer, Herriott C. *The First Presbyterian Church of Franklin, Indiana.* Greenfield, Indiana: Wm. Mitchell Printing Co., 1946.
Peckham, Howard H. *Indiana: A Bicentennial History.* New York: W. W. Norton, 1978.
Peissner, Elias. *The American Question in Its National Aspect.* New York: Negro Universities Press, 1970.
Phillips, Cliffton J. *Indiana in Transition.* Indianapolis: Indiana Historical Bureau, 1968.
Potter, David Morris. *The Impending Crisis, 1848–1861.* New York: Harper & Row, 1976.
Presbyterian Reunion, A Memorial Volume: 1837–1871. New York: DeWitt C. Lent, 1870.
Quarles, Benjamin. *The Negro in the Civil War.* Boston: Little, Brown, 1953.
Rawick, George P. *The American Slave: A Composite Autobiography.* Westport, Connecticut: Greenwood, 1972.
Ripley, C. Peter, ed. *Black Abolitionist Papers.* 5 vols. Chapel Hill: University of North Carolina Press, 1985–93.
Robbins, Coy D. *Indiana Negro Register, 1852–1855.* Bowie: Heritage Books, 1994.
_____. *Reclaiming African Heritage at Salem, Indiana.* Bowie: Heritage Books, 1995.
Robinson, Mona. *Who's Your Hoosier Ancestor?* Bloomington: Indiana University Press, 1992.
Rudolph, L. C. *Hoosier Faiths.* Bloomington: Indiana University Press, 1995.
_____. *Hoosier Zion: The Presbyterians in Early Indiana.* New Haven, Connecticut: Yale University Press, 1963.
_____. *Indiana Letters: Abstracts of Letters from Missionaries on the Indiana Frontier to the AHMS, 1824–1893.* 3 vols. Ann Arbor, Michigan: Univ. Microfilms International, 1979.
Rule, Lucien V., and Thomas B. Terhune. *History of Hutchinson Memorial Presbyterian Church of New Albany.* Pamphlet. New Albany, Indiana, 1937.
Runyon, Randolph Paul. *Delia Webster and the Underground Railroad.* Lexington: University Press of Kentucky, 1996.
Saulman, Earl. *A History of the Blacks in Harrison County.* (Unpublished).
Savage, W. Sherman. *Controversy Over the Distribution of Abolition Literature, 1830–1860.* Jefferson City, Missouri: Association for the Study of Negro Life and History, 1938.
Scribner, B. F. *How Soldiers Were Made.* New Albany, Indiana: B. F. Scribner, 1887.
Siebert, Wilbur H. *The Underground Railroad, From Slavery to Freedom.* New York: Macmillan, 1898.
Simons, Richard S. and Francis H. Parker. *The Railroads of Indiana.* Bloomington: Indiana University Press, 1997.
Smith, Page. *Trial by Fire.* New York: McGraw-Hill, 1982.
Stampp, Kenneth M. *Indiana Politics During the Civil War.* Indianapolis: Indiana Historical Bureau, 1949.
Stephens, John Vant. *The Founding of Lane Seminary.* A reprint by permission from *One Hundred and Fifty Years of Presbyterianism in the Ohio Valley.* Cincinnati: 1941.
Tappan, Lewis. *The Evangelical War Against Slavery.* Cleveland: Case Western Reserve, 1969.

Terrell, W. H. H. Adjutant General Indiana. *Roster of Enlisted Men, 1861–1865.* Indianapolis: M. Douglass, 1867.
Thornbrough, Emma Lou. *The Negro in Indiana Before 1900.* Bloomington: Indiana University Press, 1993.
Thornbrough, Emma Lou, and Dorothy Riker. *Readings in Indiana History.* Indianapolis: Indiana Historical Bureau, 1956.
Trotter, Joe William, Jr. *River Jordan.* Lexington: University of Kentucky Press, 1998.
Trudeau, Noah Andre. *Like Men of War: Black Troops in the Civil War 1862–1865.* Boston: Little, Brown, 1998.
Wade, Richard C. *Slavery in the Cities.* New York: Oxford University Press, 1964.
Williams, L. A. *History of the Ohio Falls Cities and Their Counties.* Cleveland: L. A. Williams, 1882.
Wilson, George R. *Early Indiana Trails and Surveys.* Indiana Historical Society Publication, Vol. 6, No. 3, Indianapolis: C. E. Pauley, 1919.
Wilson, Joseph Thomas. *The Black Phalanx, A History of the Negro Soldiers of the United States in the Wars of 1775–1812 and 1861–1865.* Hartford, Connecticut: American, 1890.
Wolfe, Samuel M. *Helper's Impending Crisis Dissected.* New York: Negro University Press, 1969.
Woodson, Carter G. *A Century of Negro Migration.* New York: Russell & Russell, 1969.
Wyatt-Brown, Bertram. *Lewis Tappan and the Evangelical War Against Slavery.* Cleveland: Press of Case Western Reserve, 1969.
Yater, George H. *200 Years at the Falls of the Ohio.* Louisville: Heritage Corporation of Louisville and Jefferson County, 1979.

II. Manuscript Collections and Archives

Amistad Research Center, Tulane University
DePauw University Archives and Special Collections
Duggan Library Archives, Hanover College
Eidson Archives, Iliff School of Theology
Ernest Miller White Library, Louisville Presbyterian Seminary
The Filson Club Historical Society, Louisville, Kentucky
Hamline University Archives
Howard Steamboat Museum
Indiana Historical Society Library
Indiana State Library
Indiana University Library
Maine Historical Society Archives
Minnesota Historical Society Library
Mississippi Department of Archives and History
Missouri United Methodist Archives, Central Methodist College
National Cemetery Records, Zachary Taylor Cemetery, Louisville, Kentucky
Ohio Historical Society, Library Division, Archives
Presbyterian Historical Society Library
Smith, Isaac P., private collection of letters and papers
Stuart B. Wrege Indiana History Room, New Albany–Floyd County Public Library.
University of Louisville: Black Studies Collection

III. Articles

"Address of the New York City Anti-Slavery Society." *Anti-slavery Reporter* 1, no. 5.
Bates, Alan L., et al. "Falls Cities Ferries: A Note." *Indiana Magazine of History* XCV (September 1999).
Berry, Mary F. "Negro Troops in Blue and Gray: The Louisiana Native Guards, 1861–1863." Published in Donald G. Nieman, *The Day of the Jubilee*. New York: Garland, (1994).
Blockson, Charles L. "Escape from Slavery." *National Geographic Magazine*. Washington, D.C.: National Geographic Society (July 1984).
Bogle, Victor M. "A View of New Albany Society at Mid-Nineteenth Century." *Indiana Magazine of History* LIII (June 1957).
Bovard, Freeman Daily. "Benjamin Franklin Crary, D.D." *Methodist Review*, XII (March 1896).
Collins, Mary S. Davis. "New Albany, With a Short Sketch of the Scribner Family." *Indiana Magazine of History* XVII (September 1921).
Edson, H. A. "An Indiana Pioneer," *The Princeton Review* 3d ser. VI Princeton: J. M. Sherwood (1877).
Fairchild, James W. "The Underground Railroad." *Western Reserve Historical Society* Tract 87, IV, Cleveland, an address delivered by the ex-president of Oberlin (January 24, 1895).
Filler, Louis. "Anti-Slavery Movements in the United States." *Colliers Encyclopedia* II, Crowell-Collier (1965 ed.).
Funk, Arville L. "The Hoosier Scrapbook." *Louisville Times* (October 4, 1976).
Guthrie, J. M. "Sesquicentennial Scrapbook: The U.G. Railroad." Jeffersonville, Indiana: *Jeffersonville Evening News* (February 28,1967).
"Hannibal's Retreat." *The Appeal*, A National African American Newspaper, Boston. (July 25, 1891).
Hoffmeier, James. "Israel in Egypt." *Time* (December 14, 1998).
Howard, Victor B. "Sectionalism, Slavery and Education—New Albany vs. Danville, Kentucky." *The Register of The Kentucky Historical Society* 68, #4 (October 1970).
Joshi, Manoj K. and Joseph P. Reidy, "To Come Forward and Aid in Putting Down this Unholy Rebellion: The Officers of Louisiana's Free Black Native Guard During the Civil War Era." Published in Donald G. Nieman, *The Day of the Jubilee*. New York: Garland (1994).
Kuhns, Frederick, "Slavery and Missions in the Old Northwest." *Journal of the Presbyterian Historical Society* XXIV (December 1946).
Lyons, Rev. John P. "The Attitude of Presbyterians in Ohio, Indiana and Illinois Toward Slavery 1825–1861." *Journal of Presbyterian History* XI no. 2 (June 1921).
McCoy, Lon. "Road to Freedom." *Homespun Magazine* I No. 5 (April 1949).
Money, Charles. "The Fugitive Slave Law in Indiana." *Indiana Magazine of History* XVII (September 1921).
Myers, John L. "The Antislavery Agency System in Maine, 1836-1838." *Maine Historical Society Quarterly*, XXIII, no. 2, Orono, Maine: U. Maine Orono (Fall 1983).
Newson, Vida. "Phases of Southeastern Indiana History." *Indiana Magazine of History* XX (March 1924).
Perring, Thomas Carter. "The New Albany–Salem Railroad: Incidents of Road and Men." *Indiana Magazine of History* XV (December 1919).
Poucher, John, "Social Effects of the Monon Railway in Indiana." *Indiana Magazine of History* XII (1916).
Sabin, Harold. "Underground Railroad Had Many Routes and Stations in Indiana." Indianapolis, Indiana: *Indianapolis Star* (March 6, 1966).
Smith, George Winston. "Fugitive Slave Laws." *Colliers Encyclopedia* 10, Crowell-Collier (1965 ed.).

Smith, Henry Lester, "The Underground Railroad in Monroe County." *Indiana Magazine of History* (September 1917).
Thomas, Luke W. "The Thomas Family." *Indiana Magazine of History* XXIII (December 1923).
Trout, Allan M. "The Civil War in Kentucky, 1861–1865; Louisville: A Foot in Each Camp." *Courier Journal Magazine*, Louisville (November 20, 1960).
Veasey, Tyler. "Clock in Steeple High Above Main Street Faithful After 99 Years." New Albany, Indiana: *New Albany Tribune* (1949).
Webster, Donovan. "Traveling the Long Road to Freedom, One Step at a Time." *Smithsonian*, Washington, D.C.: Smithsonian Institution (October 1996).

IV. Dissertations

Cheaney, Henry Ellis. "Attitudes of the Indiana Pulpit and Press Toward the Negro: 1860–1880." Unpublished Ph.D. dissertation, the University of Chicago, June, 1961.
Howard, Victor B. "The Anti-Slavery Movement in the Presbyterian Church, 1835–1861." Ph.D. dissertation, Ohio State University, 1961.
Kuhns, Frederick Irving. "The AHMS in Relation to the Anti-Slavery Controversy in the Old Northwest, 1826–1861." Ph.D. thesis, Billings, Montana, 1959.
Lipin, Lawrence M. "Producers, Proletarians and Politicians: Opposition and Accommodation in the Small Industrializing City, 1850–1887." Ph.D. dissertation, University of California, Los Angeles, Ann Arbor, Michigan: University Microfilms International, 1989.
Miller, Harold V. "The Industrial Development of New Albany." M.A. dissertation, Chicago: University of Chicago, 1934.
Miller, Marion Clinton. "The Anti-Slavery Movement in Indiana." Ph.D. dissertation, University of Michigan, 1938.
Zimmerman, Carl Arthur. "A History of the School, City of New Albany, Indiana." M.A. dissertation, Indiana University, 1932.

V. Newspapers

Frederick Douglass' Newspaper. Various years on microfilm.
Louisville Daily Courier. Various years on microfilm.
New Albany Daily Commercial. Various years on microfilm, Stuart B. Wrege Indiana History Room, New Albany–Floyd County Public Library.
New Albany Daily Ledger. Various years on microfilm, Stuart B. Wrege Indiana History Room, New Albany–Floyd County Public Library.
New Albany Tribune. Various years on microfilm, Stuart B. Wrege Indiana History Room, New Albany–Floyd County Public Library.

Index

(Names listed in Appendices A, C, D and E are not necessarily included in this Index.)

Abbeville District (South Carolina) 156, 158, 159
Abolition Intelligencer 183n.64
Abolition Movement: in Indiana 27; in Kentucky 35; in New Albany 47–48; and the Republican Party 26; Helperism 28–31
African Americans: cemeteries 63, 64, 68–69, 75, 77, 109; early settlement of 27, 59–66; occupations 66–68, 76; Underground Railroad 80–83
African Methodist Episcopal Church: in New Albany 69–71; in Jeffersonville 88; aid in education of blacks 70, 71
Akers, Thomas (New Albany Town Marshal) 16, 22, 92
Akin, Isaac N. 20, 121
Aldrich, John 59
Allen, Diarca Howe 183n.54
American Colonization Society *see* colonization
American Home Missionary Society 13; employees of 43, 44, 173n.44
Anderson Guards 19
Anderson, Melinda, Deed of Manumission 161
Anti-slavery: meaning of term 26; conventions 32, 88, 199n.29; societies 33, 34, 88
Armstrong, C. Q. (Kentucky slave owner) 87
Arterburn Slave Pens 6
Atterbury, The Rev. John Guest 38; as anti-slavery advocate 43, 44, 45; Pastor of Second Presbyterian Church 43, 97, 104; relationship with Levi Coffin 45, 46
Atterbury, William 43
Augusta County (Virginia) 163
Ayres University *see* New Albany Theological Seminary
Azalia (Indiana) 88, 89

Badger, Milton 44
Baeck, The Rev. Robert L. 181n.27
Bailey, Gamaliel (anti-slavery advocate) 34
Baird, Samuel John 52
Baker, James 4
Baker, Knolly 86
Ball, Flamen 163
Ballard, William 158
Baptist Church 38, 99, 100
Barnett, Lewis (runaway slave) 83
Battle Creek (Michigan) 84
Beadle, The Rev. E. R. 43
Beckwith, Charles Henry, Freedom Papers 139
Beckwith, Quinos 139
Bedford (Indiana) 25, 43, 54, 94
Beecher, Henry Ward (supporter of colonization) 32; as "political" preacher 55
Beecher, Lyman 50, 179n.6; 182n.52
Bell, David Family: Charles and Horace, as Underground Railroad agents 86
Bentley, Rebecca, Deed of Manumission 163
Bethel AME 70
Bethlehem (Indiana) 49
Betsy Jane (indentured servant) 4

Betsy and Letina (slaves) 43
"Big Ben of New Albany" *see* Presbyterian churches
Bill of Sale: explanation of 135
Bishop, The Rev. John 13, 43; Lucy 100, 102, 142
Bishop, Robert H. 52; as anti-slavery advocate 43
Bishop, Tom (runaway slave) 92
"Black Friday," Portsmouth (Ohio) 124
Black, Morgan: proof of freedom 163
"Black" Republicans *see* Republicans
Black, The Rev. John 43
Blair, John (abolitionist) 86
Bloomington (Indiana) 86, 94, 96
Blue River (Indiana) 100
Bogert, Henry 154
Boiling Spring in Floyd County (Indiana) 116
Bolivar County (Mississippi) 169
Bolivar (Tennessee) 76
Bonner, James O. (Chicago businessman) 71
Borden (Indiana) 96
Borden, William Wallace 96
Boyd, George W. (slave owner in Mobile, Alabama) 165
Boyd, Jesse and family: Sarah, Ann, Barbara, Elizabeth, Martha Ann, John Amos, Franklin, Farra Lawundia, freedom papers 158
Boyd, William (black settler) 67
Boyet, J. B.: allegiance to the Union 11
Boyle, General J. T. (commander

211

Western District of Kentucky) 76
Bracken County (Kentucky) 181n.25
Brandenburg (Kentucky) 86, 116
Breckinridge County (Kentucky) 10
Brent, Julia (black teacher) 70
Briddle, The Rev. R. R. (black preacher in Louisville, Kentucky) 187n. 42
Brook, The Rev. B. L.: mission work in New Albany 70, 81
Brooks, Arthur (slave owner in Kentucky) 65
Brooks, James: as elder at Second Presbyterian Church) 47, 49; President New Albany–Salem Railroad 47, 49, 68, 94; Assistant Quartermaster 47, 49
Brown, Jesse J. 75
Brown, John (abolitionist) 31
Brown, John (Kentucky resident) 9
Brown, Patrick, Freedom Papers 160
Brown, The Rev. Thomas J. (Kentucky AME preacher) 70
Brownstown (Indiana) 41
Bruner, John 154
Buckner, Mary: proof of freedom 151
Buena Vista (Indiana) 63
Buffum, Arnold (anti-slavery league advocate) 35
Buford, Milton (Burford) 120
Buford, Richard, Deed of Manumission 135
Burch, Adam (black farmer) 67
Burgoyne, John (judge in Cincinnati) 167
Burleigh, Charles C. (anti-slavery advocate) 34
Burnett, Alexander S. (Mayor of New Albany) 24
Burney, William A. 75
Busby, Tunica County (Mississippi) 79
Bush, William 68
Butchertown, New Albany 187n.31
Butler, Albert (early black resident of New Albany) 74
Byerly, Solomon 4
Byrne, Leonide *see* Adelade Goram

Cabin Creek, Randolph County (Indiana) 80
Cairo (Illinois) 34, 36, 66, 74
Camden (Indiana) 89

Campbell, Douglas (slave owner) 165
Campbell, Elijah and Nancy (early leaders in AME Church) 69
Campbell, J. O. (Louisville merchant) 97
Campbell, Polly (black Civil War nurse) 77
Campbell, R. H. (New Albany freight commissioner) 97, 194n.53
Canada 5, 13, 70, 80–81, 91–92, 124, 198–199n.29
Canton (Indiana) 88
Carpenter, Franklin 75, 191n.103
Carrol Parish (Louisiana) 155
Carter, Artemas (Chicago businessman) 71
Carter, Edward 127
Carter, Edward (Louisiana Native Guard) 77–79
Carter, Emanuel Moore: proof of freedom 137
Carter, George Washington 24, 46, 70, 72, 81, 96, 124–128, 147, 198n.29
Carter, Hannibal: Louisiana Native Guard 77–79; Gray-Carter Civil Rights Bill 79–80, 107
Carter, Harriett Hill 46
Carter, James 81, 127
Carter, John family: Betsy, Sarah, Sally, Carey, Betsy, freedom papers 139, 164
Carter, Jonas (black farmer) 67
Carter, Solon: early immigration of 63
Cartwright, The Rev. Peter 53, 88
Casey, Samuel, Deed of Manumission 167
Cass County (Indiana) 34
Caution, David: execution of 16
Centenary Methodist Church *see* Methodist Churches
Chambersburg (Indiana) 25, 87
Charlestown (Indiana) 80, 87, 100
Cheever, George B. 55
Chicago (Illinois) 71, 94, 107
Chilicothe (Ohio) 124
Christian Review 87
Cincinnati (Ohio) 8, 10, 33, 50, 52, 84, 88, 97, 121–122, 199n.4
Cincinnati Herald 17, 34
Civil War: enlistment of black soldiers 74–76; hospitals 19, 76, 103–104, 195n.16; 23rd Reg. Indiana Volunteers 47, 77;

38th Reg. Indiana Volunteers 25; 53rd Reg. Indiana Volunteers 77
Clapp, Dr. William Ashbel 46, 137
Clark County (Indiana) 12, 13, 16, 20, 27, 53, 80, 86, 87, 88, 89, 100, 120
Clark, James (anti-slavery advocate) 86
Clark, Milton (Underground Railroad operator from Portland, Kentucky) 91
Clark, William and Jerry (black settlers) 60, 67
Clarksville (Indiana) 12, 13, 16, 20, 27, 53, 80, 86–89, 100, 120
Clay, Cassius M. 18, 88; and Helperism 29
Clay, Henry (blacksmith) 73, 74, 81, 127, 149
Claysburg Settlement, Jeffersonville (Indiana) 88
Clement, John: and the Underground Railroad 120
Clien, John family: Polly, Jim, Sally, John, Eleanor, Ben, Elizabeth, freedom papers 156
Clipper, Rebecca: indenture of 4
Clouster, Ann Mariah: freedom papers 152–153; Joseph, Joseph, Jr., 153
Cloverport (Kentucky) 10
Cockrum, William M. 34
Codding, Ichabod (anti-slavery advocate) 34
Coffin, Levi 10, 38, 84–86, 88, 97, 167; in Clark County, Indiana 88; in Floyd County, Indiana 38, 45–46
Coldwater (Michigan) 84
Colonization 21, 29, 31–33
Colporteur 35, 181n.25
Confederate States of America 7, 74
Conner, Benjamin 158, 191n.100
Conner, William C. 137, 153
Conover, John D. (Alabama slaveowner) 161
Contraband Quarters 76
Contraband soldiers 6, 21, 76
Cook, Benjamin (black farmer) 67
Corps d' Afrique 78
Corydon (Indiana) 25, 37, 86
County Poor House, Floyd County 4
Cousins, George 63
Covenanter Presbyterians *see* Presbyterianism

Cozzins, Elizabeth (alias Buford) 135, 136
Crabb, John (slave owner) 167
Craigg, Sarah: proof of freedom 162
Crary, The Rev. Benjamin Franklin: as pastor of Wesley Chapel 13; views on slavery 54–57; conflict with *New Albany Daily Ledger* 54–55
Cravens, The Rev. William 53
Crawford County (Indiana) 35, 86
Crawfordsville (Indiana) 94
Crowe, John Finley family *183n.64*; John and Thomas 52
Culbertson, William S. 4, 152
Cummings, Jacob (runaway slave) 80–81
Cunningham, James R. 91, 123
Curry, Samuel and William (anti-slavery advocates) 86

Daniels, Col. N. W. 79
Danville (Kentucky) 16
Davis, John S. 152
Davis, Maria and Family: Jesse, William, Mary and Adeline Deed of Manumission 138,167
Davis, Squire (slave owner in Jefferson County, Mississippi) 138
Dawson, William Frank 75
Day, E. R. 137
Dayton, Caleb C. (white settler) 69
Daytown (northern suburb of New Albany) 23
Dearborn County (Indiana) 34
Decatur (Indiana) 34, 37, 84
Delany, Dr. Martin 123
Democratic Party 26, 52
Denice, William (slave owner in Mobile, Alabama) 165
Depauw Hotel 104
Devore, Peter and Porterfield 9, 10
Dickey, The Rev. John M. 88
Discrimination *see* racial discrimination
Division Street School 71
Dodson, John D. (Civil War veteran) 75
Dole, Eben (abolitionist) *178n.43*
Dole, John (anti-slavery guard) 33, 34, 36
Doll, James A. 160; member 23rd Reg., Indiana Volunteers 47, 77
Douglas, Stephen A. 26

Douglass, Frederick 123; and colonization 32–33, 71
Dove, The Rev. William A. 70
Downey, Robert: and colonization 31
Dungen, Ann: indenture of 4, 121
Dunn, Capt. W. B. 90

Edmonds, John W. *191n.103*
Edwards, Martin (black farmer) 67
Ellaville County (Georgia) 11
"Ellen," Deed of Manumission 165
"Elizabeth," Deed of Manumission 165
Elliott, John (Kentucky slave owner) 43
Emancipation Proclamation 6–7, 18, 21, 67, 84
Evansville (Indiana) 29, 36, 84
Ewing, Robert (anti-slavery advocate) 86
Exclusion Act of 1851: explanation of 20; 1852 act passed to enforce 134, 135

Fairbank, Calvin 88, 92, 123
Fairview Cemetery 68, 96, 124
Fall Creek Anti-Slavery League 34
Falling Run Creek: Floyd County 10, 88–89; baptisms performed in 69
Faris, The Rev. J. B. (anti-slavery advocate) 86
Faris, T. N. (anti-slavery advocate) 86
Farmers Feed and Supply Store *see* Sweet Gum Stable
Farmland (Indiana) 89
Farrar, Tandy R. 157
Fayette County (Indiana) 37
Fayette County (Kentucky) 28
Fee, Rev. John G.: abolitionist work 44, *183n.54*; employee of the AHMS 44
Fenwick,William, Bill of Sale, Deed of Manumission 168
Ferries, Floyd County 89–90; *see also* Ohio River
Field, Elizabeth J. (Kentucky slave owner) 168
Field, Dr. Nathaniel 15, 87, 88
Fields, Abraham (Kentucky slave owner) 27
Findley, Caesar (black farmer) 63, 147
Findley, Elias,Thomas and Andrew J. 63

Findley, Joseph (colored Republican radical) 81
Findley, Josiah and Mary (black farmer) 63–67
Findley, Peter 81–82
Findley, Robert 4
Findley, William W.: and colonization *177n.33*
Finley, Josiah: heirs *186n.18*
Finney, Amanda (servant of W. A. Clapp) 46
Finney, John (black settler) 64, 67, 81
Finney, William 80
First Presbyterian Church, New Albany *see* Presbyterianism
Fisher, The Rev. D. W. *183n.54*
Fisher, Nelson family: Margaret, William and May, Freedom Papers 167
Fitch, Mason C. 137
Five Mile Lane (Floyd County) 72, 113–114
Flinn, Samuel family: Louisa, James George, Maida, Zion, Ellendar, Ann Louisa, proof of freedom 159
Floyd, Mahala 4
Floyd County *passim*
Follin, Mrs. M. W. (slave owner in Mobile, Alabama) 165
Ft. Wayne (Indiana) 84
Fountain City (Indiana) 84, 89
Fowles, John 127
Foy, Sarah A. (slave owner in Pt. Gibson, Mississippi) 163
Framell, Dennis (slave owner) 11
Franklin County (Kentucky) 160
Franklin County (Mississippi) 155
Franklin Township (Floyd County, Indiana): black settlers 59–63, 67–68
Frederick Douglass' Paper 71, 123
Free Democratic Association 88
Free Masons *see* Masons
Free Negro Law (Kentucky) 8
Free Soil: explanation of 26; convention in Indianapolis 88; in Pittsburgh 123;
Freedmen's Aid Associations 44, 46, 57
Freedom Land *see* African American cemeteries
Fremont, John Charles 26
Frost, Israel 158
Fugitive Slave Law of 1793: explanation of 11
Fugitive Slave Law of 1850: explanation of 11, 136

Fugitive slaves *see* Runaway slaves
Fulton, John (black farmer) 67

Garrett, William H. 123
Garrison, Matthew (Louisville slave dealer) 6
Garrison, William Lloyd 26, 87
Gaslin, William H. (Kentucky slave owner) 170
Gaston, Jack and Polly Smith: court refusal to marry 20
Gatewood, Emily, Deed of Manumission and proof of freedom 168
George (runaway slave) 8
Georgetown Township (Floyd County, Indiana) 67
Gibson County (Indiana) 72, 123
Gibson, W. H. 72, 123–124
Gilchrist, Captain 93
Gillespie, J. P.: and border rangers 19, *175n.28*
Gleaves, Richard H. (Grand Master of Ohio) 72
Glenn, The Rev. Peter 116, 117
Glover, Isabella family: Rebecca, George, John G., proof of freedom 159
Goen(s), Henderson: evidence of freedom 160
Goins, Zeke: and runaway slave assistance 80
Goram, Adelade, and family: Leonide Byrne, Cornelia Young, Tom Hamilton, bill of sale, power of attorney, Deed of Manumission 162
Gordon, Samuel (anti-slavery advocate) 86
Graham, Emma (teacher for Western Freedmen's Aid Society) 44
Graham, John 5
Grainger County (Tennessee) 160
Granger, General Gordon 16
Gray, Mariah: and slavery in Indiana 3
Greeley, Horace: relationship with Hinton R. Helper *177n.20*
Greencastle (Indiana) 94
Greenley, William J. 70, 71
Greenville Township (Floyd County, Indiana) 4, 116
Gresham, Walter Q. 77
Griffin Tract (in New Albany) 62, 64, 152
Grisney, Francie (black farmer) 67

Grundy, Burrell Stapleton 109
Grundy, Charles Meredith 109, 114
Grundy, William I. (black teacher) 70
Gruyan (Marshal of New Albany) 9
Gurley, R. R.: support of colonization 31
Gwin, Josiah 11, 136; Appendix F *Passim*

Hagan, John (black farmer) 67, 156; proof of freedom 152; Rachael 152
Haines, James M. (conductor, New Albany–Salem Railroad) 94
Hamilton (Indiana) 84
Hamilton County (Ohio) 167
Hamilton, Tom *see* Adelade Goram freedom papers
Hankins, John (black settler) 67
Hanover, J. T. (alias John Hansen) 35
Hanover College (anti-slavery organization) 34
Hanover (Indiana) 100
Harding, William 72, 81, 123–124, 127
Harding, William, Jr. (black teacher in New Albany) 70
Harper, Pampia (black settler) 67
Harris, Florence, Deed of Manumission 170
Harris, Mary, Deed of Manumission 170
Harrison, James G. 136
Harrison County (Indiana) 12, 35, 36, 37, 42, 60, 63, 81, 86, 117, 120
Harry (a slave) 3
Hart, Samuel 52
Hartman, Louis 58, 109, 128–130
Hasbrook, Thomas A. (slave owner) 166
Hawkins, Cupid family: Nancy and Maria 4
Hawkins, William 86
Head, Thomas L. and Emeline M. 155
Helper, Hinton Rowan 41; as abolitionist 28; as racist 28; relationship to the Republican party 28–29
Helperism 28–31
Henderson (Kentucky) *191n.5*
Henderson, William: proof of freedom 157
Hendrick, William B. 4

Henry (runaway slave) 36
Hibben, The Rev. William W.: support of colonization *177n.35*; as "political" preacher 55
Hicklin, The Rev. Lewis (abolitionist in Jefferson County, Indiana) *184n.69*
Hill, H. R. W. (slave owner in Louisiana) 162
Hill, John 82, 127
Hill, Margaretta E. (slave owner in Louisiana) 162
Hite, John (anti-slavery advocate) 86
Holmes, Oliver Wendell *182n.40*
Hooper, Dummer (Mayor of New Albany, 1863 to 1865) 57
Hooper, The Rev. William S. 57, 58
Hooper, S. K. (member 23rd Reg., New Albany Volunteers) 57, 58
Hopkins County (Kentucky): Helperism 29
Hosea, William: arrest of 9, 123
Houston Hollow (Ohio) 124
Howard, Frank (stable owner) 106
Howard, John 13, 14
Hughes, John P. (slave owner, Bolivar County, Mississippi) 169
Huncilman, A.: recruitment of black troops in New Albany 75
Hurd, Beverly 61
Hurlbut & Mann, and construction of Second Presbyterian Church 103
Hurlbut, Edward W. 168

Impending Crisis of the South 28–31
Indenture system: in Indiana 3–4; black indentured servants listed 4–5
Indian Creek (Harrison County, Indiana) 36
"Indiana": power of attorney, Deed of Manumission 169
Indiana Theological Seminary *see* New Albany Theological Seminary
Indianapolis (Indiana) 75
Irvin, D. S. (anti-slavery advocate) 86
Irwin, Nettie (WPA interview) 90
Israel, A. F. 158
Israel Boarding House 24
Israelite 87

Index

Jackson County (Indiana) 37
"Jane" (runaway slave) 82
Jay County (Indiana) 34
Jefferson County (Indiana): anti-slavery society 34
Jefferson County (Kentucky) *passim*
Jefferson County, (Mississippi) 138
Jeffersonville (Indiana) 13, 14, 15, 17, 21, 25, 35, 69, 80, 87, 88, 92, 97, 100, *181n.28*
Jeffersonville Republican 15, 17, 87
Jennings County (Indiana) 37
Jocelyn, Jared C. (Judge, Floyd Common Pleas Court) 11, 134; Appendix E, *Passim*
Johnson, Hannah (black member of Second Presbyterian Church) 46
Johnson, Nancy 100
Johnson, Quintini: proof of freedom 151
Johnson, Rachel: proof of freedom 151
Johnson, Samuel 152; proof of freedom 169
Jones, John (Chicago businessman) 71
Journal of Christianity 87
Justice, Hugh (black farmer) 67

Kansas Nebraska Act 26
Keniday, Sarah Ann 157
Kennedy, Isaac (benefactor) 156
Kent, Phineas M. 118
Kentucky and Indiana Bridge (K & I) 68, 89, 129
Kerr, Michael C. (benefactor) 166
Key, Gwinn M. 138
Key, Isham 137
Key, Payton (Kentucky slave owner) 163
Kidnapping: of free blacks 6
Kimbrough, Pearl Grundy 68, 100, 108
King, H. A. 103
Kirkwood, Ann and William (Kentucky slave owners) 4
Knepfley, John 160
Knight, John 87
Knight, Sidney (Civil War Veteran) 75
Knoefel, August 53, 58, 111–113
Knox County (Kentucky) 43

Lacey, Charles 80
Lacey, Samuel 81
Lafayette (Indiana) 84
Lafayette Township (Floyd County, Indiana) 63–64, 67
Laforce, Benjamin 68
Lafourch Interim (Louisiana) 155
Lane Seminary 33, 43, 50–52
Lapalle, Richard 122
Lawrence County (Indiana) 138
Leeper, D. J. 89
Leonard, Somerville E. 162, 163
Letcher, William (Kentucky slave owner) 65
Lewis, Francis (Frank), Deed of Manumission 153
Lewis, Henry 65; Deed of Manumission 164
Lewis, Precilla 65
Lexington (Kentucky) 16
"Liberator" (wagon used to hide runaway slaves) 90
Lick Creek (Indiana) 25, 69, 108
Limestone County (Alabama) 156, 157
Lincoln, Abraham 74; attitude toward slavery 6–7, 18; Lincoln Campaign Club in Floyd Cty. 47–48; members *182n.44*
Lincoln County (Maine): anti-slavery movement 33
Lindley, Eli and Elizabeth 108
Lindsey, Patsy (runaway slave in New Albany) 47, 77
Lindsley, William (alias "Bill Slick"), Bill of Sale, Deed of Manumission 166
Little, The Rev. Henry (anti-slavery advocate) 44
Locklayer, Franklin: proof of freedom 156
Locklayer, Suckey: proof of freedom 156–157; *191n.103*
Locklayer, Thomas 67, 156; family: Sarah Ann, Agny, Amanda, Victoria, May, James 157
Lockwood, Benjamin 24
Louisa County (Virginia) 138
Louisville (Kentucky) 4–10, 12–13, 16, 69, 72, 94–95 126; Louisville and Nashville Railroad 10; *see also* slave trade
Loughmiller, John (elder of Second Presbyterian) 41, 49, 102–103, 141, *179n.11*
Louisiana Native Guards and New Albany men 77–79
Lucas, Sarah Ann: proof of freedom 158
Lyman, George 4

McClure, Newton (slave owner in Tennessee) 97
McCormick, The Rev. T. B. *181n.30*
McDongal, Henry 169
McGrew's Point (Floyd County) 59
McIntosh, Henson (alias Fremont) 4, 82; and family: Elizabeth, Anna, Mary F., Janie & William 120–123
McMaster, Erasmus Darwin: views on slavery 51
McQuinn, Thomas (slave owner) 166
Madison (Indiana) 3, 8, 43–44, 100
Madisonville (Kentucky) 29
Manly, Burkett and Sylvia (black settlers) 65
Manumission: explanation of 135
Marshall, James H. 5
Martin, Alexander 25, 66
Martin, Asa (black farmer) 67
Masons 72–74, 81, 114
Matthews, Lorine 4
Mauckport (Indiana) 86, 109
Melton, Alexander (black farmer) 67
Merchant, Leander (Alabama slave owner) 165
Merrill, Sarah (WPA interview) 82–83, 108
Merriweather, Jesse (black leader in Louisville) 72, 123
Methodism 12, 53–58
Methodist Churches: Centenary 46, 53; John Street 57; "Old Ship of Zion" 53, 113; Wesley Chapel 53–54
Meyers, John E. 137
Miami University, Oxford (Ohio) 43
Miensell, Luke (anti-slavery advocate) 34
Miller, Isaac T. (Kentucky slave owner) 92
Miller, The Rev. J. V. R. 55
Miller, Violet (benefactor) 162
Milton (Indiana) 34
Mississippi County (Missouri) 139
Missouri Compromise of 1820 *176n.3*
Mitchell, The Rev. James (colonization agent) 31–32;
Mitchem, Bright, Littleton, Mace, Mike, Tom and Harry 63
Mitchum, Isam 5, 147; Enos 75, 150; Jacob, arrest of 8
Mitchum, Josephine (servant of William A. Clapp) 46

Mitchum, Moses 5
Mitchum, Thompson (boatman) 63
Mitchum, Newell S.: proof of freedom 154
Mitchum, Paul & Susannah: immigration to Harrison Cty., Indiana 63
Mobile (Alabama) 161, 165
Moffett, J. A. (Mayor of New Albany) 90
Mokuna Society (New Albany literary club) 17
Monroe, China 160
Monroe County (Indiana) 86, 96
Monroe, William Henry Washington: proof of freedom 160
Montgomery, Capt. James 96
Montgomery, Robert (Kentucky slave owner) 164
Moore, Emanuel (Carter): proof of freedom 137
Moore, Richard (Louisville police officer) 93, 122
Morgan County (Indiana) 34
Morgan, John Hunt 116; Morgan's Raiders 116
Morris, Eliza Jane, Deed of Manumission 155
Morris, James H. (Louisiana slave owner) 155
Morris, Martha 138
Morris, New Year Branson, Deed of Manumission 155
Morris, William, Emancipation Papers 138
Morrison Light Guard 5, 19
Morrison, George 91
Morrow, James (anti-slavery advocate) 34
Morvins Landing (Indiana) 86
Mosee, Bill, Freedom Papers 169, *191n.103*
Mosee, Harry G. 139, *191n.103*
Mount Tabor: revival meetings 39, 50
Mukes, Rueben (black farmer) 67
Munfordsville (Kentucky) 83
Murphy, Andrew J. 49

Naghal, Lewis H. 5
National Cemetery (New Albany) 75
Nelson, William (black farmer) 67
New Albany (Indiana) *passim*
New Albany–Salem Railroad 47, 49, 82; Board of Directors *194n.53*; as an escape route 47, 94–98, 121

New Albany Theological Seminary: and abolitionism 37, 51; and Lane Seminary 50–51
New Albany Township (Floyd County, Indiana) 67, 81
New Albany Tribune 17, 54–55, 56
New Amsterdam (Indiana) 86
New Orleans (Louisiana) 6, 77, 162, 164, 167; formation of black troops 78–79, *New York Tribune* 28; and Helperism 30
Newberry District (South Carolina) 158
Newland, J. W. (Louisville slave owner) 92
Nichols, Lucy Higgs (black Civil War nurse) 76–77
Noble, The Rev. G. M. 130
Norman, John B.: attitude toward politics 18, 27, 47; toward blacks 14, 16, 17, 82, 118; threatened with assassination 20
North Star see *Frederick Douglass' Paper*
Nunemacher, Elizabeth 103
Nunemacher, John R. 94

Oakland City (Indiana) 35
Oatman, John (as slave owner) 3; George 61; Oatman Ferry 89; Oatman Plat 61, 152
Oberlin (Ohio) 50
Ohio River 3, 8, 13–14, 35; baptisms, 69; ferries 9, 89–93; as escape route 7, 68, 91, 121; permit to cross 90; *passim*
"Old Ship of Zion" see Methodist Churches
Oldam County (Kentucky) 4
Olden Street School (New Albany) 70
O'Neil (O'Neal), Matilda 4, 155
O'Neil, Walter B., Manumission Papers 155
Orange County (Indiana) 108
Ormsby, R. J. (slave owner) 168
Owen, Samuel H.: Appendix E *passim*
Owensboro (Kentucky) 6

Paoli (Indiana) 69, 86, 87
Parker, Byrd: as AME pastor; attitude toward colonization 32–33; political involvement 71–72
Parks, Willis (Underground Railroad Agent) 89
Paul, Colonel John 59

Payton, James (Payton House Hotel) 106
Pell, Alex *191n.103*
Peters, Absalom 42
Petersburg (Indiana) 84
Pfrimmer, The Rev. John George 42
Philanthropist 34
Phillips, Wendell 17
Pleasants, Andrew: proof of freedom; family: Ann, John H., Josiah, James 153–154
Port Gibson (Mississippi) 163
Porter, James 81
Portland (Indiana) 84
Portland (Kentucky) 6, 9, 74, 90, 91; ferry 36, 89, 92, 121
Portsmouth (Ohio): Black Friday 124
Powell, Benjamin and Thomas (slave dealers) 6, 12
Powell, James 63
Powhattan County (Virginia) 153
Presbyterianism 38–53, 99–105; Old School/New School differences 38–39; views on slavery 38–39; Presbyterian churches 38–41, 99, 102–103; support of mission to the poor 100–101; black membership in 46; Post–Civil War work among blacks 44, 46; Covenanters 51, 86
Price, Judy, Deed of Manumission: proof of freedom 168
Priest, James M. 52
Princeton (Indiana) 84
Proof of Freedom Papers: explanation of 135
Protectionist 35
Providence (settlement near K & I Bridge) 89

Quakers 5, 17, 37, 86–87, 108
Quinn, The Rev. William Paul 66, 69, 71
Quinn Chapel (Louisville) 69

Railroad (Ohio and Mississippi) 121
Ralph (a slave) 9
Ramsier, Fred and Henry 113
Randolph County (Indiana): Cabin Creek 80; Nettle Creek 87
Rankin, The Rev. A. T. 34
Rankin, The Rev. William C. *179n.11*
Raysville (Indiana) 89
Reeder, Joe (slave catcher) 14

Reid, Isaiah (Underground Railroad agent) 86, *192n.7*
Reineking, J. W. 168
Rensselaer (Indiana) 84
Republican 17
Republican: Party 26–27; "Black" Republicans 17, 46, 47; newspapers 17; support of Helperism 30–31
Reuben (a runaway slave) 8
Revivalist movement 39, 43
Reynolds, Elisha 92
Rice, Mary (slave owner) 4
Rice, The Rev. N. L. 51
Richard (a slave) 4
Richardson, Samuel K. (Louisville slave owner) 121
Richey, John S. 169
Richmond (Indiana) 84
Richmond (Virginia): Court of Hustings 153–154
Riddle, Thomas (steamboat captain) 105
Riots: race, in New Albany 22–25; in Jeffersonville 25; in Harrison Cty. 25; in Portsmouth, Ohio 124
Rising Sun (Indiana) 134
River Road (Floyd County) 113
Roberts, Sarah 5
Robison, William (livery stable owner) 106
Rochester, Sarah 109
Rockport (Indiana) 84
Rogers, Lewis 161
Ross, Henry 153
Ross, Peter, Sr., family: Peter, John, Thomas, Saul, Rome, Eli 67, 139, 147, 153
Ross, Peter, Freedom Papers 153
Rucker, James P. (Kentucky slave owner) 135
Runaway slaves: 8, 14; in Floyd County 11–12, 13, 16, 21, 95–96; *see also* Underground Railroad
Rush County (Indiana) 37
Russell, George (black settler) 67
Russell, John (anti-slavery advocate) 86

Sabin, E. H. 57
St. John Lutheran Church, Greenville Township (Floyd County) 116–118
Salem (Indiana) 69, 86, 96
Salem Weekly Times 17
Sanders, John W. 74, 81, 82, 121, 127

Saunders, Morgan *177n.22*
Scioto County (Ohio) 124
Scott, John (white settler) 27
Scott, Robert 4
Scott, Wesley G. 27
Scribner, B. F. 10, 25, 41, 151
Scribner, H. S. 70–71
Scribner, William A. 50, 137, 161
Second Baptist Church 99
Second Great Awakening 128
Second Presbyterian Church *see* Presbyterian churches
Selma (Indiana) 89
Seward, Austin (anti-slavery advocate) 86
Seward, William H. 30
Seymour (Indiana) 88, 93, 122
Shaw, Jonathan 87
Shelby County (Kentucky) 135
Shields, Henry B. 50, *194n.53*
Shields, Patrick: as slave owner 59
Shields, Pleasant S. 50
Shiloh, Battle of 104
Shrader, John (spiritualist) 53
Shrader, John (undertaker, furniture craftsman) 124
Siebert, Wilbur H. 10, 88, 131
Silver Creek (Indiana) 81, 89, 128; as Underground Railroad route 16, 88, 89
Sims, James (slave owner) 152
Sims, Rachel, Manumission Papers 152
Sims, Sarah: proof of freedom 154
Skoats, B. S. (slave owner) 165
Slaughter, Atticus (slave owner) 167
Slaughterhouses in New Albany *187n.31*
Slave catchers 6, 12, 13, 15, 43; kidnapping of free blacks 6; police as slave catchers 15–16
Slave trade 5–7
Slavery: in Indiana 3, 4, 8; attitudes toward 7, 10, 15, 17; resistance of *172n.12*; in the city 7–8; hiring out 4, 8; running off slaves 9–10; stories of *see* George; Harry; Henry; Ralph; Reuben; Richard; Tamar Sloan/Bicknell House 118–119; Dr. Sloan 104
Sly, Philip: proof of freedom 154–155
Smith, Caleb B. 27
Smith, Isaac P. 27, 47, 119; Quartermaster, 23rd Reg. 47, 77; as Republican 47; as architect 27;

Abby H. Campbell Smith 46, 77, 97, 103; James and Samuel 10
Smith, The Rev. John C.: views on slavery 55–56
Smith, Thomas (anti-slavery advocate) 86
Smith, W. C. (anti-slavery advocate) 86
Smyser, Jacob L. (slave owner) 3
Sneed, Rev. Samuel K. 5; revivals 39, 50; views on slavery 143–145, 155–156, 167–168
South Bend (Indiana) 84
Spaulding, Bishop Martin J.: as slave owner 9
Speake, William 154
Spencer, The Rev. Thomas *181n.27*
Springville (Indiana) 41
Stanton, Edwin McMaster 47
Stanton, Henry B. 33
Stausbery, Baryemon (slave owner) 162
Steamboats 76; B. J. Adams 8; Baltic 92; Brown 66; Commercial 19; Interchange 93; Monarch 23, 66; New York 81; Peytona 92; Pike 8; Silver Moon 97; Vichsburgh 77
Stevenson, John McMillan 55
Stinson, Charles, George and Nancy (black farmers) 63–64, 67, 75
Stotsenberg, John H. 166
Stowe, Calvin *179n.6*
Stowe, Harriett Beecher 29, *179n.6*
Stroud, Mr. (New Albany ferry) 89
Stubblefield, Jemina (Mina) 28; Deed of Manumission 159; Samuel 159–160
Stute, Thomas (Kentucky slave owner) 153
Sunard, Martha 158
Sweet Gum Stable 105–107

Talbott, Hannah: and the Underground Railroad 87
Talson, John 15
Tamar (a runaway slave) 88
Tappan, Lewis 29
Terre Haute (Indiana) 84
Thirteenth Article of the Indiana Constitution *see* Exclusion Act of 1851
Thompson, James L. 88
Thomas, John 88–89
Thomas, Thomas E.: views on slavery 51–52

Thompson, Margaret M. 97
Thompson, Mary Ann, Freedom Papers 166
Throgmorton, Isaac (runaway slave) 91–92
Thruston, Charles M. (slave owner in Louisville) 161–162
Thurston, The Rev. David 33–34
Tina, Deed of Manumission 165–166
Town, R. R. 162
Town, Salem P. 166, 169
Transylvania Presbytery 42
True American (Lexington, Kentucky) 29
Trueblood, Martin 59
Trueblood, Thomas H. *174n.13*; *192n.7*
Tucker, James M. (Mississippi slave owner) 155
Tuly, M. D. 151
Tunnels 118–119; Second Baptist Church 103–104, 119
Tydings, John N. 164
Tyng, Beecher 55

Uncle Tom's Cabin: as best seller 29; dramatized in New Albany *179n.6*
Underground Railroad: explanation of 5, 10; in Floyd County 86, 88–89, 120–121; in Clark County 86, 87; in Harrison County 86; in Kentucky 121; methods of escape 89–90; routes of escape 84–89; after the Civil War 103, 106–107; myths, 131–132; *passim*
Utica (Indiana) 87, 100

Van DeGraff, Jane (Kentucky slave owner) 28
Vance, William O. 75
Vance, William R. 168
Vicksburg, (Tennessee) 47, 77
Vincennes (Indiana) 84
"Vinegar Hill" (in New Albany) 68
Violett (runaway slave) 36

Wainwright, Luke 165
Waldo, F. A. 163
Walker, Willis and family: Mary J., Olivia J., Samuel D., Shelby W., Stephen M. 68–69
Walnut Ridge (Indiana) 86
War of 1812 5
Warren House 104
Warring, Harriet (Louisiana slave owner) 164
Washington County (Indiana) 37, 88–89
Watson (Indiana) 100
Wayne County (Indiana) 34, 37
Weakley County (Tennessee) 152
Weaver, The Rev. John S., Peter, Mary, Gale 34, 35, 67, 75
Webb, Margaret 99
Weekly Review (Floyd County black newspaper) 75
Welch, John 63; Levi 46; Eli 63, 67
Weld, Theodore 33–35, 37, 50, 52
Wells, Ashbel S. 42, 47
Wells, Rachel family: Horrace, Sarah, Evline, permission to cross Ohio River 90
Wesley Chapel *see* Methodist Churches
West Haven Cemetery 75, 100, 108
West Union 44, 68, 76, 82; racial tension 16, 22, 24
Western Anti-Slavery Society 34
Western Freedmen's Aid Society 44
Whalan, William, and the Underground Railroad 120
Wheeler, George (slave owner) 3
Whig/Republicans 12, 17, 47
White, Allen (Civil War veteran) 75

White, The Rev. Henry 70
Whiten, Peter (black settler) 67
Whitten, Hetty (formerly "White"), Deed of Emancipation 161
Whitewater Anti-Slavery Society 34
"Wide Awakes" and Lincoln 26
Willett, Elsie (a slave) 42; Deed of Manumission 167–168
Williams, Vance (Civil War Veteran) 75
Williams, William 8, 149, 154; James 75; Laben 154
Wilson, Joshua 61; family: Ludson, Pendleton, Allen, Louise and Cynthia 62
Wilson, Samuel G. 136, 151
Wilson, William W. ("runner" for slave dealer) 6
Wilson, "Yellow" *see* Joshua Wilson
Winchester (Indiana) 84
Winthrop (Mae) 33
Woodruff, Charles 50
Woodruff, Seth 27; as slave owner 28, 159
Woodson, Alex (early member of Second Baptist Church) 99
Woodward Hall 86
Worth, Daniel: and Helperism 29
Wright, James (Kentucky slave owner) 160
Wright, John F. 162–163
Wright, Oswald 63

Yeager (Yeater), A. J. 53
Yocum, Dr. 120
Youman, Willis L. (slave owner) 165
Young, Cornelia, Freedom Papers *see* Adelade Goram
Young Men's Christian Association 17
Young, Octavious: proof of freedom 163